ADVANCE PRAISE

"Ruby Jo Walker's seminal work transcends trauma clinicians and serves as a blueprint for enhancing all therapeutic relationships. This should be essential reading for all therapists who are geared towards helping clients find more resilience. Walker, with profound clinical acumen, employs PVT to demonstrate the paramount significance of self-regulation and co-regulation in achieving optimal well-being, as she elucidates the synergistic interplay and connection between PVT and attachment theory. This book holds value for all sentient beings."

—**Bruce Gottlieb, MSW,** therapist, presenter, and mental coach to professional and Olympic athletes, specializing in self-regulation with a polyvagal emphasis

"Ruby Jo Walker's book is a remarkable contribution to the field of trauma recovery. Her years of investment as a clinician, supervisor, presenter, educator, and researcher make this book relatable, practical, and supportive. She masterfully presents theory and application that has deepened my skills and effectiveness in nurturing growth and resilience in my clients. The beautiful embodiment exercises for the clinician have truly helped me to be more regulated and present in my sessions."

—**Michelle Trosclair, LPC, LMHC,** Certified Hakomi Therapist

"This work marks a genuine evolution in the clinical applications of Polyvagal Theory in therapy, bringing its principles to life in ways that are both accessible and truly transformative. Ruby Jo Walker's *Applied Polyvagal Theory for Resilience and Post-Traumatic Growth* stands out as a masterwork—integrating the art and science of attuning to the nervous system through specific maps, advancing our understanding of deactivation pathways, strengthening essential clinical skills, and elevating parallel processes of tracking and working with the nervous system to a new level. With decades of expertise as a trainer shaping her approach, her voice shines as a therapist-whisperer, revealing the healing potential of embodied presence and guiding readers toward clarity, confidence, and lasting change. This remarkable book is a gift to clinicians. I learned so much from this invaluable resource—thank you."

—**Stephanie D'Angelo, MA,** director of organizational training and facilitation at the Polyvagal Institute and developer of *Polyvagal-Informed Embodied Mindfulness*™ (PIEM)

"Taking a wide, wise view of life challenges, Ruby Jo Walker offers invaluable practical tools to help clinicians guide clients beyond the pain and trauma trapped in their dysregulated nervous systems to fulfill their potential as human beings. Walker teaches how to help clients move beyond healing their wounds and locate inner support in their unconditioned human nature where access to loving kindness and other resources can lead to a life of fulfillment and joy."

—**Julia Dengel, LCSW,** psychotherapist and
Diamond Approach teacher

APPLIED POLYVAGAL THEORY
FOR RESILIENCE AND
POST-TRAUMATIC GROWTH

APPLIED POLYVAGAL THEORY FOR RESILIENCE AND POST-TRAUMATIC GROWTH

A CLINICIAN'S GUIDE

RUBY JO WALKER
LCSW, SEP, CHT

Norton Professional Books

An Imprint of W. W. Norton & Company
Independent Publishers Since 1923

Note to Readers: This book is intended as a general information resource for professionals practicing in the field of psychotherapy and mental health. It is not a substitute for appropriate training or clinical supervision. Standards of clinical practice and protocol vary in different practice settings and change over time. No technique or recommendation is guaranteed to be safe or effective in all circumstances, and neither the publisher nor the author(s) can guarantee the complete accuracy, efficacy, or appropriateness of any particular recommendation in every respect or in all settings or circumstances.

All patients referred to in this book are composites. Any URLs displayed in this book link or refer to websites that existed as of press time. The publisher is not responsible for, and should not be deemed to endorse or recommend, any website other than its own or any content that it did not create. The author, also, is not responsible for any third-party material.

For information about permission to reproduce selections from this book, write to
Permissions, W. W. Norton & Company, Inc., 500 Fifth Avenue, New York, NY 10110

For information about special discounts for bulk purchases, please contact
W. W. Norton Special Sales at specialsales@wwnorton.com or 800-233-4830

Manufacturing by Versa Press
Production manager: Gwen Cullen

ISBN: 978-1-324-08298-9 (Paperback)

W. W. Norton & Company, Inc., 500 Fifth Avenue, New York, NY 10110
www.wwnorton.com

W. W. Norton & Company Ltd., 15 Carlisle Street, London W1D 3BS

Authorized EU representative: EAS, Mustamäe tee 50, 10621 Tallinn, Estonia

1 2 3 4 5 6 7 8 9 0

For Mama and Charles, for modeling post-traumatic growth for me.
For my child, for being my biggest teacher.
For Tamola, for all of the support along the way.

You are all part of my resilience and post-traumatic growth.

Contents

Foreword

The journey of Polyvagal Theory began not with a map, but with a question—a physiological curiosity about how the human nervous system navigates the world of safety, threat, and connection. It began with a simple observation: that beneath the complexities of behavior and emotion lies a deeply embedded neurophysiological architecture, one that determines not only how we survive but how we connect, love, grieve, and heal.

In this volume, Ruby Jo Walker brings forward a clinically grounded, deeply humane interpretation of Polyvagal Theory. Her work is not merely a restatement of scientific principles, but a vibrant synthesis of theory and practice. It is a book shaped by compassion, lived experience, clinical presence, and embodied scholarship. What emerges is a guide not only for therapists but for any practitioner seeking to accompany others through the labyrinth of trauma toward a horizon of hope.

Over the past three decades, Polyvagal Theory has evolved through dialogue—across disciplines, clinical settings, developmental contexts, and, crucially, with those who have suffered. It is in that relational field that its concepts take form. The theory's scaffolding—neuroception, the hierarchical organization of the autonomic nervous system, and the role of the ventral vagal complex in enabling social engagement—offers more than academic insight; it provides a language for human experience, especially the often wordless experiences of threat and safety.

Ruby Jo Walker's clinical work demonstrates how theory can become a felt sense—a therapeutic presence. She understands that resilience is not a trait, but a capacity that arises from a state: a neurophysiological condition of safety that allows flexibility, adaptability, and growth. Her therapeutic framework attends to the body's implicit memory, and to the fundamental truth that trauma is held not only in stories but in viscera, breath, posture, and tone.

In this book, the nervous system is not presented as a set of circuits to be regulated in isolation but as a living, relational system that is coregulated within the therapeutic encounter. This distinction is critical. The neural platform for healing is not activated solely through technique, but through the presence of another who has attuned, who has softened their own physiology to offer safety to another. The process of healing becomes reciprocal, rhythmic, and responsive.

Ruby Jo Walker has crafted a structure that honors the science while speaking to the soul. Her delineation of the autonomic hierarchy is at once accessible and precise. She captures the ventral vagal state not as a theoretical endpoint but as the embodied expression of trust, connection, and presence. She recognizes that dorsal states—of collapse and withdrawal—are not dysfunctions to be eradicated but ancient survival strategies that must be honored, understood, and gently transformed.

The therapeutic journey, as she articulates it, is the process of shifting defensive immobilization—marked by fear, dissociation, and withdrawal—into an accessible state of feeling safe enough to be held in the arms of another. It is the transformation of immobilization with fear into immobilization without fear: the physiological substrate of intimacy and trust. This is the core of what it means to reclaim our capacity to connect.

One of the significant contributions of this text is its integration of post-traumatic growth. By linking Polyvagal Theory with the processes of transformation following adversity, Ruby Jo gives language and structure to the often nonlinear path from suffering to strength. She shows that post-traumatic growth is not the denial of trauma, but its transcendence. It is not bypassing but reorganization—a re-emergence of agency and authenticity as the nervous system gradually begins to trust again.

The tools and strategies Ruby Jo offers are grounded in what I have often described as the biology of safety. Her work affirms that our nervous system responds not to the cognitive content of words, but to the prosody of voice, the micro-movements of face and gesture, the rhythm of interaction. She invites clinicians to embody regulation, not merely to instruct it. In doing so, she elevates the therapeutic process from intervention to invitation.

The narratives and vignettes woven throughout this book serve not as case studies in the traditional sense but as lived illustrations of how autonomic state shapes behavior, meaning, and possibility. They remind us that behind every symptom is a story of adaptation, and behind every adaptation is a nervous system striving to survive.

It is also important to acknowledge that Polyvagal Theory has, in some circles, been misunderstood or overly simplified. Ruby Jo addresses this with integrity and clarity. She does not reduce the theory to colors or catchphrases. Instead, she restores it to its scientific and relational roots, offering a nuanced understanding of the autonomic nervous system that respects both complexity and clarity.

In the field of trauma therapy, we are witnessing a shift—from models of correction to models of connection. Ruby Jo's work is part of this evolution. It invites clinicians to move beyond pathology into presence, beyond fixing into witnessing, and beyond reactivity into regulation. It honors the wisdom of the body and the healing power of relationship.

This book is a gift to clinicians, educators, and clients alike. It is a practical guide, a theoretical map, and a compassionate companion. It reflects the heart of Polyvagal Theory—not as a doctrine, but as an evolving framework through which we can understand the human experience in all its fragility and resilience.

As you enter these pages, I invite you not only to read but to feel—to notice your own physiology, your breath, your posture, and your sense of connection. For it is in these subtle cues that the work begins. May this text support you in your own journey of growth, and may it serve as a guide as you support others.

—Stephen W. Porges, PhD

Acknowledgments

I always read the acknowledgments of books and have been struck by all the recognition offered to others. Now, I have the embodied awareness of why that occurs as I feel inside myself how so many others are in the scaffolding of this book, both in the content as well as the writing process. All of you noted here are in the foundation of these pages, and I want to thank you and acknowledge you for your support of me and the evolution of this book.

I must first thank my mentor from afar, Dr. Stephen Porges, the founder of PVT. His seminal work on the nervous system has transformed me as a psychotherapist and shaped how I approach clients. Dr. Porges, your contribution of PVT to the psychotherapy world both reinforced and guided the development of my approach in PVT-informed therapy, resulting in more effective clinical work with my clients. Thank you, Dr. Porges, for your powerful influence on me.

I also want to thank the Polyvagal Institute (PVI). Under the leadership of Randall Redfield, PVI gave me an opportunity to teach what I love—the clinical applications of Polyvagal Theory, the basis of this book. Randall, along with Suzie Cavassa, backed me and allowed me the exciting opportunity to be part of the PVI teaching team. Randall and Suzie, sharing the passion regarding the power of PVT has been so fulfilling. Thank you both for all the kindness and care along the way in working together. I also want to thank Stephanie D'Angelo for being both a kindred spirit and for seeing what I have to offer. Stephanie, as a natural leader at PVI, is gifted at championing others, and I have benefited from this gift. Stephanie, your belief in me has been so meaningful. You have made my teaching more nourishing with your allyship. Thank you, for our personal and professional connection and for so much laughter and fun. From the beginning of my course, Regan Desautels, as the education programs manager at PVI, brought so much regulation and ease. Regan, collaboration with you has been gift. Your warmth and helpful feedback have helped make me a better trainer. Thank you, Regan. I also appreciate the rest of the PVI team—Caroline, Jen, Jerry, Lovinah, and Mac, who brought the infrastructure to for success in my course. I have great appreciation for each of you—thank you. I truly love the partnership with all of you at the Polyvagal Institute!

There are parts of my training and education that are woven into this book. My roots in Hakomi Mindful Somatic Therapy are such an embodied part of me that it is often hard to pull apart and differentiate the strands of that work within myself. My personal teachers all have had a strong impact on me. It started almost 3 decades ago with Dr. Mark Fallon-Cyr, who I first heard say, "The issues are in the tissues," as he coaxed me into studying somatic work. Thank you, Mark. My trainers, Cedar Barstow, Phil Del Prince, Deepesh Faucheux, Melissa Grace, and Morgan Holford, I am grateful to all of you. Beyond skills, you taught me the heart of therapeutic work. I am a better therapist because of your teachings and your gifts of presence. I carry each of you in the therapist I am today. Thank you.

My other deep roots are found in Somatic Experiencing® (SE). Bruce Gottlieb is the person who inspired me to learn SE, and I will always be grateful for that nudge. Thank you, Bruce. Mentors, Berns Galloway and Twig Wheeler, thank you for enhancing my knowledge of SE and the nervous system. Berns and Twig, I appreciate you both so much. Twig, I never would have gotten PVT without your tutoring. You were one of the first people to have a deep understanding of PVT decades before it was very well known. Sharing your knowledge about the power of PVT was critical to get me here today. Thank you, Twig.

At the core of writing this book there are several key individuals I want to thank. First, I want to acknowledge Laura McClenny, my initial editor. From the very beginning, Laura believed in me and encouraged me as we worked together. Her steady presence was incredibly meaningful and boosted my confidence. I never could have completed this book without Laura, along with her expert input and craft in writing. Unlike me, Laura is a true writer, and her professional writing skills were evident all along the way. She often gave feedback starting with the words, "A reader wants . . ." which was incredibly helpful. She found ways to help me understand the necessary components of the writing process. She also encouraged me to express myself more as I wrote, which was essential to reflect my authentic voice. Thank you, Laura. I am so grateful for the gifts you have in this area and how you shared them with me. Laura, you are an integral part of this book, and you helped set the groundwork for the structure of this book today.

Next, I want to thank Emily Newcomer. Although I once provided clinical supervision to Emily, we reversed roles as I started learning from her. She approached me after assisting with a training, letting me know she had ideas on how to improve it. Through this offering, she became my curriculum development consultant for Southwest Trauma Training. Emily's genius mind helped me break down complex concepts in my trainings. I often called her "my pre-frontal cortex" because she had an extraordinary ability to take my ideas and make them clearer. She made a real difference to me, resulting in me being able to teach with greater precision and depth. As I wrote, Emily's voice stayed close, asking, "Can you break that down more?" Emily, your influence is woven into many of my teachings. You remain the person I want to talk to as I am organizing new concepts in my mind. You always bring your ability to ask the right questions that lead me to gaining the necessary clarity. Thank you, Emily, for your contribution in helping me grow as both a teacher and a writer.

I also want to thank Jenny Mason, my citation coach. I hired Jenny to help me with formatting, and she became so much more as I wrote. Thank you, Jenny, for all your dedication and your regulated presence.

I want to recognize two of my readers whose feedback and writing skills were so important—M Carrasco-Songer and Michelle Trosclair. Both M and Michelle are lead teaching assistants in my trainings, and their brilliance stood out all along as I integrated their powerful perspective into my text. As great writers themselves, they had a unique role in helping me with many concepts; their understanding of my work from our years together has been so useful. Thank you, M and Michelle. M also enhanced this book with some separate discussions to refine concepts. This was so important in creating even more coherence. Thank you, M, for this added assistance.

Finally, Cindy Atchinson elevated all of my ideas into graphics through her work. Thank you, Cindy, for bringing these concepts to life through your creative lens. I love how you always brought your artistic self to the graphics, and you made my ideas all the better.

I also want to acknowledge my readers of the initial drafts: Charles Stacy, Robin Craig, Stephanie D'Angelo, and Blake O'Connor. Charlie and Robin contributed a somatic expertise with their thoughtful feedback, which enriched this book. Thank you, Charlie and Robin. Stephanie and Blake played a vital role in offering refinement in both PVT knowledge and language throughout the manuscript. Thank you to both of you, Stephanie and Blake!

I am also grateful to my team at Norton. Jamie Vincent recognized that I had a book inside me after working together on another book project. Her invitation to work with her was a lovely gift to me. She, along with McKenna Tanner, Olivia Guarnieri, and Mariah Eppes, offered me much practical help as I was on my learning curve of writing; they also provided crucial editing and vision. I would have been lost without their expertise. Thank you to the whole team at Norton for taking a risk on me and seeing that I had something to share.

My own personal experience is what led me to explore post-traumatic growth. With that in mind, I want to acknowledge my family and friends who walked with me personally as I navigated my post-traumatic growth path. Family members, John, Jane, Kat, Joe, Alana, Tamie, and Brad, I hope you know how much I appreciate your love and encouragement throughout the years.

Tamie, I especially want to thank you. I can't imagine having made this journey without you. The depth and constancy of your support are beyond words—you stand in a category of your own. You showed up in every way a person possibly could. I will always be grateful that you were with me on this path. I also want to thank my sister, Kat. More than my sister, you are a great friend. Thank you, Kat. I must also shout out my big brother, John. Your kind words and genuine pride in me meant the world to me in my writing endeavors. Thank you, big brother! Brad, your help has softened many aspects of my struggle, and I appreciate that you continue to be in my life. My friends are also part of my personal journey. Cecile, Mel, Patricia, Laura, and Jen, thank you for your care throughout the years as I negotiated my challenges. Your friendship helped me expand and grow. With generosity, my Tucson friends, Pam and Denise, supported me in my writing by allowing me to be in their lovely home in the warmth of the desert. My time with you was a welcome reprieve, offering me the space to write. Thank you both! I also want to say thank you to my dear neighbors, Lumi and Leila, who brought me so much joy at our shared tea parties that consisted mostly of whipped cream with a little hot cocoa. Lumi and Leila, thank you for being in my life and making me smile so often. I love watching you grow up.

Also on my personal evolution are some professionals who helped me find and strengthen my own resilience: Linda Kerr, Dr. Michael Hoffman, and Cheryl Sanders. Having your guidance and anchoring influence is a huge part of my post-traumatic growth, and I appreciate your help throughout the years. I hope you know how grateful I am for your role in helping me find my way.

To all of my teaching assistants, who have assisted at trainings throughout the years, I appreciate all of you so much! My lead teaching assistants, Chrishana Woody, Lisa Donelan, Michelle Trosclair, Karin Lee Hughes, and M Carrasco-Songer brought embodied ventral vagal energy and wisdom to the participants in my classes. Thank you for being true leaders in learning with me and for the many ways you have been committed to me and the students. I want to especially recognize Chrishana and Lisa. I love how you both are helping me now carry this work forward in so many different ways with your special interests and gifts. Thank you, Lisa and CJ, for your dedication and love of this work.

Last, but not least, I want to thank my clients. Trusting me to work with you has been a privilege. Your courage and vulnerability have been inspiring to me. You were always the reason I kept growing, the driving force that kept me stretching myself as a clinician. I have learned and grown along with you in my process. Thank you.

Introduction

My journey and interest in post-traumatic growth began at a young age. During my first year of high school, I faced the heartbreaking loss of my mother to cancer. She was a single parent raising my five siblings and me. At that time, outdated rules and attitudes regarding visitation for hospitalized patients were in place; kids were not allowed to visit. As a 14-year-old, I was allowed to see my mom, but my ability to see her depended on whether I could find a ride. Unfortunately, transportation was not consistently available to me. This created a significant loss for me, as I couldn't spend much time with my mom during her dying process in the hospital. This loss marked the beginning of all the painful losses and trauma that would follow.

It was challenging not to be able to see my only available parent. At that time, there was little understanding about death, coupled with a stigma about even talking about it. As the oldest girl in my household in the 1970s, I had some responsibility to attend to my younger siblings. It was a lot for a 14-year-old girl. The weight of this complicated struggle added to the burden of my grief. I felt lonely and overwhelmed, in addition to tremendous sorrow.

The loneliness was one of the most challenging aspects of this process for me. It was the biggest event of my young life, and no one was talking to me about it. I wondered why people didn't ask how I was doing and why they seemed to avoid discussing my mom's dying. Relatives, neighbors, and friends knew that my father had been abusive. With my mom's death, he came back into our lives, along with my stepmother, to raise us. The people who had been part of our lives before Mom's death found it difficult to interact with him due to the awareness of that abuse. Because of those feelings, they stayed away. This just added to my loneliness and grief.

Two events happened that led me to my early path of post-traumatic growth. One occurred as I read the book my mom had given me before she died. *On*

Death and Dying, by Elizabeth Kübler-Ross, was a recently released book, and my mom had read it while she was dealing with her recurrence of cancer. The book helped me to understand that my feelings were normal; I also began to understand how important it was to be connected with others while grieving. Recognizing that bereavement was both normal and necessary to move forward, I realized that I needed to have room for my feelings. This was profound for me. These insights were incredibly supportive to my grief journey. The second big event was meeting a social worker who started coming to our school every other Tuesday. I looked forward to those visits; they made a difference for me because I received support. Meeting with her also helped me know I wanted to help others with loss. At the age of 15, I committed to being a social worker as my profession, and I wanted to specialize in serving others who were coping with death.

These life-changing events reshaped everything for me and gave me a new meaning and focus. I understood that I might have something to offer kids who lost a parent. I knew how to talk to people. I understood how loss and trauma felt. This gave me a purpose and a direction. I remember saying to myself many times, "This pain has to count for something." That phrase became a guide for me, and it gave me regulation and a semblance of peace. Realizing I could ease another person's loss made my difficult experience useful; this meant everything to me. This was probably my first foray into settling my nervous system with embodied agency through meaning, but I did not understand that just yet. Finding this meaning gave my grief a pathway forward; the mantra of "this pain can count for something" are the words that helped me go forward to try to help others with their grief. With this renewed purpose, I moved from depression to my path of post-traumatic growth.

Years later, I had the privilege to meet the mom who would unofficially adopt me. We had an adoption that was not legal, but it was of the heart. Mama (also known as Nancy) was the epitome of post-traumatic growth. She greeted every challenge she ever had in her life with "How do I grow through this?" Mama experienced physiological trauma symptoms due to burns suffered as a child after a house fire. With true acceptance, her remaining scars were simply part of her; there was no self-consciousness or awkwardness. Mama was never a victim concerning anything that happened to her. Instead, she reinforced the opportunity for growth. It was both how she lived and how she encouraged me to live.

My stepdad, Charles, also played a role in my firsthand experience of learning about post-traumatic growth. He had an accident and broke his back at age 38. For the rest of his life, he was in a wheelchair. Charles did not let physical limitations define him, which is a hallmark of post-traumatic growth. He found a new profession in psychotherapy when he could no longer do the physical job of being a roofer. Nurturing his love of nature, he found a way to camp regularly on his own into his early 70s. When spending time around him it was easy to forget he could not walk. What radiated out of Charles was wholeness, compassion, and an enlivened sense of being.

Acceptance of the event that changed his life, coupled with his commitment to fullhearted living, was always evident. He used to say that although he would not wish for the accident to happen, he was glad it did because of how it changed him. He acknowledged how much he had changed after breaking his back; this included his personal growth and evolution in his movement toward wholeness. Charles has since died, but I still remember him as the most present person I have ever met. These two role models were instrumental in my finding my path. I didn't realize it then, but they were preparing me for the most significant trauma I would ever face in my life.

Sitting in my living room years later, I read an email about a student recruiting volunteers for a survey on post-traumatic growth. I was stunned to read that there was even a topic called post-traumatic growth, and I knew immediately it was for me. As I sat on the couch that day, I was in the struggle of my lifetime as a single parent of a child with mental illness. (I do have permission from my child to share this information.) Things were escalating on many levels for her, both socially and at school. She was adopted and had in-utero crystal meth exposure as well as poor prenatal care. There is a cultural naivety concerning adoption as well as the impact of in-utero experiences. These experiences can create major repercussions that many people do not understand. Loving a child well is *not* enough to shift the imprint on the nervous system and brain development. Although love is not enough, it is also the only thing you can do. Children who are adopted and exposed to drugs have challenges because of their perinatal and epigenetic experiences. Not having that understanding can lead to judgment from others. This judgment is painfully aimed at both the child and the parent.

My daughter, with her history of adoption, crystal meth exposure, and poor prenatal care did not have a normal or neurotypical nervous system. She was diagnosed with severe mental illness as an eighth-grader. She required long-term hospitalizations. I could only visit her by traveling long distances. Visiting these facilities required either driving for hours by car or taking flights; this created a significant roadblock just to get to be with my daughter. Facilities also kept limiting visiting hours, another example of visitation regulations not matching a very human need. I needed to be with my child as much as she needed me to be there.

Despite all the interventions for her, there was no evidence that she was improving. Facilities often could not keep her safe, and yet, she could not be safe at home. Even in the treatment centers, she was sexually and physically assaulted. She also had two overdoses while in treatment, one that was almost lethal, resulting in her being airlifted to a larger pediatric hospital in another city. The issues went on and on, and it felt horrible that I could not help her or find a way to protect her.

One of the most painful and surprising parts for me of having a child in a psychiatric hospital was how the facilities often initially blamed me for her mental illness. This blame occurred despite documented extensive early supportive interventions and a history of in-utero trauma. As a committed parent, this was quite traumatic for me; I was not being seen accurately. I was putting every resource I knew into supporting her, and both of us were being mistreated. This stretch of time was the hardest thing I have ever been through. It seemed to mirror the challenges of my earlier life.

Another parallel awakening for me was the realization that people are not generally skilled at talking about the fact that a child has a mental illness. It is not intentional, but society does not approach children with mental health issues in the same way as children with physical health issues. In addition to finding reluctance to talk about what was happening, other kinds of supports were also lacking that are customarily part of having a sick child. There are no fundraisers or meal trains to offer support to families, even in situations like mine that went on for years. With history repeating itself, others were hesitant to question how she and I were both doing. Instead, I experienced the same avoidance from others as when my mom died. It was incredibly painful for me.

Feeling scared, helpless, and ashamed, I asked myself, how could I, a skilled and successful mental health professional, not be able to help more? I could not fathom that I could not do more for the person who meant the most to me in the world—my own child. My past traumas resurfaced in the form of wondering if I was to blame in some way; I kept wondering what else I could have done. Over time, I also regressed into wondering if I deserved some of the bad treatment I was experiencing. These issues just added to my struggle. I now had a very stressful outer world with a sick child, and it was being matched with a very stressful inner world as I was hitting more of my traumatic core wounding.

Furthermore, I was not having a positive experience with the mental health system in general. I viewed my role as an advocate for my child, but that was not embraced at all. I often felt I was just holding on to get through the challenge of caring for a sick child and navigating a difficult mental health system and insurance issues, all while lacking enough support. There was no consistent advocate for me, and managing things on my own was often very overwhelming, again a replay of my earlier life.

After a few years, it became clear that my daughter's mental health was not going to improve quickly. As her primary parent, the advocacy and support for her care were mostly on me. At one point, my clinician said an important phrase to me: "You have simply gotten through things before, so I wonder if you focused on expanding this time, if it would be helpful to you." Those words, combined with receiving the earlier email asking about post-traumatic growth, were both inspiring and comforting to me. I knew her invitation to expand meant that I needed to do more than just survive the challenge. That call to evolve was the moment I started my journey toward post-traumatic growth. It was very similar to my time as a teenager; I suddenly knew there was a route for me to find my way through the struggle. Finding agency in these words propelled me and regulated me more. As in my earlier life, I started feeling better once I found this focus.

As part of this commitment to expand myself, I read everything I could about both post-traumatic growth and resilience. My personal work became about working on my limiting core beliefs in a deeper and whole new way. I had to grow to do more rather than "just get through it" and survive. I knew how important it was to commit to being my truest and best self. This meant working on my sense of value and of "being enough" and learning to take in more support. I also needed to see myself in a system where I was not being seen accurately. Working with my negative limiting core beliefs that had been stirred up, I viewed my struggle to move more into my own Essence—who I was without my adaptations from earlier trauma.

At that time, I had already studied Polyvagal Theory (PVT). As a trauma specialist, I knew that PVT offered game-changing information affecting the trauma treatment field. Years before, I had hired a tutor to more deeply understand Stephen Porges's first book, *The Polyvagal Theory: Neurophysiological Foundations of Emotions, Attachment, Communication, and Self-Regulation*, which led me to start teaching PVT to different groups. My learning direction then changed to apply PVT to resilience and post-traumatic growth, and I began teaching the very topic of this book. "We teach what we need to learn" became my motto as I committed to helping others and myself grow. It was regulating to my nervous system to keep my focus on my expansion and growth. I was still in the throes of trauma, but I was on my path to my evolution with post-traumatic growth as I found renewed purpose again.

USING THIS BOOK

This book was written to help trauma clinicians find more effective ways to work with trauma using the lens of Polyvagal Theory. It will cover understanding the nervous system and its role in the cultivation of resilience and post-traumatic growth in your clients. This book is being written directly for clinicians, as it is how I have applied the material. I know other kinds of trauma practitioners might also be utilizing this information, including coaches and body workers. Even with this awareness, I will be using the term "clinician" when I am referring to the trauma practitioner.

This book is divided into three sections. The first section provides an overview and maps of interventions in working therapeutically to promote resilience and post-traumatic growth through the lens of Polyvagal Theory. The second section covers applications for each of the deactivation pathways. The third section is integration in therapy, including the change process, phases of treatment, and the clinician's expansion of self for deepening presence.

Throughout the book, there will be reflections, practice tips, and clinician embodiment exercises for supporting the clinician. You might find some exercises will resonate, and others will not. Let this awareness simply be information as to what feels right to you as you attune to yourself and your regulation. There is no good, bad, right, or wrong answer in terms of your response to the embodiment exercises. More than anything, they are designed to support your nervous system as you support your clients.

You might be tempted to skip right over these exercises. If you are interested in applying this content to your work, I would encourage you to instead try them to support your own deepening. Tzipi Weis, associate professor at LIU Post, says that one of the biggest factors in promoting post-traumatic growth is just having contact with someone who has grown. Our work with ourselves will always be a way to support our work with clients. We become better allies for their healing journeys.

EXAMPLES AND STORIES DISCLAIMER

This book comes from years of clinical work in the field. It is important to note that the clinical information presented in examples and stories is clinically accurate but all client examples are composites.

APPLIED POLYVAGAL THEORY
FOR RESILIENCE AND
POST-TRAUMATIC GROWTH

SECTION I

OVERVIEW AND MAPS OF INTERVENTIONS

CHAPTER 1

Introduction to Polyvagal Theory, Resilience, and Post-Traumatic Growth

Post-traumatic growth shines a light on a person's Essence. It encompasses a sense of vitality and often opens the door to one's most expanded version of themselves.

OVERVIEW

Trauma work has completely changed in the three decades of my career. The early lens of trauma treatment started with the belief that simply hearing the story would shift someone's experience and that symptoms would change, which did not always happen. Now, with so much available information about trauma's influence on neurobiology, clients' outcomes have improved. Working with the body and applied somatic and neurobiological interventions has been profound in offering clients a path not only to symptom reduction, but also to more fullhearted living. This chapter will explore the new ways to understand and work effectively with trauma through the lens of the nervous system. It will also focus on both strengthening resilience as well as creating the neurobiological platform for post-traumatic growth.

Because trauma is a primary issue that clients bring to treatment, learning ways to work with clients to support resilience is a critical skill for trauma clinicians. According to Stephen Porges, resilience is defined as having the ability to go through challenges with ease (2022). Cultivating resilience is a fundamental part of working with clients; it can serve as an antidote to moving beyond trauma, leading to smoother life experiences despite challenges. In resilience, there is a sense that one can meet the moment of whatever is happening. As espoused throughout the work of Rick Hanson, renowned resilience expert, resilience can be learned through positive neuroplasticity and intention, by applying the necessary skills (2009). Not everyone will have access to post-traumatic growth, but almost anyone can develop resilience.

Different than resilience, post-traumatic growth is the transformation that can occur after trauma (Calhoun & Tedeschi, 2013). Both resilience and post-traumatic growth are built on the neural platform, or the neurobiological underpinnings of the state of *safety* in the nervous system. This state of safety, as explained by Polyvagal Theory, is required for any kind of growth and expansion (Porges & Porges, 2023).

Polyvagal Theory explains the underlying foundation of neurobiology, using the lens of the nervous system (Porges, 2011). In supporting trauma recovery and healing, Polyvagal Theory is perhaps the most impactful information to have been applied to the field of trauma, as it explains the neurobiology of both trauma and resilience. It emphasizes the concept of our physiological state in our functioning (Porges, 2011). Our physiological state is our mode of being that reflects how safe or threatening our nervous system perceives the world to be; it is at the heart of trauma symptoms, leading clients to seek help.[1] Polyvagal Theory provides the schema for the change process of shifting physiological states.

Learning to apply Polyvagal Theory directly in trauma work will be the focus of this book. The goal of any kind of trauma treatment is to shift the physiology of symptoms and barriers to the neural platform that allows more access to resilience and/or the possibility of post-traumatic growth. This chapter will expand on these concepts, starting with an explanation of Polyvagal Theory.

POLYVAGAL THEORY

Polyvagal Theory (PVT) is a framework for understanding the nervous system's organization, which highlights safety as a primary foundation for health, growth, and restoration (Porges, 2011, 2022, 2024). To grasp this more fully, it is essential to understand the nervous system's role in determining one's physiological state, which then impacts behavioral and emotional states. These states are the influential and intervening variables in dictating whether there is access to the neural platform of safety (Porges, 2022) that can foster resilience and post-traumatic growth. Flexible nervous system responses exhibit resilience and contribute to post-traumatic growth. To gain a deeper understanding of attaining safety on the neurobiological level, it is necessary to explore the fundamental states of the nervous system.

Our autonomic nervous system (ANS) has three primary states: the ventral vagal complex (VVC-green zone) associated with *social engagement*, the sympathetic nervous system (SNS-yellow zone) responsible for *mobilization, which includes fight-or-flight,* and the dorsal vagal complex (DVC-red zone) which underlies immobilization, as part of *freeze* and *shutdown.*[2] Each of these states will be discussed in greater detail below. These states are influenced by a process of neuroception, which is the unconscious threat detection system in the body (Porges, 2011, 2024).

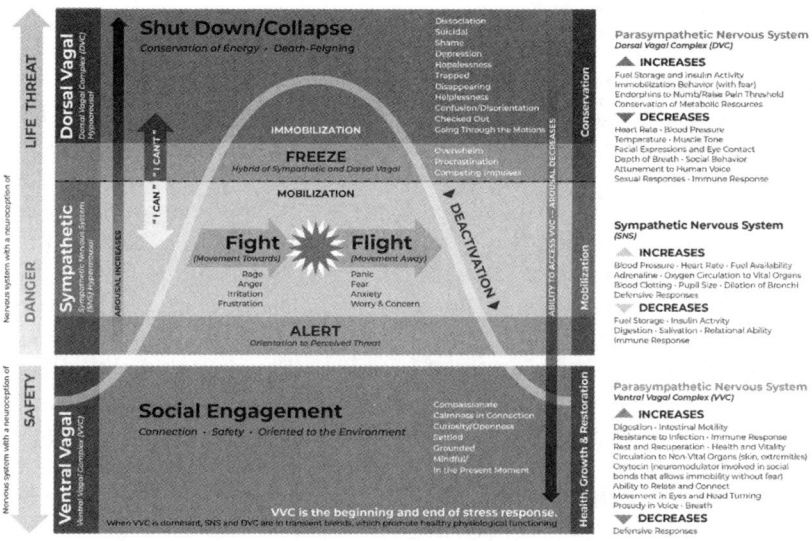

FIGURE 1.1:   Neuroception   Credit: Ruby Jo Walker with ideas from Cheryl Sanders, Peter Levine, Anthony "Twig" Wheeler, and Stephen Porges; graphic by Cindy Miller Atchison Design & Art

Neuroception is "a neural process, distinct from perception, capable of distinguishing environmental and visceral features that are safe, dangerous, or life-threatening" (Porges 2021, p. 82; see Figure 1.1). Neuroception is not cognitive and determines one's state without awareness that it is happening. It can be seen as the body's built-in radar system. As part of human survival, it shifts physiological states to respond to threats in the environment. Neuroception detects across three fields simultaneously: internal (through body sensations), external (signals from the environment), and relational (cues from social interactions).

With input from these three streams of information from neuroception, the physiological state is determined. Internal information is the signaling from inside the body, which includes rhythms of heartbeat and breath as well as organs, particularly digestion. If one's heartbeat starts to go faster, it can increase a sense of threat, particularly if it occurs unexpectedly. External information refers to the environment, which includes the current place one is in at the moment, as well as the other influences of the world. An example of the external stream is experiencing the neuroception of threat while walking to one's car at night in a dimly lit, unfamiliar parking lot; conversely, a neuroception of safety might be present in walking into a welcoming, sunny, warm office. The external environment will signal neuroception, leading to shifts in physiology. Relational information is the nervous system sensing what is occurring between people (Dana, 2021). Relational threat might occur in recognizing that someone is defensive or angry, eliciting a threat state; on the other hand, relational safety might occur when someone is authentic and present, leading to a state of safety. In this amazing radar system, neuroception occurs constantly, moment by moment, from all three streams of information.

All three neuroceptive streams work together, with one potentially becoming more prominent depending on the situation. When anticipating attending a new group activity, one might feel unease as a bodily sensation such as a clenched stomach or an increased heartbeat because neuroception detects danger. If, while attending this group, one is immediately greeted by a friend, this might signal a sense of safety, leading to easy breathing, along with softening in the face and eyes. In the above example of neuroception of threat while walking to one's car at night, neuroception of threat might shift to safety if one were walking with a group of friends in the same dimly lit, unfamiliar parking lot. Conversely, in the same welcoming, sunny, and warm office, if the receptionist is angry and impatient, the relational signal from the receptionist may create a sense of threat, even in an otherwise positive environment. These streams of neuroception continually occur below awareness; one might be just picking up on one of the signals: internal, external, or relational. The signals weave together and will determine our physiological state of safety, danger, or life threat. These physiological states will have corresponding and predictable behaviors and emotions that will be talked about more fully in this chapter; these states are the intervening variables in determining both behavior and emotions (Porges, 2022).

Neuroception is focused on survival. It has an evolutionary function to keep us prepared for the right kind of needed action, which might be *immobilization* (DVC-red zone), *mobilization* for action (SNS-yellow zone), or *social engagement* (VVC-green zone). Polyvagal Theory highlights an autonomic hierarchy based on the evolution of the mammalian nervous system we have today. The hierarchy refers to the way the nervous system evolved, originating with the dorsal vagal complex (red), then evolving to the sympathetic nervous system (yellow), and lastly, evolving to the ventral vagal complex (green). This hierarchy also refers to the way the nervous system is used. Humans first use the newest system, if possible, which is the VVC-green zone, then the SNS-yellow zone, and lastly, the DVC-red zone as described by the Jacksonian principle of dissolution (Porges, 2011). The three evolutionary circuits are the building blocks of the nervous system (Porges, 2011, 2024; see also Dana, 2021). With neuroception always actively working in the service of survival, our body gets neuroceptive signals which determine our physiological state along with what kind of action is needed to be safe. These states are automatic and connected to survival and occur without conscious decision making. If there is a neuroception of a life threat, shutting down (DVC-red zone) supports survival. Or, if neuroception detects danger, mobilizing by fighting or fleeing (SNS-yellow zone) can be a useful action. Lastly, if there is a neuroception of safety, we can be in connection using social engagement (VVC-green zone).

The vagus nerve is central to neuroception (see Figure 1.2). As a major conduit for bidirectional communication between the brain and body, it serves as the principal pathway for interoceptive signals, which is the sensory information from the body. This information is relayed from the body's internal organs to reach the brain, particularly areas involved in autonomic regulation and emotional processing (Porges, 2011, 2024). This bidirectional communication involves afferent fibers carrying information from the body to the brain and efferent fibers regulating autonomic functions such as heart rate, respiration, and digestion (Porges & Porges, 2023). The vagus nerve helps maintain homeostasis across major physiological systems via this dynamic feedback loop.

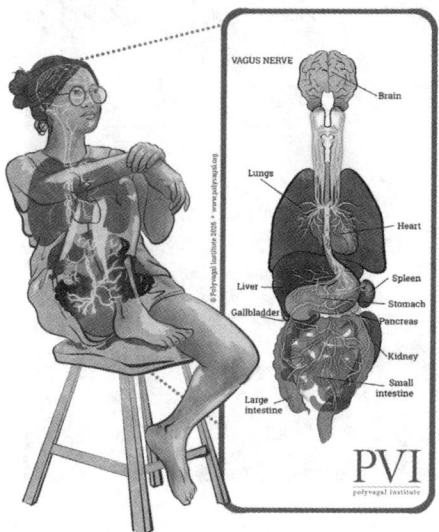

FIGURE 1.2:   Vagus Nerve   Credit: Illustration by Alexis Cruz Gómez, "Anatomy of the Vagus Nerve," Polyvagal Institute

Neuroception can be either accurate or faulty. Faulty neuroception occurs frequently after experiences of nervous system dysregulation such as childhood trauma, events, illnesses, or any experience that creates threat states. Accurate neuroception informs the ANS on how to respond with the best action for survival. When neuroception is faulty, clients then tend to oversee or undersee danger.[3] Overseeing danger is often part of SNS-yellow dominance, and in contrast, underseeing or misreading danger can be part of DVC-red zone dominance (see Figure 1.3 in the text and on the color insert).

> *Reflection:* Keep in mind that we all have some degree of faulty neuroception because of our negativity bias, which serves our drive for survival. Nervous sys-

tems often respond as if we are facing a saber-toothed tiger when we are cut off in traffic, ignored at a meeting, or feeling pressured to respond to emails. This is the normal human condition.

Because neuroception is an unconscious process, it is also important to note that we can impact it by bringing consciousness to it. When we learn to track our state, we can bring awareness that we are in threat and that we are experiencing *faulty neuroception*. Sometimes, that awareness can shift our state.

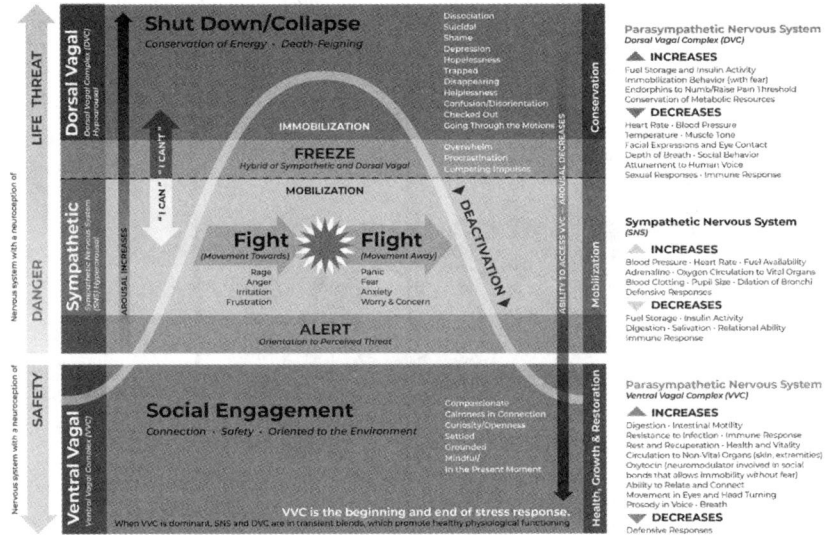

FIGURE 1.3:   Polyvagal Theory Chart of Trauma Response   Credit: Ruby Jo Walker adapted from Cheryl Sanders, with ideas from Peter Levine, Anthony "Twig" Wheeler, and Stephen Porges; graphic by Cindy Miller Atchison Design & Art

DORSAL VAGAL COMPLEX (RED ZONE PHYSIOLOGY): IMMOBILIZATION

In the hierarchy, the oldest circuit is the dorsal vagal complex (DVC-red zone). This is the neural platform that is elicited with the neuroception of life threat.[4] When this occurs, the nervous system moves to conservation physiology or immobility (DVC-red zone), which is supportive when faced with a life threat but not supportive of being able to take protective action or to be in connection (Porges, 2011, 2024; see Figure 1.4). In the animal world, this might be observed when a deer is being chased by a mountain lion and eventually falls to the ground, "playing dead." This term refers to the non-conscious, automatic nervous system reaction of shutdown for survival. In humans, it might be reflected by someone experiencing a significant traumatic event that leads to a shutdown, like fainting (Porges, 2011, 2024). According to Scaer (2005), this physiological state has many benefits, including the evolutionary function of being still; being still in the wild often leads predators to be less interested, promoting survival of the prey. Secondly, if the predator is seeking food for its young, it might leave the area to "gather its brood," giving the prey time to flee the area (Scaer, 2005, p. 44). Lastly, there is an analgesic effect associated with the DVC-state as it induces "the release of large amounts of brain endorphins, allowing injured prey to refrain from nursing its wound" (Scaer, 2005, p. 44). As prey can move on quickly, another attack can be thwarted. The numbing effect associated with the DVC-red zone is useful as it acts as a buffer against pain. This is a deeply embedded survival strategy in the nervous system that is necessary for life-threatening situations (Porges, 2011, 2024).

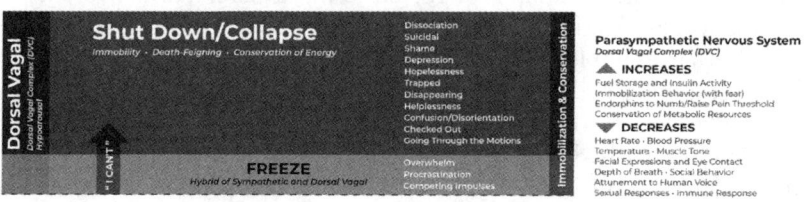

FIGURE 1.4:　Dorsal Vagal Complex　Credit: Ruby Jo Walker adapted from Cheryl Sanders, with ideas from Peter Levine, Anthony "Twig" Wheeler, and Stephen Porges; graphic by Cindy Miller Atchison Design & Art

In humans, the neural platform of the DVC-red zone state can lead to a variety of behaviors. They range from going through the motions, feeling less present, confusion, disorientation, disconnection, depression, and dissociation. Other indicators can be memory issues and difficulty interacting with others. In this state, the capacity to attune to the human voice is diminished, which contributes to the difficulty in relating to others. The DVC-red zone is inherently a low-energy state, leading one to feel lethargy or tiredness. Additionally, there can be a desire to disappear. Collapsing into submission or resignation can also be part of this presentation in severe or cumulative life threats. From a survival standpoint, the threat physiology of the DVC is highly useful, but it gets in the way of truly living.

In recent years, Porges has been delineating *freeze* (orange zone) from *shutdown* (red zone) as different physiological states (Porges & Porges, 2023). You will see that *freeze* is both part of the DVC-red zone, as well as the SNS-yellow zone. It is a transition from the SNS-yellow zone to the DVC-red zone and

I have named it an orange state. It is considered a hybrid state, and it often has markers of an SNS yellow-zone state (e.g., high blood pressure, quickened heartbeat, pupil dilation, and muscle tension) coupled with the immobility of the DVC-red zone.[5] At the base of freeze are competing impulses: "I want to take action" and "I can't take action." Indicators of a freeze-orange state can include overwhelm, procrastination, and lack of motivation as the physiology feels stuck.

Life threat detection can occur in response to threats that we may not consider to be traumatic events. In PVT, there is less emphasis on the events of trauma and more on neuroception and its impact on states. Having longer-term challenges or ones that are excessive and intense can also lead to the DVC-red zone being the dominant state; the accumulation sends the nervous system into higher levels of arousal. An example of this might be having childhood illnesses and/or invasive procedures that result in reduced peer interaction and missing school. This accumulation of experiences could lead to DVC-red zone dominance. Another example might be losing a parent, which often brings about many other kinds of losses; this also could result in DVC-red zone dominance. Other examples include having early medical issues, falls, or strong perinatal experiences. In these situations, there is little agency and resources are underdeveloped, which sets the stage for the nervous system to become sensitized to move to the DVC-red zone more easily. In summary, DVC-red zone dominance can result from any form of trauma that poses a real or perceived life threat, and/or any challenging experiences that are intense or prolonged.[6] Challenging experiences characterized by intensity or prolonged duration often lead to heightened levels of arousal, resulting in DVC-red zone dominance (hypoarousal) within the ANS.[7]

When clients get stuck in the DVC-red zone, they can tend to lead lives that feel low quality; they will not feel enlivened or present. It is common to report struggling to feel a connection with oneself and others. It is also harder to have hope, as the nervous system is in a state of "I can't," which leads to giving up; effort toward change can be even more difficult in this state. Resilience and post-traumatic growth are then hard to attain. Because the role of threat and its impact on agency is often not understood, clients can be very self-critical and judgmental about their inability to take action, rather than understanding that it is connected to their physiology.

It is also important to acknowledge that the DVC-red zone can be connected to emotional neglect. It is a life threat not to have emotional attunement as a child. Because we are wired for connection and to be responded to as part of caregiving, not receiving the necessary soothing and comforting from a caregiver creates a threat state. "It is through this ongoing interaction with the social engagement circuit that the neurophysiological 'platforms' are consolidated and strengthened, providing the foundational requirements for resilience and access to healthy regulation" (Kain & Terrell, 2018, p. 67). An underdeveloped sense of self is another outcome connected to DVC-red zone physiology, as awareness and connection to oneself are less clear. These other types of examples can be crucial for providing psychoeducation to clients, since they often lack the memory or understanding to recognize why they have a DVC-red zone dominant state. Providing psychoeducation can help prevent shame and encourage self-compassion and self-kindness.

As part of DVC-red zone physiology, neuroception is always occurring, but it can appear to be offline, as clients might not sense danger. You may recall clients who seem to get into dangerous situations without awareness. In this case, although neuroception is happening, it is inaccurate. This inaccuracy is based on either the signals being muted and not detectable as part of conscious awareness, or previous conditioning has made the cues of danger not recognizable. As an example, in abuse situations, there is often no action available to the client, which leads to less awareness of the cues of threat over time. This is both common and adaptive in clients with histories of abuse; paying attention to their neuroceptive signals during abuse was not useful to their well-being, as it could not lead to a protective action.

> *Practice Tip:* Many high-functioning clients will be operating in *functional shutdown* as part of the DVC-red zone. This describes clients who are still living their lives despite underlying DVC-red zone physiology, and their behavior often seems calm to others. Because of their strong capabilities, it is important to distinguish if a client is simply coping well or struggling with DVC-red zone dominance.

SYMPATHETIC NERVOUS SYSTEM (YELLOW ZONE PHYSIOLOGY): MOBILIZATION

The SNS-yellow zone of mobilization, with its well-known fight-or-flight circuit, is associated with the neuroception of danger. In this state, the physiology is in mobilization, primed and ready to take action to attain safety (Porges, 2011, 2024).[8] In the animal world, this state is demonstrated by fleeing from a predator as a first response in the nervous system or trying to fight if that is not an option. Different from DVC-red zone dominance, there is a sense of "I can" in the nervous system, but with limited options; the only options are fight or flight in this threat state (see Figure 1.5).

In humans, the SNS-yellow zone physiological states lead to emotions that go from *worry* all the way to *panic* (flight) or from *frustration* all the way to *rage* (fight). With the flight response, as activation in the nervous system increases, the state can move higher in intensity from worry and concern to anxiety, fear, and finally, panic, the highest level of flight activation. On the fight side of the SNS-yellow zone, as activation in the nervous system increases, it starts with frustration, moving up to irritation, anger, and then rage, the highest level of

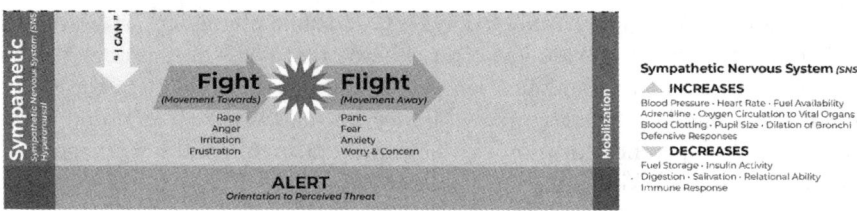

FIGURE 1.5:   Sympathetic Nervous System   Credit: Ruby Jo Walker adapted from Cheryl Sanders, with ideas from Dr. Peter Levine, Anthony "Twig" Wheeler, and Dr. Stephen Porges; graphic by Cindy Miller Atchison Design & Art

fight activation. Other indicators of SNS-yellow zone include being anxious or frustrated as a baseline state. The SNS-yellow zone is also the root of anxiety disorders and anger issues.

This SNS-yellow zone state is the basis for being reactive rather than responsive. This physiological state creates difficulty in accessing resilience and post-traumatic growth. Additionally, it can be hard to rest in this state as there is a bodily sensation of urgency. The need for action and movement can be in the foreground in this state, creating a lack of relaxation due to mobilization (Porges, 2011, 2014).

Relationships are also challenging in this state; relational capacity is diminished or limited when the neuroception of danger is present. In a very human way, when we struggle with stress or trauma, it is normal to want someone to be on our side. In the state of defense from the SNS-yellow zone, we often negatively misinterpret others' intentions and assume they are not supportive. It is challenging to connect with warmth and care when the physiology is mobilized. When our state is SNS-yellow zone dominant, the associated actions reflect our least skillful social self. The SNS-yellow zone is also evoked when we feel judged. Along those same lines, when we judge others, we also move into the SNS-yellow zone. We are so deeply wired for connection, that judgment becomes a threat to our social self.

> *Practice Tip*: It often helps clients to understand that their least skillful behaviors are connected to threat physiology. None of us are our best selves while in threat states. Teaching this to clients helps to soften their judgement and can bring in compassion for others as well as themselves.

Similar to how certain experiences can create DVC-red zone dominance, SNS-yellow zone dominance also occurs. Early experiences that result in the SNS being in a more fixed state can sensitize the nervous system to see danger in the absence of actual threats, reinforcing the physiology of the SNS-yellow zone. Examples of this include a wide range of behaviors such as feeling anxious in undeniably safe situations (flight response). It may also involve having phobias rooted in irrational fears and panicking as an exaggerated reaction (flight response). Instances of the fight response may include displaying overly angry reactions to situations or maintaining irritability as a baseline state. When this type of neuroceptive sensitization occurs, the nervous system defaults to SNS-yellow zone physiology and is predisposed to see danger whether it is present or not. This leads to exaggerated responses of the mobilization physiology, like being overly anxious when someone is late, or being irate about a traffic jam.

Additionally, it is critical to understand that systemic oppression can also contribute to the nervous system's activation of threat states; this activation is not an overreaction and is an example of accurate neuroception. Oppression is a very real threat to the nervous system. Additionally, clients' behaviors or fears can get misinterpreted as irrational, leading to further activation of threat states. It is crucial to validate clients' nervous system responses, because systemic oppression can operate in invisible or covert ways. In addition to validating, it is also important to explore clients' real lived experiences of marginalization through racism, sexism, classism, and ableism. For people in marginalized groups, a lack of safety is a real experience for their nervous system.

> *Reflection:* In this book, I am discussing the nervous system in threat states, as it is the foundation of trauma and nervous system dysregulation. There are also nonthreat states of DVC and SNS, including hybrid states that won't be discussed in detail. DVC in nonthreat includes intentional, comforting solitude, daydreaming, meditative states, and nonsleep rest. SNS in nonthreat states entails mobilized energy for activity, excitement, and purpose-driven motivation. Playing and dancing together are hybrid states of nonthreat states of VVC and SNS. As social behaviors, intimacy and breastfeeding are hybrid nonthreat states of VVC and DVC.

VENTRAL VAGAL COMPLEX (GREEN ZONE PHYSIOLOGY): SOCIAL ENGAGEMENT

The newest circuit in the hierarchy is the ventral vagal complex (VVC-green zone), and it is a specialized branch of the vagus nerve. It regulates the muscles of facial expression, vocalization, and middle ear function (Porges, 2011, 2024). These functions are foundational to a key component of Polyvagal Theory, the social engagement system, which supports calm states and interpersonal connection described as the green zone (Porges & Porges, 2023). When the VVC-green zone is active, individuals are capable of co-regulation, communication, and prosocial behavior (see Figure 1.6).

Polyvagal Theory posits that the VVC evolved as part of the mammalian nervous system. To care for offspring, mammals need to be in connection, which occurs through the social engagement system of the VVC-green zone.

This is very different from other species, whose survival is more about how fast they can run or swim, or if they can fight off a predator. Mammals are born dependent and require nurturing to survive, often forming strong bonds that involve mutual care and support (Porges, 2011, 2014). Humans require the longest caregiving period of all mammals, with babies only surviving if their needs are attended to by others for years. Beyond the needed closeness in breastfeeding, babies need connection and relationships to grow.

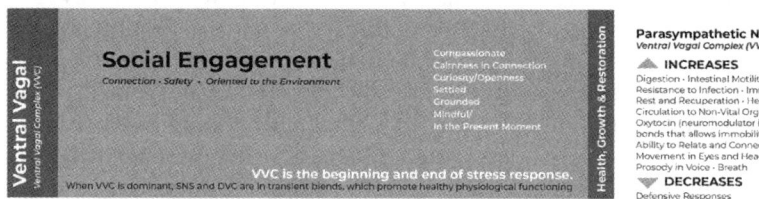

FIGURE 1.6:   Ventral Vagal Complex   Credit: Ruby Jo Walker adapted from Cheryl Sanders, with ideas from Dr. Peter Levine, Anthony "Twig" Wheeler, and Dr. Stephen Porges; graphic by Cindy Miller Atchison Design & Art

The VVC-green zone is part of our hunter-gatherer origins and is a necessary component of the prosociality needed to thrive in a community. VVC-green zone supports both connection and collaboration in communities. The communal focus on supporting others in society is ingrained in our survival. The benefit is a society that collaborates effectively for the greater good of the entire group. The VVC-green zone reflects a prosocial principle and often embodies the best aspects of humanity. Prosocial behavior is defined as "voluntary behavior intended to benefit another" (Eisenberg et al., 2006). This includes expressing kindness and compassion, as well as offering help to others, including practical ways that support accomplishing tasks. These prosocial behaviors contribute to creating a sense of safety in the community, which is an outcome of working together in a unified manner for the good of all.

Another prosocial aspect of the VVC-green zone is to offer co-regulation to another being. Co-regulation is the reciprocal sending and receiving of cues of safety, facilitating connection and regulation (Porges & Porges, 2023). Co-regulation is a crucial aspect of the VVC-green zone as it is how we establish a sense of safety in the world. When struggling, we are wired to reach out to another person. It is part of our humanness to be in connection when we struggle to get regulated; this process creates the foundation for future self-regulation. Co-regulation is challenged when we are stuck in the non-relational states of the DVC-red zone or SNS-yellow zone states, as we are unavailable (DVC-red zone) or defensive in connection (SNS-yellow zone). Both DVC-red zone and SNS-yellow zone dominance will make co-regulation more difficult as reciprocity is lessened. The concept of co-regulation will be examined in more detail in Chapter 5, as it is also a *deactivation pathway* for the autonomic nervous system.

VVC-green zone is the foundation of regulation. For those suffering from post-traumatic stress or other nervous system dysregulation issues, the VVC-green zone is not readily accessible, and there is limited fluidity between states. Fluidity is connected to the VVC's impact on regulating the heart rate using the vagal brake. The vagal brake is the VVC-green zone's influence on the sinoatrial node of the heart, slowing the heart down while in a safe state. The vagal brake is involved in every breath we take. Each inhalation requires sympathetic activation, which happens as the vagal brake is released, and the VVC-parasympathetic engages the vagal brake with each exhalation, supporting a feeling of ease when the brake is engaged. Being able to experience ease and safety is the foundation of well-being, as the body is rooted in "health, growth, and restoration" (Porges & Porges, 2023, p. 97).

Unlike the SNS-yellow zone, when "I can" only has limited options of fight or flight, in the VVC-green zone "I can" has options. "I can" with options is at the heart of agency; as part of green zone physiology, this is the foundation of empowerment. It is only when we have access to the VVC-green zone physiology that we can move to resilience and post-traumatic growth. In resilience, we can move between these states with fluidity in response to various external stimuli (Porges, 2024). This fluidity is reflected in the nervous system's ability to downregulate through deactivation to the VVC-green zone after the challenge moves the nervous system into a threat state. This downregulation from deactivation refers to the transition from the red or yellow zone to the green zone. The speed and manner in which this process occurs contribute to the adaptability and flexibility of the ANS and will be reflective of access to resilience. The faster the autonomic nervous system can return to the green zone after moving from the red or yellow zone, the more resilient it is.

> *Reflection*: It is important to note that we cannot always be in the green zone and it is actually not even the goal. The goal is to have access to the green zone and to have fluidity and movement between the nervous system states. It helps to know this for ourselves and for our clients.

Learning to identify which state is dominant, as well as applying deactivation pathways to access the VVC-green zone, is a cornerstone for effective treatment. The deactivation pathways will be covered more in subsequent chapters and they include the interventions that downregulate the nervous system. In therapy, clinicians are actively noting whether the client is in red, yellow, or green zones and noting the kinds of shifts occurring. The Polyvagal Theory Chart of Trauma Response (see Figure 1.3 in the text and on the color insert) lists general indicators that assist in knowing which nervous system state is most present. The clinician can get clarity by paying close attention to the identifying characteristics of red, yellow, or green states to determine the dominant state. In addition to the behavioral and emotional indicators, it is important to track the body. This includes tracking breath: Is it shallow and fast (SNS-yellow zone) or imperceptible (DVC-red zone)? Tracking eyes can include noticing if they are open wider (SNS-yellow zone), heavy looking (DVC-red zone), or gazing softly (VVC-green zone). Watching the face for indications of relaxation and availability for connection (VVC-green zone) can also determine state; the face can seem flatter in DVC-red zone dominance and tighter in SNS-yellow zone dominance. At all times, these states are tracked to determine both interventions and their effectiveness for polyvagal-informed therapy.

> *Reflection:* My passion for Polyvagal Theory (PVT) came directly from understanding that our human neurobiological responses of the nervous system had little to do with coping and strength; instead, they were connected to our threat system. It became clear immediately that PVT is at the heart of depathologizing responses. One way I find myself working with clinicians is to help them normalize their own experiences and feelings. This includes embracing whatever our dominant nervous system state is without judgment. Offering the concept that there is no good, bad, right, or wrong seems to soften their judgment of themselves, which is always the goal. The more lovingly we can hold ourselves, the more lovingly we can hold others in their therapeutic work. From our nervous system to our clients' nervous systems, clients will feel how we hold ourselves and this adds to their sense of safety.

ESSENCE

Because trauma and nervous system dysregulation can limit options, having options is a connection to one's true self, or *Essence,* whose home is in the VVC-green zone. Essence can be defined as the core self with agency. Essence represents a connection to the holistic blueprint of our being. Essence is our authentic self; we can access personal agency and be in the fullness of all of who we truly are and not in the limits of our dysregulation, co-regulation capacity, and/or limiting core beliefs. Being in Essence can range from simply being in touch with what brings aliveness and vitality to life to oneself; it can also include the sense of being our best selves, the most expanded version of who we can be. Both post-traumatic growth and resilience work are aimed toward reconnecting and restoring Essence.

Essence will manifest in clients as their genuine impulses toward wholehearted living. Vitality and a sense of aliveness are the primary indicators of one's Essence. Much of clinical treatment is trying to restore clients to this state, which lives in green zone physiology. Too often, clients have had their nervous system get stuck in yellow or red, and/or they might have had to adapt in a way that supported their early life experiences. Both yellow and red zone states will constrain the type of life a client may embody. As the objective in therapy is a more enriching and satisfying life, moving toward one's Essence is the path to resilience and potentially to post-traumatic growth.

> *Reflection:* Your Essence is already in you. A deeper connection to Essence arises from paying attention to what nourishes and fulfills you. This creates the path to restoring the impulses of your holistic blueprint.

REGULATION-DYSREGULATION AND AUTONOMIC FLEXIBILITY

A *regulated nervous system* is the bedrock of having access to resilience and post-traumatic growth (Porges, 2024). While in regulation, we have a range of responses and access to all three nervous system states. Access to and fluid shifts among all three autonomic states reflect autonomic flexibility, which is a hallmark of resilience and post-traumatic growth. Flexibility is key to resilience, and it is necessary to move back and forth between the different states (Porges & Porges, 2023). Vagal efficiency supports this process by enabling the nervous system to regulate quickly and appropriately in response to changing demands.

In regulation, our nervous system responds appropriately to what is needed, rather than being stuck from a past response that got us through a challenge or traumatic event. This stuckness is connected to being in fixed states of mobilization of the SNS-yellow zone or immobilization of the DVC-red zone.[9] The fixed states lead us to have an automated response instead of a fresh approach to a situation, to make a choice from a regulated state. The autonomic response is influenced by physiological cues rather than the actual context of the current situation. A response driven by conditioned physiology instead of the reality of a situation demonstrates stuckness, as it is based on neural wiring from past experiences. It encompasses both physiological activation and the imprint of past neural patterns, which is an autonomic stuckness. Being anxious or angry while waiting in a line is an overreaction if it is merely an inconvenience; there is no real threat present. This often occurs in fixed physiology as a reaction because of the sensitization in the nervous system to move easily to threat states.

Sensitization can come from either of the two main threat states, DVC-red zone or SNS-yellow zone. Due to this sensitization, DVC-red zone or SNS-yellow zone dominance becomes the primary nervous system response, leading to trauma symptoms. These trauma symptoms occur as a result of what Levine (1997) named "undischarged arousal." When either of these states is dominant, it is often the default state and becomes an automatic response, resulting in less choice. Instead of choosing a response, behaviors and emotions are determined by the influence of the physiological state of the SNS-yellow zone or the DVC-red zone. When the physiological states of SNS-yellow zone or DVC-red zone become automatic, we might tend to react with anger or anxiety (fight-or-flight or NS-yellow zone dominance), or be prone to being immobilized by freezing (orange zone dominance) or shutting down (DVC-red zone dominance). This makes accessing regulation difficult.

In dysregulation, the ANS has limited responses. It is not responding to the current situation but instead to the body cues from the physiology of the SNS-yellow zone or DVC-red zone. If a client is mobilized and stuck more in the flight response of the SNS-yellow zone, you might see the primary reaction in stress states as being anxious and avoidant. If they are mobilized and stuck more in a fight response, there is typically more anger and irritation. There is no autonomic flexibility if a client is responding from a stuck system, as it is more of an automatic reaction than a response. These survival-based reactions are not based in the present moment, as they come from fixed states in physiology. These fixed states of mobilization or immobilization with no autonomic flexibility are at the heart of dysregulation as they limit the physiological range of behavior. Fixed states are a key piece of trauma presentation; this again reflects the nervous system *activation* that is not moving into *deactivation*, which is the return to the baseline of the VVC-green zone. Effective trauma treatment needs to support nervous system deactivation that downregulates survival responses and restores access to the VVC-green zone. This shift helps release the system from the stuckness that underlies trauma symptoms.

The stuckness or fixed state in the ANS leads to having less access to one's true Essence, which is part of the VVC-green zone physiological state of safety. As noted, this sense of safety creates the platform for growth and expansion, a true connection with self and others, including a gateway to vitality and aliveness. Emotional and behavioral repertoires are limited when we are mired in a trauma state. Shifting the physiological fixed states of the nervous system is part of all effective trauma work, as it also shifts trauma symptoms. It is only when clients have some access to the VVC-green zone that they can move to resilience and post-traumatic growth. "While our resilience is innate, it is not fixed" (Porges & Porges, 2023, p. 97). This leads to the necessity of strengthening the VVC-green zone state for any kind of growth and expansion (Walker & Newcomer, 2025).

Strengthening the VVC-green zone does not guarantee that we will never experience dysregulation. It is normal to encounter dysregulation, and it can happen multiple times even within a single day. Rather than aiming to avoid dysregulation entirely, we need to establish a base in the green zone to maintain a connection to the VVC-green zone. Since experience is what alters the brain, developing templates for downregulation into the VVC-green zone is a vital component of trauma treatment and the genuine application of Polyvagal Theory in trauma therapy. In addition to being a treatment goal, oscillation from activation (SNS-yellow zone and DVC-red zone states) to deactivation (VVC-green zone) is part of regulation. Clients benefit greatly if downregulation of the nervous system occurs regularly in session work, supporting the overall physiology. Over time, this process of downregulation teaches the nervous system to have a new option of an access-point into the VVC-green zone, resulting in a doorway to resilience. The objective of treatment is for the nervous system to have a template to support deactivation from dysregulation into regulation (Walker & Newcomer, 2025).

The model of the window of tolerance describes the optimal state of the ANS as threading the center between hyperarousal (sympathetic nervous system—yellow zone) and hypoarousal (dorsal vagal complex—red zone) (Ogden et al., 2006; Siegel, 1999). This concept is often described as not having too much hyperarousal (SNS-yellow zone) or hypoarousal (DVC-red zone) present in the nervous system to keep the client between the two states. However, both the DVC-red zone and the SNS-yellow zone can be mediated to function optimally by having an entry into the VVC-green zone (Walker & Newcomer, 2025). Having some access to the VVC-green zone keeps the nervous system from going out of its threshold and allows effective management of the trauma state. With this knowledge, it is critical to strengthen pathways to the VVC-green zone. This will be the major focus of this book, because developing and/ or having more regular access to the VVC-green zone is the cornerstone of trauma work.

RESILIENCE

Resilience is defined as the capacity to withstand or to recover quickly from difficulties. It includes having the capacity to hold the challenging experience, while having some access to agency. Recovering quickly is connected to the nervous system's ability to move back into the green zone from dysregulation. It is important to note that resilience can be learned (Porges & Porges, 2023; Roberts et al., 2017; Walker & Newcomer, 2025). For trauma work, this is good news, as it means cultivating resilience can be a means of supporting clients through their trauma processes, leading to more capacity to hold the challenges in their lives. Strengthening capacity leads to more agency in skillfully handling our lives, which is another marker of resilience. Having resilience reinforces the sense of capability.

Inherent resilience is seen in many ways with clients. It can be a client who has a sick family member and still finds a way to do their job and handle their life effectively. It can also be seen in a client who loses their job and can keep a focus on managing their life as they look for a new job. Or maybe it is a client who is in a domestic violence situation and can attend to her children's needs, despite the stress and trauma around her. Examples of resilience are endless and are seen every day in the offices of clinicians working with clients experiencing trauma. Having access to resilience creates the capacity needed to continue living one's life with some effectiveness and ease.

Because not all clients may naturally possess resilience, focusing on developing it is important and will be further discussed in this book. As capacity is strengthened, so is resilience. Resilience and capacity are naturally connected. As stated earlier, resilience will always be a component of post-traumatic growth, although post-traumatic growth may not always be a part of resilience. What is most important is being in alignment with what might be possible for each client. Honoring each client's innate strengths and self-determination is key. This book will cover how to strengthen the capacity for resilience in clients.

POST-TRAUMATIC GROWTH

Trauma can be a portal into post-traumatic growth, particularly when it is used to expand beyond one's limitations and adaptations. Post-traumatic growth has been defined as "positive change that the individual experiences as a result of the struggle with a traumatic event" (Calhoun & Tedeschi, 1999). Certain qualities are often associated with these positive psychological changes (Brunet et al., 2010; Calhoun & Tedeschi, 2013; Taku et al., 2008; Tedeschi & Calhoun, 1996):

- Increased inner strength
- Increased sense of purpose and meaning
- More reliance on others and more intimacy in relationships
- A greater appreciation of life—more gratitude and more presence
- A stronger sense of spirituality
- Openness to new experiences—enhanced creativity
- A new narrative unfolds

Post-traumatic growth is not ignoring the pain and being optimistic in an unrealistic way. It is not trying to just be positive about a traumatic challenge. Instead, it is not allowing the trauma to define oneself (Schwartz, 2020). It is about examining the questions: "How can I grow through this?" and "How can I live life now with what has happened?" These questions shift the trauma and victim state to a potentially thriving state of post-traumatic growth. There is often a shift in identity as priorities and life focus become redefined. This identity shift often connects us to our Essence, noted above, with less of our limits of conditioning and nervous system dysregulation and with full access to vitality and aliveness.

The path to post-traumatic growth requires the courage to face the pain of whatever is occurring, as well as letting that pain truly be part of the experience. Being truly present with the loss and trauma can break a person's heart open to one's deepest self, bringing in the awareness of what is most important in life itself; it transforms one's sense of being and life path. This often leads to a shift in perspective, bringing new priorities and a renewed way of seeing life.

As current trauma often unearths past traumas, which carry old, limiting core beliefs, it can also lead to facing these long-held, painful beliefs. Limiting beliefs become more alive with the current trauma. An example might be someone who grew up with beliefs about inherent lovability or deservingness based on early abuse. After losing a spouse, in deep grief, an unhealed scar is opened up. As they grieve the loss, part of their pain becomes questioning: Did they ever deserve love? This hidden wound is now brought to light to be transformed. In post-traumatic growth, the old wound is given a chance to be transformed. The wound has always been there, and the person was living with it; in current time, it presents as an undeniable pain that needs to be faced. This is the opportunity and challenge of post-traumatic growth.

Post-traumatic growth does not need to be the goal of trauma treatment, yet it is critical to hold this possibility for each client without any preconceived limits on how clients can grow. If the neural platform of post-traumatic growth is created, personal expansion can be attained. Clinicians never really know how clients can change in their lives, so staying open to their potential for expansion is important.

There are so many ways that post-traumatic growth happens in clients. Examples of this include someone who grows up with abuse and goes on in life to help others by being in the field of human services, to make a difference for others. Or it might be someone who has an accident that limits their life physically, and they find a way that their physical limit does not define them by finding what else makes them feel whole. Or it might be someone who lost a child to addiction who then supports other parents who have struggled with the same kind of loss. Some people go through extreme situations and trauma and find a way to be authentically grateful for any goodness in life. They also find agency through meaning as part of their new path.

> *Reflection*: As humans, we seem to be deeply touched when witnessing post-traumatic growth in others. It inspires us and brings us into the VVC-green zone as we feel the shared humanity of pain and growth. As you experience this wonder with your clients, take time to feel the beauty of being part of another's journey to support your access to the VVC-green zone.

As noted earlier, post-traumatic growth seems to connect humans to move beyond their Essence, to their most evolved self, without the limits of dysregulation in the nervous system and limiting core beliefs. It has also been noted that this kind of expansion will not occur naturally for everyone; it also is not necessary for everyone. However, the conditions for post-traumatic growth can be created to support this expansion beyond trauma. The fundamental conditions for both resilience and post-traumatic growth are a regulated nervous system and the embodiment of positive states. These foundational elements become the primary focus in treatment and are the clinical applications that support trauma recovery for both resilience and post-traumatic growth.

Reflection: Most trauma clinicians have already developed post-traumatic growth. They had some experience that led them to say, "I want to help others, and I want to make a difference." Your awareness will make it easier to support the process in others. Take a moment for self-appreciation of your path to post-traumatic growth, owning that aspect of yourself.

SUMMARY

The development of resilience and post-traumatic growth is connected to the physiology of safety from the VVC-green zone. Threat physiology hinders access to the platform of the VVC-green zone; instead, either the SNS-yellow zone or the DVC-red zone becomes dominant. Understanding Polyvagal Theory is crucial in supporting the neural platform of health, growth, and restoration to attain this expansion. Although post-traumatic growth is not an option for everyone, anyone can develop resilience. Creating the conditions for both includes a regulated nervous system and the embodiment of positive states. There are several deactivation pathways that support this underlying process, which will be covered throughout this book.

VVC EXERCISE: ACCESSING THE GREEN ZONE

Let yourself put your hand on your heart as a way to bring a heart-centered connection to yourself. You might notice the up and down movement of your chest, recognizing how it is connected to yourself. As you feel this connection to your heart, bring awareness to one of your qualities that supports your ability to connect with others. This might be your compassion, your curiosity, your openness, or your ability to hold the pain of another. As you bring this to your awareness, let yourself say a phrase to yourself about this, "I am . . ." naming the quality that came up for you. Notice how it feels in your body as you acknowledge this aspect of yourself, possibly noticing more relaxation or warmth or another kind of pleasant sensation. Allow yourself to savor the positive sensations in your body, paying particular attention to how this feels good. Notice the changes that occur in your body.

This exercise can support access to the VVC-green zone and can be repeated to strengthen this state.

CHAPTER 2

Maps of Attunement and Deactivation Pathways

Attunement is in our nature. We are wired to read another nervous system.

The days of being a blank slate as a trauma clinician are long behind us. Thanks to Polyvagal Theory, we now understand that creating a sense of safety, the foundation of effective therapy, starts with being human first. It's not just about technique; it's about connection. When we lean into our humanness, we support the healing process in a deep way. This chapter will explore how attunement, a natural part of our mammalian wiring, along with key therapeutic approaches of applying deactivation pathways, can help regulate the nervous system and foster lasting change.

The first part of this chapter will discuss the attunement process, including identifying how to offer effective presence, moment-to-moment tracking, and utilizing perception to inform interventions, all leading to responses to support resilience and post-traumatic growth (Walker & Newcomer, 2025). All effective treatment requires attunement, as it provides the underpinnings of co-regulation (Siegel, 1999); it also downregulates the nervous system. Attunement creates resonance in order to find the most impactful intervention. This chapter will cover these concepts in depth.

The second part of this chapter will discuss deactivation pathways for downregulating the nervous system. (See Figure 2.3 in the text and on the color insert.) This is the foundation of PVT-informed clinical applications in trauma treatment. Deactivation pathways are the interventions that downregulate the nervous system from the DVC-red zone and SNS-yellow zone to the VVC-green zone, creating the neural platform to support post-traumatic growth, resilience, and the cultivation of enlivenment and vitality or Essence.[10]

Over time, applying deactivation pathways with clients can train the nervous system and promote flexibility.

ATTUNEMENT

Attunement is "the process of focused attention and clear perception," and it is the foundation of how we form relationships (Siegel, 2010b, p. 35). When we attune to others, we resonate with the internal and external experiences of others. This resonance is "a state of alignment" in which "two individuals experience a sense of joining" (Siegel & Hartzell, 2014, p. 61). It creates the sense of "feeling felt," which supports connection and the development of relationships (Siegel, 2010b, p. 55). Humans need attunement to feel safe and connected. It is the cornerstone of any effective trauma work. The attunement process informs positive parenting and relationships and is at the heart of the therapeutic process. Attunement includes four parts: *presence, tracking, perception,* and *response* (Blaustein, 2019; Hatcher, 2015; Walker & Newcomer, 2025).

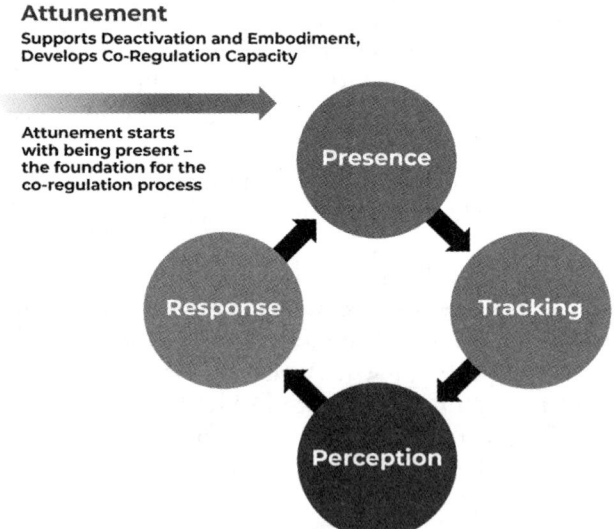

FIGURE 2.1: Attunement Chart   Credit: Ruby Jo Walker with concepts from Margaret Blaustein; graphic by Cindy Miller Atchison Design & Art

The four parts of attunement provide the road map for putting forth the type of interventions that will most effectively support the client in shifting their trauma symptoms. Attunement leads to clarity for accurate and potent responses to clients. When in attunement, clients have the experience of feeling safe, as well as feeling seen and met. Attunement itself is powerful and can serve as a reparative experience for clients. To be attuned to by another person is a healing experience and inherently settling to the nervous system. When clients feel seen, gotten, and heard, it can feel corrective to other experiences in their lives. It is a basic human need to feel a connection and resonance with another human, and attunement brings this to life. As Dan Siegel posted on Facebook:

> Presence, attunement, and resonance are the way we clinically create the essential condition of trust. As our patients feel this healing love without fear, as they come to the neuroceptive evaluation of safety, trust is created within their subjective experience. (Siegel, 2013)

Being in attunement through resonance is the VVC-green zone in action.

> *Reflection:* We all know attunement when we feel it. We feel seen, heard, and understood. Take a moment to look at a time this has happened. How does it feel in your body? How is this something you are offering others?

PRESENCE

A clinician's *presence* is the pillar of trauma treatment as it sends a signal of safety to the client, and it cannot be underestimated (Siegel, 2010b). Presence can be defined as being in a state of loving-kindness, holding the essential goodness of another while offering trust in their journey (Kurtz, 1990). It includes being embodied and having an intention to be there for the other person (Geller, 2018; Geller & Porges, 2014). True presence is the platform for effective work in any helping role, including parenting and clinical work. Sending the signal of safety through presence relays a message to the client that they are safe; this safety assists the client in being with their own experience and allows their organic unfolding (Kurtz, 1990). As the client feels supported in their process, they receive needed attention from another to explore challenges while also feeling connected and valued by another. With the role of mirror neurons and social brain networks, we are wired to perceive and sense, interpret, and resonate with one another. In addition to reflecting our highly relational wiring, mirror neurons point to how one's state can affect the state of another (Cozolino, 2006; Siegel, 2010b). With this in mind, being able to track one's state and keep it in awareness is important. It also requires that the clinician cultivate accessing their green zone physiology (VVC-green zone) as part of the therapeutic process. Offering a loving-kindness presence is inherently regulating for clinicians and feels wonderful, making it rewarding while creating reciprocity in the therapeutic relationship.

OFFERING PRESENCE EXERCISE

Let yourself start by grounding yourself by feeling whatever part of your body is easiest to feel in the moment. As you stay with that awareness, allow your attention to move into your heart, feeling your true heartfelt desire to help another person. Allow recognition that this desire to support another person's healing journey is part of your Essence. As you think of your client, begin to focus on your wish for them to have ease, as well as the true desire for the life they want. Notice how this feels now in your heart area as you hold this for your client. It might feel more warm, open, or softer and bring awareness to this shift as it happens. Let yourself also take in that this person, like you, has had quite a journey in life. Allow a true appreciation to surface inside you for how they needed to adapt to get through their struggles. Notice that sense of appreciation as sensations in your body. Bring into awareness that this person holds an essential goodness inside, and this might not be something they even know yet; you are holding this about them. Feel the appreciation of their essential goodness in your heart. Let yourself pay attention to how it feels to honor another person in this way. Notice how the sensations in your body feel now, paying attention to the shifts in your eyes and face, perhaps noticing a sense of more connection and ease. Allow yourself to savor the sweetness of this con- nection and ease between you and this client. As you move into closing, feel a sense of loving-kindness emanating from your heart, noticing the reciprocity of this experience.

Come back to this exercise as often as needed to guide yourself to be able to offer presence.

Barriers to Presence

Clinicians bring their human selves to their work, and that includes their nervous system and personal responses. These same issues that are a focus of clinical work can impact the clinician and cause dysregulation, leading to a lack of presence. Thus, not being able to remain present is common, and it is always the objective to return to being present. Because one's presence is always tracked, clinicians need to find a way to attend to their nervous system. This usually means knowing what the "felt sense" (Gendlin, 1996) of embod- ied presence feels like in the body as in the Offering Presence Exercise. That embodied knowledge of presence in the body helps us to know when it has gone offline. When in presence, clinicians might notice that their body is relaxed, and they might feel warmth with an ease of movement in their face, including a soft gaze. They find it easy to care for the client with a feeling of their heart being open.

When presence is less available, clinicians might note an increase in their heart rate, a feeling of anxiety or confusion, or a ruminating thought that competes with being present. Examples of thoughts they might have include: "I have no idea how to help right now," or "I don't feel I am skilled enough for this client." This presence struggle can also be demonstrated by emotions of judgment, anger, or anxiety (SNS-yellow zone), or feeling checked out (DVC-red zone). Knowing these body indicators of both having embodied presence and losing access to it is key to being able to hold it effectively. This awareness creates the map of how to work with cultivating a presence for your clients.

Barriers to presence are often based on countertransference, which is the range of emotional reactions and attitudes toward the client. These feelings often stem from personal history and experiences, both conscious and unconscious. They can be both positive and negative and can interfere with being present as the clinician is hijacked into their own experience, rather than staying in the current moment with the client. Additionally, the clinician's nervous system tendency toward SNS-yellow zone or DVC-red zone, their co-regulation capacity, and their limiting core beliefs can also limit presence. This will all be explored more fully in Chapter 15.

Besides the personal barriers that can occur, current challenges in life can lead to the clinician being dysregulated. Having the intention of offering a state of loving presence for clients requires the critical skill of always paying attention to your state. It helps to ask, "Am I in a green, yellow, or red state?" If green is not the predominant state, you can learn to work with your nervous system regulation to get back to the VVC-green zone. In addition to awareness, this takes time and, again, practice.

> *Reflection:* It might feel daunting to bring awareness to red and yellow zone
> physiology dominance in yourself, and you might even feel fearful of your abil-
> ity to shift your state enough to be present. It is important to remember that
> the VVC-green zone is your natural state; presence is already a part of you and
> your true Essence. Simply *wanting to be in service of your clients* is the necessary
> anchor to access your VVC-green zone. This ability for presence is in you now
> because of the career you picked as a helper. Presence simply requires that you
> keep attending to your offer of loving-kindness, benevolence, and service in your
> sessions. Remember that you can have red or yellow zone dominance in your
> ANS and still have the embedded sense of service to another human to connect
> to the VVC-green zone. Knowing this capability is an inherent part of your being
> is important to bring into awareness as you work on strengthening your skills in
> offering presence.

In addition to incorporating the meditation listed above, other things that can help include:

- Acknowledging to oneself the struggle to be present. This mindfulness practice of "name it to tame it" (Siegel, 2017) can be highly useful in shifting the state. Often, just the acknowledgment of what is happening can soften the experience. An example might be feeling sad, and just naming to oneself: "I feel sad," or "I am not feeling good about my interaction with my boss today," or "I am having a hard time being away from my new baby right now." This simple recognition of the challenge within oneself can be useful. It might not work for every person every time, but it does bring in congruency, nevertheless, and congruence itself can enhance presence.
- Offering oneself self-compassion around the dysregulation. This can also sometimes shift physiology, leading to access to the green zone of VVC. Self-compassion is often particularly important if a clinician is feeling that they made a mistake in the session. Because self-compassion includes how we hold ourselves, this can convey self-kindness to the client even when it is not spoken about directly. We often feel how others are holding themselves, making self-compassion a benefit to both the client and the clinician.
- Leaning into the general benevolence of wanting to offer help to another and/or to feel the essential goodness of your client. This can also be regulating to the clinician's nervous system. If the clinician is losing their way with presence, simply embodying the benevolence of truly wanting to help and/or appreciating the client's essential goodness is inherently a green zone self-intervention; it promotes connection.
- Using a mantra like "I am enough" or another needed statement that can come from triggers in session work. "Feeling enough" as connected to worth is a common theme for clinicians who place such value and importance on doing a good job. A simple mantra can be a way to embody the outdated belief that might be hijacking presence at the moment.
- Finally, doing daily doses of neural exercises that create regulation. These can also support clinicians, especially when applied regularly and not just when we are struggling with presence. This can include anything that helps support your nervous system into the VVC-green zone: breath work, humming, being outside in nature, physical activity, music, social engagement, meaningful conversations, and yoga. Because we are all different, it helps to know what is most effective to your access to green zone physiology.

Additionally, it is important to model to clients what we want from them, including acting in a way that demonstrates that mental health is as important as physical health. This could include an occasional cancellation of an appointment; this does not imply sharing the reason with the client, as it is more about attending to yourself. Even with personal work with your regulation, there may be times when being present is too much. Not pushing through and instead tak-ing care of yourself is important. The goal will generally be to find your base in green to be present for clients, while honoring your limits when it is necessary.

Occasionally, it can help to name to the client why being present is hard. Because authenticity is often settling to another nervous system, this can be useful for some clients. This is very dependent on the client relationship and the nature of what is happening with the clinician. Topics such as recovering from an injury, having a relative who is ill, or recently moving are generally less concerning to clients and may elicit a milder reaction, depending on the client. More personal issues often will be triggering to the client in some way, like going through a divorce or the death of a loved one. Care needs to be taken to make sure it is in the best interest of the client to share the information. With the right clients, it can often relieve them because they feel something is wrong, and not knowing what it is can be unsettling. The naming can help the nervous systems of both the clinician and the client.

> *Reflection:* In my journey, I sometimes let clients know my child was in the hos-pital, as it affected my schedule so frequently. There are clients with whom I did not bring it up because I had concerns that it would dysregulate them. For the clients with whom I did disclose, I know it helped me to be more present. It is important to use your clinical judgment. The good news is that if it does trigger the client in some way, you simply go back to the basics of attunement to support the client back into regulation with the necessary therapeutic interactions. When clients do get triggered, *it will still be about them*, and you will have gained some clinical information about the client and possibly your relationship. If you dis-close something and the client says they are worried about you, they can get the reparative experience of integrating that it is not their job to take care of you, and that you do not need for them to attend to you, or whatever pattern comes up that is part of the client's history.

Different strategies will assist in helping different clinicians at different times. It is important to make regulation practices a priority in trauma work as they lead to an ability to work more effectively and to be nourished by the work. It is essential for clinicians to regularly work toward their own regulation. This includes learning to attend to personal struggles and being dysregulated, and then, finding the capacity to restore a bridge to the green zone of the VVC. This can be developed and strengthened with practice. It requires having your foothold in two places, in both dysregulation and regulation. This is a very nec-essary job requirement.

This cultivation of presence remains the ongoing intention in every session. Offering presence means that the clinicians start in this state from the moment they meet the client. They might need to begin with checking in with them-selves before they even bring the client to their office or go online to meet with them. The signal of safety from the clinician is critical at the very first moment of contact for clinical work to be effective. It sets the stage for all the work because "safety is [the] treatment" (Porges quoted in Badenoch, 2018; I added "the").

> *Practice Tip:* Some clients might bring a challenge that makes the therapeutic relationship not feel like the right match. There is no need to push through to make something work if you believe you cannot fully be present. Honoring the impulse to refer the client to another clinician is also a connection to regulation in your nervous system. Many years ago, when my caseload was way too full, I was trying to determine which clients to refer and which ones to take on. A wise psychiatrist, Dr. Mark Fallon-Cyr, told me, "Just take on the clients you know you can love." That was very helpful to me. As I would listen to the client talk on the phone message, and I happened to have an opening, I would check in with my body. If I felt open and warm, I knew it was a right fit; if I felt any hesitation at all, including if I could love them, I referred them to another clinician. This was no reflection on the client and their actual lovability, as it was more of a way for me to learn which clients were the ones I could most easily offer presence.

One of the beauties of working with the offering of presence to clients is that it feels wonderful both ways, as it is part of our true nature and Essence. More positive news is that offering presence regulates us as well as the client. Presence means our nervous system is in the VVC-green zone, and the loveliest aspects of our humanness are available to our clients and ourselves. I often think the cultivation of presence is the best prevention of burnout, as we are nourished by the reciprocity of our work.

> *Reflection:* There is a myth out there that because we are clinicians, we never get dysregulated in sessions. The dysregulation is not the problem. Instead, the guiding principle is to learn to have a foothold in the green zone. This can be fostered over time, strengthening the capacity for presence.
>
> Can you lovingly consider that it is normal to lose a sense of presence? What are your indicators? What helps you find your way back to the green zone if you lose presence? Is there anything else you might want to try to support yourself?

TRACKING

The next part of the attunement process is *tracking*. Tracking includes paying attention to many things, including indicators of nervous system functioning, the ability to co-regulate, adaptive patterns stemming from earlier life indicating inaccurate and limiting core beliefs, and anything that reflects the therapeutic needs of the client. (Three Nervous System Maps for Treatment are covered later in this chapter and in Figure 2.2.)

In tracking nervous system states, clinicians note which threat state is most dominant. Observing body indicators of the client's posture, as well as how they move and talk, can help clarify this. If a client is in the SNS-yellow zone, there is more body movement in general, and clients can feel speedy. If the client is DVC-red zone dominant, they might have fewer body movements and talk more slowly. Emotionally, in the SNS-yellow zone, clients might exhibit anger or anxiety (mobilization with fight-or-flight), and their bodies might seem braced and tense. For DVC-red zone presentations, clients might appear to be low energy, flat, and/or depressed. They also might come across as confused and disconnected from themselves. Their bodies could be flaccid or still. All of this is relevant information to hold about the client's nervous system dominance or "their home away from home" (Dana, 2021, p. 70). Dana (2021) uses this phrase to acknowledge the adaptive survival state, as opposed to one's real home in the VVC.

As part of tracking the nervous system, it is also important to note what is happening in the face and body in general. This includes watching the breath, emotions, and facial expressions. In the SNS-yellow zone, there might be tension in the face, and the eyes might seem wider and narrowly focused. Breathing might be shallow and quick. These are all indicators of the SNS-yellow zone. In the DVC-red zone, the face might appear flat with little movement, and the eyes might have a heaviness to them with smaller pupils. Breath might be imperceptible or slow as part of DVC-red zone physiology. Paying attention to all of these indicators can help the clinician understand which state is dominant and how it may relate to the issue for which the client is seeking help.

If a client is expressing concerns about anxiety or depression, the clinician should be mindful that these symptoms are related to the client's physiological state. With more tracking and information, the clinician can incorporate this into their understanding of the client's overall condition to provide the best interventions as part of attunement. Attunement includes tracking as the means to perceiving what is happening in order to provide an effective response.

Because so much research points to the therapeutic relationship being the most fundamental factor in any kind of therapy, tracking aspects of the relationship is front-and-center in its importance. Attending to the safety of the relationship is a prominent step in the first phase of any trauma work. Part of tracking co-regulation capacity involves monitoring the therapeutic relationship and how the client is connected to the clinician. This includes observing the level of safety the client experiences during interactions, as well as how these interactions feel to the clinician. This kind of observational tracking may or may not be vocalized, but it is informative for the clinician. It includes monitoring how the relationship evolves over time as the therapeutic work progresses. Tracking can also include paying attention to the reported content that indicates how the client might be operating in their relationships around their needs, wants, and boundaries. This content gives the clinician information about how the client is experiencing themselves in relationships.

The clinician might be tracking that the client seems very distant and seems to withhold information when asked questions. They might use short answers and not respond to the positive support offered. Or they might seem to be non-responsive to the clinician. Contrarily, the client might seem very at ease with the clinician and forthcoming about their concerns. They might relax even more when they are offered a supportive comment or validation of their feelings. These observations are not judgments and are simply information about co-regulation capacity. When clients show availability for connection in the therapeutic relationship, their co-regulation capacity is more developed; these clients are less in threat state at that moment. On the other hand, if the clients are not accepting of these same offerings for connection, they are indicating they have less co-regulation capacity at that moment; they are more in a threat state. It is important to emphasize that tracking brings awareness of the impact of the physiological state and any changes that might be occurring. The client might demonstrate less co-regulation capacity in a particular session; the clinician might observe this by noticing the client feels more distant. This would indicate a state change that would need to be explored through the attunement process, checking further into what caused the change. This might mean exploring avenues with the client: Was there a rupture in the relationship between the client and clinician? Did something happen recently that affected the client moving into more yellow or red zones as indicated by avoidance, defensiveness, or shutdown? Likewise, the client might seem more available relationally. This could mean delving into what might be supporting more safety in the session. Is the client trusting more? Does the client have another life shift occurring that has stabilized their nervous system? These tracking indicators provide the information leading to the most effective therapeutic interventions for expanding co-regulation capacity.

The content of relational material is also tracked. The client might be reporting that they feel their needs are not met while also stating that they have a hard time asking for what they want. This kind of juxtaposition gives the clinician information that can lead to the perception of the needed response, that is, the intervention. The client might need to explore the barriers to asking for what they want. This exploration might include emotions about needs, connection to needs, and experiences with having needs met. Tracking the barrier of asking for what they want is key to being able to change the pattern. The client might state that they wish they had better boundaries while also saying how scared they are to name them. Once more, the relationship between these two disclosures emphasizes a direction for inquiry. What is the client afraid of? What experiences led to this fear? In this example, content is tracked as a step toward having the best understanding of how to support the client more effectively and to note any impediments that get in the way of the client having reciprocal relationships.

The clinician is also tracking any ties between the therapeutic goal the client states and how the client is presenting in the therapeutic relationship. Is the client saying that their relationships are not feeling very fulfilling, but they are not offering authenticity and vulnerability in the sessions? Or is the client saying they never feel safe, while they exhibit fear and anxiety when talking to the clinician? This kind of observation can be useful as the clinician begins to work with the client, targeting what is being presented in the therapy itself. The clinician could share the observation, "I know you want more fulfilling relationships, and I notice it is hard for you to be vulnerable here with me," while helping the client understand how those two things might relate. The clinician could reflect this by saying "I know you have talked about not feeling safe, and it looks like that is happening here now with us." Pointing out the correlation between what the client says they want and how they are interfacing with the clinician provides an opportunity to bring to life the tracked content. It is tracking the relational patterning that might be their therapeutic concern. This information can be very valuable because it is occurring in real time, providing the footing to work directly with the pattern.

Clients also present adaptations from childhood wounding that reflect the underlying limiting core beliefs; those beliefs often become the default way of being. This is explored more fully in Chapter 7, but briefly, clinicians notice what the client is telling them without words. Ron Kurtz emphasized tracking the storyteller, not the story (Kurtz, 1990). This begins with noting how the client interacts with the clinician. Do they look to the clinician for approval? Do they seem to feel they can't get help, or that the clinician won't be able to understand them? Maybe they try to take control of the therapy, making it hard for the clinician to intervene. They also might try to prove that they are a good client by trying to do what they think the clinician wants in the session. These behaviors are indicators of adaptations.[11] They point to beliefs the client is holding and will be part of the road map to support expansion in the client. When clients are in an adaptation, they are in a default way of being in the world. This default will get in the way of being in their true Essence and will show up in sessions. Tracking these adaptations begins to provide the clinician with a sense of a limiting core belief that might need an intervention to support expansion.

Using comprehensive tracking provides information about the client's state, their co-regulation capacity, their protective adaptations from limiting core beliefs, and their patterns. There is no judgment, as the focus is on utilizing the observations to provide attunement to the client. Tracking is information-gathering to support perception and response to ensure the client's wants and goals in therapy are being met. It will guide the clinician to their *perception* of needed interventions. *Tracking* and *perception* often oscillate back and forth as part of getting clarity for needed interventions that are part of the response. Tracking the various nuances across different realms will lead to increased attunement, supporting more effective interventions as part of the presence, tracking, perception, and response cycle.

> *Practice Tip:* When learning to track others on a nervous system level, it often helps to simply observe without an immediate goal of engaging with clients' nervous system states. As you practice, releasing this agenda can be beneficial as it frees you to track without pressure. Another option is to observe when you're in situations unrelated to clients such as at the grocery store, in a class, or in a waiting room. Tracking without the expectation of needing to work with the observations can strengthen this skill.

PERCEPTION

Perception uses the information from tracking to determine the best intervention to help the client. Perception identifies the map that might be most effective to support shifting the trauma presentation of the client into a new pattern; the three main maps are: *general nervous system functioning, co-regulation capacity,* and *limiting core beliefs* (see Figure 2.2 in the text and on the color insert). These three areas are often a primary focus in the aftermath of trauma and underlie why people come for therapy. We have discussed the map of body indicators of general nervous system functioning in the section on SNS-yellow zone and DVC-red zone nervous system states. These other two maps of co-regulation capacity and limiting core beliefs also have underlying nervous system activation that needs attention. *Perception* uses observations and clinical assessments to determine the most beneficial interventions. Co-regulation capacity will be discussed in Chapter 5, and limiting core beliefs will be discussed more in depth in Chapter 7. Here is an overview now of them both.

Co-regulation capacity can be seen as green, yellow, or red zone dominant. VVC-green zone dominance means there is reciprocity and ease in connection; in this state, one is available and open to connect. In the SNS-yellow zone dominance, the state of mobilization will limit connection as there is more defense, making any connection challenging. And in the DVC-red zone, it might even be hard to feel connection or to have relational availability (Porges & Porges, 2023). When the clinician is in the VVC-green zone, they can use their nervous system to identify how the relationship feels between the client and themselves.

The map of developmental wounding will be evidenced as the client both directly and indirectly points to their core beliefs (Kurtz, 1990). Indirect examples of this can be that the client might seem to do their therapy on their own and not let the clinician work with them, or the client might indicate that they cannot ask for help. Maybe they live life in a way that demonstrates

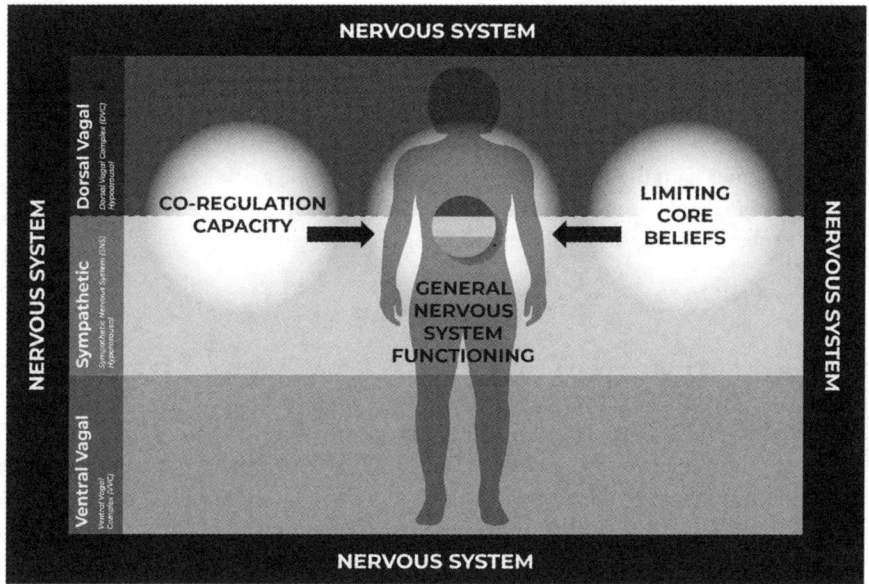

FIGURE 2.2:   Three Nervous System Maps for Treatment   Credit: Ruby Jo Walker; graphic by Cindy Miller Atchison Design & Art

that they do not feel freedom in their choices, or they withdraw from others because of a fear of belonging. Direct examples are when the client identifies what they want from therapy, like saying they feel unsupported and want more reciprocity in their relationships, or they might bring up feeling pressure to live a certain way, saying that they do not feel very satisfied. Both indirect and direct presentations offer the clinician the information to try an intervention to shift a limiting belief and its matching adaptation. *Perceiving* includes getting clear on how the client is adapting, what led to the adaptation, and deciding how to intervene. The clinician uses all the information that they have tracked to decide what would be most useful to the particular client. Again, tracking limiting beliefs from developmental wounding is discussed fully in depth in Chapter 7.

Perception uses the knowledge of the clinician to understand what is tracked (Blaustein, 2019). This knowledge includes educational learning as well as knowledge about who the client is and their goals for themselves. Additionally, our life experiences can also help with perception, as we use our humanness in relating to the client. We all know how it is to love and lose a loved one, to feel shame, to fail, and to grieve; countless life experiences inform us about life, including our journey with everyday struggles. These very human experiences can be allies in utilizing perception for the best intervention.

Practice Tip: Although our life experiences can help create a map of understanding a client's experiences, it is important not to project our experiences onto the client. Although a clinician might tap into their connection to loss in their own life as a client relays an experience of loss and grief, the clinician needs to be aware of the different ways clients grieve. This perception keeps the focus on the resonance with the client, which honors their unique journey. Again, the more the clinician has self-awareness and has worked with their own tendencies, the clearer the perception will be in working with the client.

RESPONSE

Response follows perception (Blaustein, 2019) and is defined as applying the intervention. After a response, it is necessary to track to see how the intervention impacts the client. Trauma interventions are the responses that shift the nervous system into downregulation; they attend to the issue the client brings to therapy. These skills will be covered in Section II: Downregulating the Nervous System Through Deactivation Pathways, as they describe avenues to shift the nervous system into the VVC-green zone. Each different pathway is based fully on client presentation and needs, using tracking and perception.

In the cycle of attunement, a response is mostly designed to bring in more regulation as a gateway to the VVC-green zone. Responses can vary as to what might be most useful based on what is tracked and perceived. The next chapters will discuss deactivation pathways for downregulation in detail. Deactivation pathways are some of the most effective passages to regulation, teaching the nervous system a new way of being. Providing deactivation in sessions creates a pattern of downregulation of the VVC-green zone. Accessing the VVC-green zone also supports clients, as it is inherently a state with clarity. With clarity, clients often find agency; simply put, in regulation, they know what they want to do and often do not need input.

Practice Tip: Responses are designed to be invitational, to get consent, and to support agency. With most interventions, I am checking in to see if the client is interested and/or the direction we are going feels right to them. I generally preface interventions (as responses) with, "I am interested in this, and I wonder if you are?" "I am getting a sense of . . . [an observation] and I wonder if this feels right to you?" "Is [this] okay to try now?" In addition to supporting cooperation, it is also empowering for the clients, which can cultivate more safety in the relationship as well as agency. Clarifying the direction of therapy with clients' interest invites them to check in with themselves, offering the added benefit of more self-awareness and self-attunement.

In the examples above as part of response, consider the client who is blocking the clinician's help by staying self-reliant in the session and not engaging with the clinician. The clinician could utilize a relational intervention to strengthen the relationship: "I really want to be there for you right now and support you." Conversely, the clinician might avoid this type of intervention as it might be too intimate for some clients' co-regulation capacity and history. In this case, the clinician could consider a general intervention that could be "I notice you seem to do the therapy on your own, and I wonder if that is a familiar pattern for you?" This intervention might be more useful for a client struggling with intimacy. Alternatively, the clinician might decide that stretching the client relationally would be optimal for their process and use the relational intervention. Either intervention could be useful and effective. The choice of intervention would be based on the *perception*, based on *tracking*. The intervention would be the *response*. Chapter 7, on offering reparative experiences, will provide a more in-depth exploration of interventions for developmental wounding as part of the response in the attunement cycle.

> *Practice Tip:* Responses are designed to be followed up with more tracking, continually asking, "How was this for you?" or "What is it like for me say this?" Consider bringing this question to each intervention. Being intentional about this process strengthens co-regulation. In real time, you will be sending the client the message that you are with them and you are getting the necessary feedback for more effectiveness, while also supporting the attunement. Even after all of these years in therapy, I am often surprised by what the client says when I do this kind of check in. It is particularly important to check-in with clients who have had to adapt by hiding their true feelings.

SUMMARY OF ATTUNEMENT CYCLE

This progression of attunement—presence, tracking, perception, and response—is both fundamental and familiar, as it is part of connected relationships. This begins with birth. The parent works toward being with the baby with presence, and when they hear the baby cry (tracking), they try to get a sense of the baby's need (perception). They want to meet the need, so they offer to feed the baby (response), and see that the baby is not hungry (tracking). They then pick up the baby (response), recognizing the baby simply wanted contact (perception and response).

The attunement cycle can occur very quickly. The clinician might track some dysregulation, perceive a need, and respond. The clinician might notice the client being hesitant to speak (tracking) and see that the client does not feel permission to bring in the concern about their marriage (perception). The response then is, "This is your session, and the focus gets to be on you. You have permission here to discuss whatever is important to you." If this were an attuned response, the client would show a visible relaxation, a deeper breath, or possibly an emotion (tracking)—some signal of moving toward green zone physiology, which addressed the client's concern (perception).

In the course of working with a client, the clinician might try several interventions based on tracking, perception, and response as they are moving toward the most effective intervention for the client. Just as with the baby, the goal is to find the response that is the most effective. In one session, this might occur many times, or it might occur only once. This process of attunement, with its back-and-forth process, becomes a way to get clear what the client needs and what is important for them. Attunement both supports the therapeutic work and builds more safety and connection in the relationship.

> *Reflection*: Ed Tronick, who created the Still-Face Experiment, together with colleague Andrew Gianino, calculated how often infants and caregivers are attuned to each other—and they found that it's surprisingly little. Even in healthy, securely attached relationships, caregivers and babies are in sync only 30% of the time. The other 70%, they're mismatched, out of synch, or making repairs and coming back together. (Divecha, 2020)

Let this information be a comfort to alleviate pressure to always be right; instead be willing to shift directions and/or offer repair. (We will talk more about repair in Chapter 7.)

Attunement Example 1

A new client comes into the office and is visibly nervous, with minimal eye contact or sense of connection, short sentences, and obvious body tension. Right away, the client states that a previous clinician never believed them when they described abuse in their relationship. The clinician attunes to the client first with presence; this is followed by tracking the client's content and anxious state. Using perception, the clinician wonders if the client feels this might happen again. With this in mind, the clinician says, "I am so sorry this happened to you. It sounds really horrible. It must have taken courage for you to come here today" (response). This response also underscores the client's resilience, which is integrating a positive state, a deactivation pathway that will be discussed later. By recognizing and remarking on the client's courage, a positive and resilient trait, the clinician is also building rapport, helping the client feel seen, and building trust.

Staying in presence, the clinician tracks the response for continued attunement. The clinician could notice the client relaxing (tracking); it seems the comment helped the client (perception). Checking this out, the clinician states, "I noticed you relaxed a little" (response), indicating resonance. The client nods and shows more eye contact (tracking). The clinician notes that safety is increasing (perception) and that the client can respond to the safety cues offered (perception). This interaction demonstrates both some relational capacity (tracking and perception) and an ability for the nervous system to settle easily, utilizing co-regulation (tracking, perception). The cycle of attunement continues: presence, followed by tracking, perception, and response. This can take some time over many sessions, or it might occur quickly within each session.

Attunement Example 2

A new client comes into the office holding a lot of eye contact, shaking the clinician's hand, smiling, and asking, "How are you today?" (tracking). Observing this relational and focused behavior toward the clinician (perception), the clinician also senses that there is a deeper pattern, and there might not be enough safety to talk about this yet (tracking, perception). Through attunement, there is a wondering about feeling a possible threat in the connection (tracking, perception). This threat, which seems under the surface (tracking) might be leading the client to focus outwardly (perception) as part of appeasement or fawning/placating. The clinician knows that focusing attention on another person could be a pattern in the client's relationships; it might also be happening in the current client-clinician relationship (perception). For this client, the clinician might hold back the interest in exploring this potential relational pattern until a later time, with continued tracking behaviors in session, as well as content that might relate to this pattern. Even without actively working on this issue, the clinician is in presence, tracking, perception, and response as part of the attunement cycle. This attunement includes what brought the client to treatment and what the client might be ready to examine more closely as safety in the therapeutic relationship develops over time.

Attunement Example 3

In a longer-term therapeutic connection, the clinician might notice that the client is quieter, seems more inward than usual, and looks expressionless. This is very different from other sessions (tracking). As the client speaks, they do not mention content that matches their body or facial expressions, offering only a general summary of their week (tracking). The clinician then recalls that in the last session there was challenging feedback offered about the client's relationship with their adult children. During that session, the clinician reflected that it was not their children's job to regulate them or meet their needs. Because having their needs met was what the client wanted, this was upsetting feedback; during the session, the client and clinician processed these feelings (tracking, perception, response). The processing included acknowledging to the client that this concept felt bad (tracking, perception); psychoeducation and empathy were offered regarding the client's concerns (response). When the session ended, the clinician assumed the relationship was intact and that the client understood and was accepting of the feedback, even if they did not like it (perception). As the clinician remembered this, they inquired if there was anything left over from the week before around the issue with the client's adult children (tracking, perception, response). The client then expressed feeling hurt and abandoned, stating that the clinician seemed to be siding with the children. The clinician offered validation to the client about their feelings, while talking with more sensitivity about the role of children with their parents. This interaction had been caused by misattunement, which led to a rupture in the relationship; this impacted the sense of safety, as the client felt judged (perception and response). From this interaction, safety was reestablished using attunement, presence, tracking, perception, and the response of repair.

This cycle of attunement happens regularly in healthy relationships and is part of the co-regulation process. Attunement regulates the person being tracked, perceived, and responded to, creating a sense of reciprocity; reciprocity leads to feeling rewarded in relationships. Attunement is the key to being able to support clients as it provides the road map to approach interventions. The interventions are the topic of the next section on deactivation pathways, which are the primary ways for downregulating the nervous system.

DEACTIVATION PATHWAYS FOR DOWNREGULATING THE NERVOUS SYSTEM

Deactivation pathways are the interventions that a clinician can use to shift the nervous system to VVC-green zone physiology (Walker & Newcomer, 2025). Deactivation refers to the process of downregulating the nervous system from the SNS-yellow zone and the DVC-red zone states of arousal.[12] Applying these techniques in sessions begins to teach the nervous system a new pattern, the neural pathway of not being entrenched in threat states of the SNS-yellow zone and the DVC-red zone (Walker & Newcomer, 2025). As mentioned earlier, deactivation in the ANS happens in two primary ways: embodiment of resilient states and applying deactivation pathways for downregulating the ANS. (See Deactivation Pathways, Figure 2.3 in the text and on the color insert.) Both of these are mechanisms that can shift the physiology and create access to the VVC-green zone, but they also prime the ANS to have a new pattern (Walker & Newcomer, 2025).

This movement to access the VVC-green zone state is profound for clients in trauma, as this pattern changes their relationship with life. As noted earlier, three main areas are targeted during treatment. The first area of *general nervous system functioning* is shifting the nervous system state from SNS-yellow zone or DVC-red zone dominance to having a pathway into the VVC-green zone. This VVC-green zone portal creates more immersion in life, leading to more ease (the SNS-yellow zone being less pronounced) and a sense of aliveness (as the DVC-red zone is less dominant). The second targeted area is co-regulation capacity. Supporting relational capacity changes the types of connection possible, as a co-regulation with another can become a safe haven, part of both resilience and post-traumatic growth. This will be explored more later in the book; this effect is life-changing for trauma clients, as relationships can be deeply impacted by trauma. The third area of focus for deactivation is working with *limiting core beliefs* from a nervous system lens. Core beliefs color our worldview and have a measurable effect on our lives. If we believe we "do not deserve to belong," we are "not lovable," or we "do not get to be authentic," it will limit the choices we give ourselves. These three major areas are critical to reshaping for more fullhearted and high-quality living.

As part of moving toward greater fulfillment in life, deactivation of the ANS restores healing impulses essential for regulation and growth. Physiological red (DVC) and yellow (SNS) threat states can block natural, life-enhancing impulses. When these threat states are fixed, they narrow one's life and restrict access to these healing options. Reestablishing these reorganizing impulses changes experiences, providing a sense of agency through newfound access to the VVC. As agency develops, patterns encouraging both regulation and expansion often emerge; strengthening resilience, they can be a gateway to post-traumatic growth. Restoration of healing impulses occurs as new impulses are recognized, which are *different* from the current pattern. New healing impulses usually feel inherently alive as they are integrated and embodied. This process is elaborated throughout this text as deactivation pathways are explored.

Weaving this concept into the *three maps of the nervous system,* in *general nervous system functioning,* restored thwarted impulses are often indicated by *actions* that can lead to regulation. To take regulating actions, one must be able to utilize general body cues (or interoceptive information). These cues signal the need to attend to oneself in a body-oriented way for more comfort, such as putting on a sweater when cold, resting, or taking a break when tired, as well as protective actions that re-engage fight/flight and/or the orientation responses. Emerging nervous system healing impulses can also include the development of boundaries and the expression of inhibited emotions. In *co-regulation capacity,* thwarted impulses are linked to inhibited *relational responses,* which in turn affect co-regulation capacity. When the thwarted impulses are restored, broader relational responses become available; this can include reaching out for comfort and/or connection through co-regulation, asking for one's needs to be met, experiencing reciprocity, and/or balancing autonomy versus connection in relationships. Underlying *limiting beliefs* are experiences of unmet needs, which lead to necessary adaptations to survive. Impulses associated with having these needs met become repressed. Restoring these thwarted impulses of repressed needs requires *awareness and attending to authentic needs,* often made evident and articulated through longings linked to the unmet need. As the need becomes integrated, healing impulses are restored to support choice and wholeness. Examples are countless, but can include the integration of feeling a sense of belonging, accessing needs for support, using one's voice or sense of personal power, and owning one's inherent worth and lovability.

Thwarted impulses emerge throughout the therapy process and are often underneath the client's presenting issue(s) and/or visible in the body. These impulses become more apparent and provide deeper levels of healing as the increased safety is established through access to the VVC. When these impulses emerge, they indicate the client is experiencing less inhibition from adaptations and fixed nervous system states. Instead, these healing impulses will provide the client with more agency and access to vitality and full-hearted living. As clients reclaim and embody these restored impulses, their lives change positively. There is access to actions to support general nervous system functioning, relational responses that strengthen co-regulation capacity, and awareness and attending to authentic needs, which can shift limiting beliefs; this results in nervous system regulation and connection to one's Essence.

> *Reflection*: The restoration of thwarted impulses is key in nervous system regulation work, as it improves access to the VVC. There are also broader ways of categorizing thwarted impulses, discussed in the chapters on *offering reparative experiences* and in *completing motor plans of protective actions*. This will be discussed later, but to summarize now, the client's longings will often identify the needed reparative experience; *longing* is the awareness of the thwarted impulse. Additionally, the client's body will demonstrate thwarted impulses of motor plans of protective actions; these will manifest in the body through movements of thwarted impulses; they are targeted directly as a deactivation pathway.

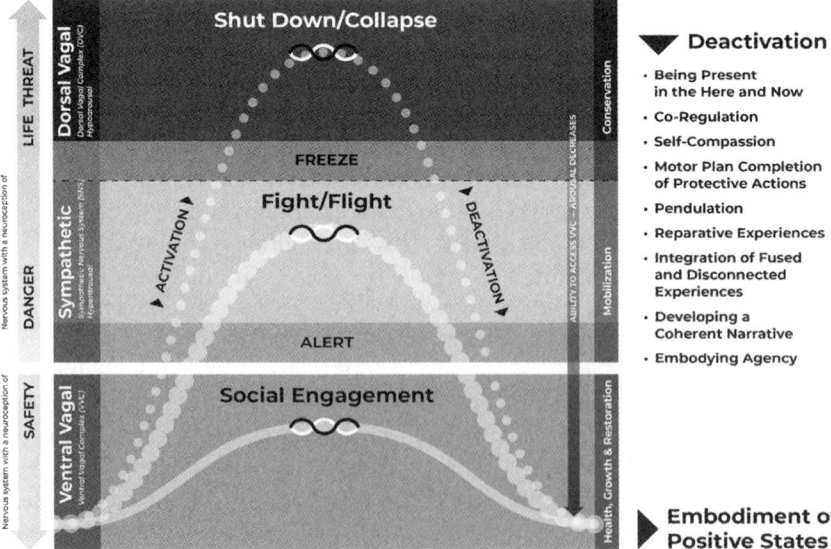

FIGURE 2.3:   Deactivation Pathways   Credit: Ruby Jo Walker with the general concept of activation and deactivation from Peter Levine and Somatic Experiencing®; graphic by Cindy Miller Atchison Design & Art

As these two deactivation pathways shift the nervous system to the VVC, they also bring about the identification of new thwarted impulses for even more growth and expansion. For the deactivation pathway of offering reparative experience, concepts discussed in the map of treatment for limiting beliefs often occur. For completing protective motor plans of action, concepts discussed in the map of treatment for general nervous system functioning often occur.

You might note that these deactivation pathways seem somewhat directive. This is purposeful, as nervous systems in dysregulated states often need an interruption to really change; otherwise, the client will stay in fixed states. The more dysregulated a nervous system is, the more it will need assistance with more targeted interventions for interventions in deactivation. What follows is an overview of each of these deactivation pathways; they will be filled out more clearly and expanded in the following chapters.

Deactivation Pathways

Embodiment of Positive States. The embodiment of any positive state starts steering the ANS to the VVC-green zone. Embodiment is having a "felt sense" of the experience (Gendlin, 1996). Different from an affirmation, embodiment brings the experience into the body. It refers to feeling the body from the inside out, rather than thinking about it. Because of the negativity bias, clients will often not notice what is neutral or going well when they are in a trauma state. Positive states tend to be bypassed, and clients will notice instead what is not going well. They might not integrate the aspects of trauma that are not traumatic, like the kind and attentive nurse who stayed with them during an accident or perhaps being supported after a domestic violence event occurred. Attending to what is going well or even just okay can change the nervous system state. This movement in attention can support priming the nervous system toward noticing things that are not about the trauma state. This can promote resilience and integration (Levine, 1997).

Being Present in the Here and Now. Being able to be in the present moment is a struggle often seen in trauma symptoms. Being present in the here and now includes orientation, which is being in the environment (Somatic Experiencing®, personal communication, 2009–2011), and interoception, which is connected to sensing and being in one's body. Both orientation and interoception are part of *being present in the here and now*. Trauma hijacks present-moment awareness and affects where attention is placed, making the skills of orientation and interoception critical. The ability to move toward being present in the here and now is the first step in trauma treatment.

Co-Regulation. Co-regulation is part of the social engagement system (VVC-green zone) and refers to the process of reciprocally sending cues of safety, resulting in regulation (Porges & Porges, 2023). Having co-regulation capacity is a hallmark of both resilience (Porges, 2011, 2024) and post-traumatic growth. This is offered as an intervention for deactivation in sessions and also to provide the experience to strengthen relational capacity in clients.

Self-Compassion. Self-compassion is linked to regulation and ease in the nervous system. Clients are often critical of their adaptations to survive trauma, leading to distortions and judgment. This self-criticalness makes trauma hard to accept and integrate. Many traumatic events and situations require applied self-compassion to have the experiences fully integrated, offering a route into the VVC green zone.

Motor Plan Completion of Protective Actions. Motor plan incompletion of protective actions is often at the heart of being stuck in dysregulation. They refer to the impulses for action that remain in the body when the needed protective action was not able to be completed (Somatic Experiencing®, personal communication, 2009–2011). They include survival responses of mobilization (fight-or-flight) and immobilization (freeze or shutdown). These survival responses in the body stay alive and are part of fixed nervous system states because they were not completed (Levine, 1997, 2010; Ogden et al., 2006). Completion of these motor plans of protective actions by the client through using movements can down-regulate the nervous system. Symptoms are often connected to these incomplete motor plans because the nervous system continues to send cues for the SNS-yellow zone or DVC-red zone, the basis of trauma symptoms. Leading the client to complete motor plans of protective action through movements deactivates the nervous system into the VVC-green zone, resulting in physiological completion (Levine, 1997, 2010; Ogden et al., 2006; Somatic Experiencing®, personal communication, 2009–2011).

Pendulation. In pendulation, the client oscillates between different sensations, feelings, images, and beliefs. This process often leads the challenging sensation, feeling, image, or belief to become metabolized, creating more ease in the body and leading to more regulation in the nervous system (Levine, 2010; Somatic Experiencing®, personal communication, 2009–2011).

Reparative Experiences. Reparative experiences are a necessary pathway to deactivate the nervous system after misattunements as well as significant traumas such as childhood abuse and developmental wounding. Reparative experiences can range from offering social engagement to simply offering of the client the experience of being witnessed or soothed by another, as well as support in changing limiting and inaccurate core beliefs. These offerings often include an embodied reeducational experience that provides the client with a new experience of themselves, relationships, and the world in a way that creates more options for getting their needs met (Kurtz, 1990), thus deactivating the nervous system.

Integration of Fused and Disconnected Experiences. In trauma memory, the channels of experience include affect, image/memory, meaning/beliefs, and somatic sensations (Kurtz, 1990; Levine, 2010). In the SNS-yellow zone, these aspects get fused together. A client might have a memory, a feeling of tightness in their chest, and a belief that "it is my fault." These aspects of trauma occur quickly and occur together as one unified experience. This fusion keeps the nervous system in activation. On the other side of things, in the DVC-red zone, experiences are not connected; a client may have a feeling with no memory or a feeling with no body sensation. This fusion in the SNS-yellow zone and the disconnection of the DVC-red zone keep the nervous system in deactivation as the trauma is not integrated (Siegel, 2010a). As experiences become linked and differentiated (Siegel, 2010a), deactivation can occur.

Developing a Coherent Narrative. The coherent narrative creates emotional regulation as the *story* is part of the person's history, leading to the ability to be more present. This includes having accurate beliefs and understanding of what has occurred. The coherent narrative is associated with being in the present moment and having one's story integrated, which are both hallmarks of regulation (Siegel, 2010a).

Embodying Agency. Embodied agency offers regulation and access to the VVC-green zone after a traumatic experience. It involves the shift from feeling victimized to feeling in control of one's life, and possibly even empowered in one's choices. Through purpose, embodied agency bridges being truly victimized to being a survivor, leading to being a thriver. When clients find a way to have their traumatic experience support a purpose through meaning, it regulates the nervous system. Restored agency promotes deactivation, strengthening the "I can" mindset and physiology.

Deactivation Pathways as Bottom-Up Work

In trauma treatment, both bottom-up work (which is somatic and body-oriented) and top-down work (which is cognitive) are utilized. Deactivation pathways are a highly effective application of bottom-up strategies when applying the PVT lens (Walker & Newcomer, 2025). Bottom-up interventions downregulate the nervous system threat states, shifting the clients' physiology (van der Kolk, 2014). When yellow and red states are changed through the bottom-up deactivation of the nervous system, clients have less need for top-down interventions

(Walker & Newcomer, 2025). Changes tend to be deeper when there is a shift to the neural platform of the VVC-green zone, which is at the core of Polyvagal Theory applied therapy. The deactivation of the ANS can create more ease in attaining regulation in general; this means less effort will be needed to move to regulation, as some access to the VVC-green zone is already present. VVC-green zone access through bottom-up changes tends to create the changes that clients are generally hoping for in treatment such as less anxiety, less depression, and fewer relational issues, because they change the physiological underpinnings that are part of the struggle. This book focuses on the application of these bottom-up polyvagal-informed strategies to support more resilience and post-traumatic growth in clients.

Although having a bottom-up shift in a nervous system will generally support therapeutic change with less need for top-down interventions, top-down interventions have their place in treatment. Common ways to apply top-down principles include downregulating threat states through addressing thoughts; this includes learning to think differently or shifting a narrative about a situation (Ord et al., 2020). It also might consist of using past experiences and knowledge to approach working with a problem. These top-down offerings can be very helpful interventions and are common in cognitive behavioral therapy (CBT). However, it is often easier to combat distorted thoughts if the nervous system has access to the green zone. CBT interventions tend to be most useful when applied to a more regulated nervous system through the application of bottom-up changes.

If a client gets sensitive feedback when they are in the yellow zone with their corresponding mobilization physiology, they might get defensive. The clinician could encourage working with this defensive state by inviting the client not to take it personally. This is a useful and reasonable top-down intervention and applies CBT to the situation. The client might apply that approach to the problem by using self-talk, saying, "This is not personal" when thinking of the feedback; however, this top-down technique of working with self-talk might not change their body state. The client might still feel defensive about the feedback. The mobilization state of the yellow zone will likely require more direct effort from the client as they continue to work with their thoughts. In this example, a bottom-up approach to shift mobilization would be the focus to reduce defensiveness so that not personalizing is easier.

In this same example, a bottom-up approach would use a deactivation pathway to shift the physiological state. When the client's body state is changed to the green zone of safety from an applied deactivation pathway, they might be able to be curious about the same feedback instead of defensive. In the green zone, being less defended physiologically, they can decide if it is something to examine or if it is better to let go and not personalize. They might even conclude that the situation really *is not* personal; this might occur more easily and naturally because of their sense of safety. This leads to less effort for the client as they do not need to keep working with their thoughts of trying not to personalize the situation to feel better. Additionally, the CBT lens can often be more readily applied in this state, and it can reinforce the desired way of thinking.

Another example of how bottom-up work can affect a presenting issue is having a client come into a session with anxiety about setting boundaries in a relationship. They could report sensations of a clenched stomach or increased heart rate, even considering the idea, reflecting an SNS-yellow zone dominant state. If the nervous system is downregulated to the VVC-green zone, this might seem like a challenge, but it could also feel doable; the activation in their nervous system will no longer be the same kind of barrier to taking action. This creates agency. If the client can have a toehold in the green zone, they can find that setting a boundary is not as daunting. Another intervention could be that the client would need to embody their rights such as expressing feelings, being authentic, setting boundaries, or taking care of themselves. This is different from top-down strategies that might use a CBT approach of telling themselves they "have a right to set the boundaries." The top-down strategy is still useful, but if the physiology is changed to a VVC-green zone, the symptoms might diminish enough that the embodiment of their rights is more available to them. The client can then consider their whole self in making decisions that keep them in regulation, including their rights. From this place, setting the boundary keeps regulation on board for the client. This results in a deeper sense of knowing and restoration to Essence.

Another example is a client presenting with overwhelm as part of freeze-orange zone or DVC-red zone physiology and stating that life is feeling "too much." If the ANS is targeted for downregulation to the VVC-green zone, the client will often still feel that they have a lot to do, but it could seem more doable to accomplish. In the VVC-green zone, clients have more access to agency, leading them to take needed action, rather than being frozen in taking needed steps. While a CBT approach might include breaking down the steps and cognitively restructuring what might be too much, changing the physiology is simply more efficient. Again, the top-down intervention of CBT is very useful, but in changing the physiological state, it is often not necessary to offer the top-down intervention to the client. Additionally, the client is connected more to their Essence, where there is true clarity of their capabilities, rather than being swept up in the power of freeze-orange zone or DVC-red zone physiology.

The gateway to the green zone changes the body's physiology, which in turn changes the symptoms and often the presenting issue as well. When it is rooted in the VVC-green zone, downregulation shifts the physiology to the agency of "I can" with choices and empowerment supporting the right and needed action. (This is different than SNS-yellow zone, as the "I can" in threat is only for mobilization of fight-or-flight.) Part of downregulation is restoring impulses that are about protecting oneself and being true to oneself. These clinical skills will be covered in depth throughout this book as pathways to downregulation are filled out.

Another benefit to moving clients into regulation is that they discover their own answers. Dysregulation creates internal confusion, but when access to regulation is available, the client knows what is best for themselves. This regulation, which includes access to the VVC-green zone, creates empowerment and choices from their true Essence, the authentic self, without conditioning and chronic dysregulation in the nervous system. Some of these choices come from having a regulated nervous system, which provides flexible access to all three states. The flexible access results in clearer thinking as well as access to one's internal resources and Essence. When clients are in the green zone, they have clarity about the issues they bring to therapy. They know what they need to do, how they feel, and what is important to them. They have less need to have the clinician even give feedback, as regulation leads to more self-knowledge.

In summary, top-down approaches tend to be more effective if there is some foundational access to the VVC-green zone. Just as the physiological state can limit the efficacy of top-down work, bottom-up work can facilitate more effectiveness. If the green zone is available to the client, openness and curiosity result in less effort to regulate; they won't have to do self-talk to shift their perspective. It is simply easier for clients as it is less work; access to the green zone supports them. This is the power of applying bottom-up techniques to assist clients. Changing the nervous system states through bottom-up work leads to the most direct access to a neural platform for change (Walker & Newcomer, 2025).

True Deactivation Versus
Faux Deactivation of the Nervous System

Faux deactivation strategies will interrupt bottom-up work and true deactivation.[13] They include behavioral and emotional adaptations designed to avoid feeling the physiological effects of threat states. Faux deactivation adaptations help manage the discomfort of the red and yellow zone states; you could view them as reactions to get relief from distress. They include adaptive behaviors that have a range of repercussions to clients, and can have both immediate and less immediate negative consequences. These adaptive behaviors might best be seen on a continuum since many start with less harmful immediate consequences but can have an escalating adverse effect over time. Most importantly, they are simply not effective in meeting deeper needs for connection and agency.

As an example, it is clear that overeating and substance abuse are commonly identified as harmful state management behaviors for coping with threat states. Because they are utilized to avoid feeling threat physiology, they lead to *faux deactivation* rather than true deactivation. Other adaptive strategies are more subtle and may or may not cross from less harmful to more harmful over time. Examples are exercise, drinking water to push down emotions, repeating the mantra "it does not matter" when feeling hurt, and possibly physically stretching or shifting breath to not feel the rising tension of an SNS-yellow zone threat state; these adaptations are a means to bypass feeling uncomfortable threat states. As my colleague Amber Redhouse says, "They are a solution, and they do not solve the problem" (personal communication). Although these solutions are both adaptive and useful at the moment to feel better, they do not create real physiological shifts to deactivate the nervous system. They are a temporary reprieve from the discomfort. As noted in Figure 2.4, the arrow for faux deactivation goes back down the same side as activation, because the sense of completion associated with deactivation does not occur.

Because these adaptations are not true deactivation, the nervous system remains stuck. To accomplish trying not to feel distress through these management behaviors, the adaptation will need to be repeated indefinitely since the state never truly changes through deactivation. This is faux deactivation versus true deactivation. Faux deactivation includes both adaptive management through behaviors as well as adaptive management of physiological responses.

It is very common for clients to use adaptive management through behaviors after developmental wounding. Behavioral/emotional faux deactivation adaptations are an attempt to avoid feeling the emotional pain of a difficult situation (Kurtz, 1990). (This will be covered more fully in Chapter 7.) One example might be the way a client adapts to not having childhood needs met. The client might deny their needs to protect their hurt and loss, or they might find a way to have others take care of their needs. Both of these adaptations assist the client with not feeling the pain of unmet needs. However, neither adaptation is the true deactivation that might shift the physiology and lead to not utilizing the adaptive behavior. True deactivation might include the client embodying that their needs were always okay and that the problem was with the caregiver, supporting the integration of accepting their needs. Alternatively, true deactivation might be learning to feel safe to reach out to others or possibly learning to lovingly accept and attend to their own needs.

The clinician will need to pay attention to this possibility for the most effective work with clients to ensure true deactivation. As opposed to the diagram of faux deactivation (see Figure 2.4), deactivation is a process that shifts physiology and is more lasting and stable. Since the goal is always true deactivation, it is crucial to recognize and pursue it.

As an example of faux deactivation through physiological management, a client with SNS-yellow zone dominance after childhood trauma might utilize breath work to shift their physiology to get through their day. When there is true deactivation to the VVC-green zone, breath work might be consciously used as support for a challenge, but it is not used regularly to cope throughout the day. In this example, the client must keep their effort and focus on their management strategy of ongoing breathwork. Because they are stuck in SNS-yellow zone physiology, they would have to repeat this regularly. Often, this kind of breathing pattern becomes habituated, and the client has no awareness of how they are managing their state. Over time, this practice could shift their root physiology somewhat, but it would not address the underlying issue that keeps their nervous system stuck. If the root issue gets addressed through the necessary deactivation pathway, the client will not have to actively manage their state.

In this same example, in developmental wounding, bottom-up work might assist the client in embodying "it is not my fault. I did not deserve this to happen." When this statement is integrated through embodiment, it can shift the physiology back to the VVC-green zone, as lack of integration of this belief is what kept the nervous system in activation. Through this embodiment (and embodiment is always bottom-up), the client might have solid access to the VVC-green zone throughout the day. Not being stuck in the yellow zone, they would no longer need to do constant breath work. Identifying the best deactivation pathway to truly shift the physiology is the bottom-up work that can change the neural platforms enough to eliminate the need for a management strategy. This is the power of bottom-up work. Utilizing these deactivation pathways is the focus of the next section of the book, so this will become clearer as you read on.

In identifying faux deactivation, the clinician is observing movements or processes that seem either forced or effortful. Aside from obvious examples like addiction, it can take time to see this kind of process occurring in the moment; it also takes observing true deactivation to see the difference. Clinicians will often have a sense that something is not quite right, that something is missing, or that something is below the surface. When this occurs, it is important to trust your gut and get curious. This approach often begins to bring clarity, even if it takes several sessions to achieve. As part of attunement, this sense gets refined over time.

> *Reflection:* My most skilled clients use faux deactivation, as it does support regulation. Even with all of their skills, it is often occurring without their conscious awareness. It is important to see that this ability is part of their resilience; they will access even more of their natural resilience if they are not working so hard, as their effort is a marker of faux deactivation behaviors. As you work more closely with deactivation shifts in physiology, clients can have more ease and true regulation.

Countless other adaptation strategies are utilized to support adverse childhood experiences. Although adaptive, they do interfere with true nervous system deactivation. *What gets one through a struggle will almost always get in the way at some point.* Painful emotions are generally unavailable or frozen (Carter, 2011) in faux deactivation. Dealing directly with the underlying issue that drives an adaptive management strategy leads to more connection to accessing the VVC-green zone, the platform to Essence. The clinician will need to pay

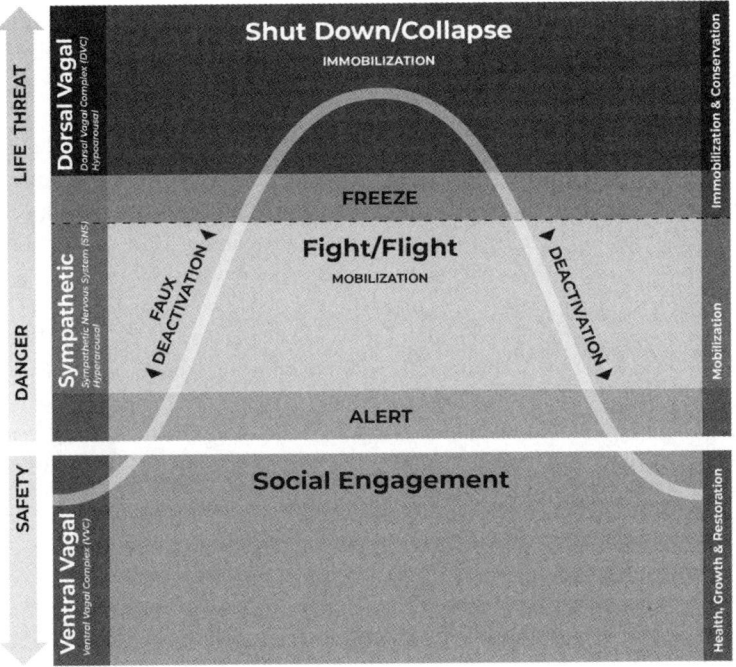

FIGURE 2.4:   Faux Deactivation   Credit: Ruby Jo Walker inspired by the "faux window of tolerance" developed by Kathy Kain and Stephen Terrell; graphic by Cindy Miller Atchison Design & Art

attention to indicators of faux deactivation and adaptation strategies for the most effective work with clients.

SUMMARY

Applying interventions to utilize deactivation pathways is key to shifting the physiology of trauma and will lead to supporting clients more effectively. Clinicians need to seek the pathway that addresses the symptoms as presented by the client, along with their requests for help. Some clients will need several deactivation pathways to achieve regulation in the nervous system, and some clients will need only one. Attunement skills are necessary for the clinician to identify which interventions will be most effective. The clinician also needs to recognize faux deactivation to ensure true deactivation is occurring instead of only temporary relief.

By using the attunement of presence, tracking, perception, and response, the clinician gets clarity about what may be most helpful for the client to shift. This process is the basis of clinical judgment. Through attunement, the clinician identifies the pathway(s) that could be most beneficial. Each of the pathways offers a different angle to work with the nervous system. This process underlines the individuality of each client's needs. These pathways will be explored and filled out in the following chapters.

> *Reflection*: Clinicians often feel they *have to know* what is going on to help the client. This loving wish comes from truly wanting to be of service. It is tricky, as it is the job of the clinician to help, yet it also puts pressure on the clinician. One of my great teachers, Phil Del Prince, once told me, "The only option is to not know." That both scared and relieved me, but it was mostly scary for a while. I kept a note on my desk next to my chair with those words for about 2 years. I also practiced saying "I don't know" at least once per session for a long time to help my body get more comfortable with not knowing. Today, not knowing is lovely, as I trust the process and love finding my way with the client. But it was not where I started. Remember that clients feel our intention for them. You truly do not have to know, and you get to experiment. Knowing will occur over time when it is necessary as you are with your client.

DOWNREGULATING THE NERVOUS SYSTEM THROUGH DEACTIVATION PATHWAYS

CHAPTER 3

Embodiment of Positive States

Trauma is unintegrated resources.

—Steve Hoskinson, Somatic Experiencing®

For a long time, the trauma field mainly focused on the event itself, without fully understanding how it impacts the physiology in the body. The emphasis was often on everything that went wrong rather than on how to support the nervous system in finding balance. As a result, meaningful change in clients' symptoms was hard to come by in therapy. Fortunately, this has been evolving, bringing new hope for helping clients experience more ease and vitality, which are key signs of a well-regulated nervous system. In this chapter, we'll explore a fresh and unique approach to supporting clients on their healing journey.

When trauma occurs, there are various responses. Clients can return to their baseline again, equipped with the same capacity. They can also get stuck in a trauma state (with symptoms of SNS and/or DVC), having minimal access to their previous life before a traumatic event or natural inner resources. As discussed earlier, clients can also become more resilient and transform into an expanded capacity of post-traumatic growth. This chapter is focused on supporting the substructure of the VVC through the embodiment of positive states for the attainment of resilience and potential post-traumatic growth. Embodiment of positive states is a primary deactivation pathway for downregulating the nervous system (Walker & Newcomer, 2025). The process of the embodiment of positive states establishes the groundwork to shift the nervous system as it strengthens the resiliency vortex. Through strengthening the resiliency vortex, there is a shift in the threshold of a person's capacity to hold challenging experiences. When the resiliency vortex is strengthened, the trauma is still present, but the increased capacity makes it easier to hold the experience. Over time, as capacity is increased and deactivation occurs, the trauma becomes integrated and part of the client's narrative. Embodying positive states provides a direct experience of the VVC (Walker & Newcomer, 2025). This experience of the VVC changes the physiology of the nervous system and supports more overall fluidity in the ANS (Porges, 2022; see also Dana, 2018; Walker & Newcomer, 2025). We will now explore a deeper understanding of this important deactivation pathway.

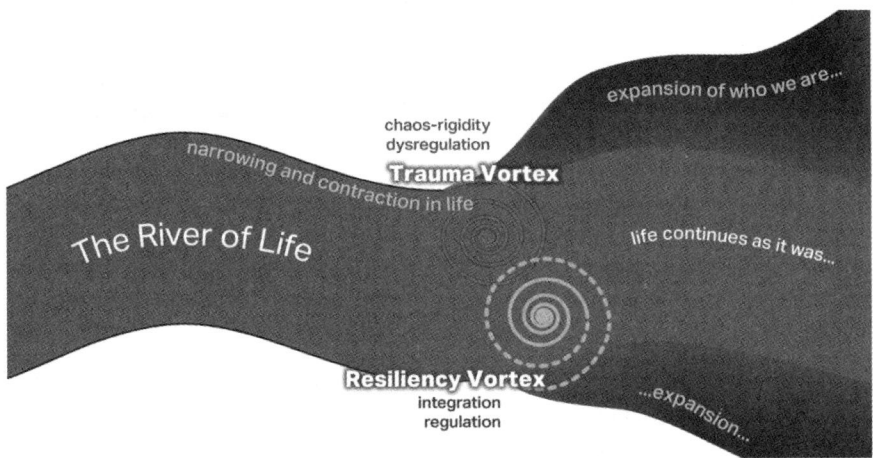

FIGURE 3.1:   Post-Traumatic Growth Chart   Credit: Ruby Jo Walker with concepts from. Peter Levine, Somatic Experiencing®, and Stephen Porges; graphic by Cindy Miller Atchison Design & Art

THE TRAUMA VORTEX AND THE RIVER OF INTEGRATION

The *embodiment of positive states* rarely occurs naturally in trauma. Traumatic events and corresponding nervous system states of SNS and DVC have compelling physiology. They do not just limit expansion and growth; they also limit where attention can be placed. Peter Levine's work on the trauma vortex (1997) and Dan Siegel's work on chaos, rigidity, and integration (2010a) offer a framework for understanding the process of how clients get stuck in these states. We will be combining these two frameworks as a lens to understand how to support the nervous system more fully to access the VVC and support changing the fixed states of stuckness to support integration, the goal of trauma treatment. Both models from Levine and Siegel highlight the concept that the lack of integration is central to trauma symptoms. Trauma is considered integrated when the story becomes part of one's narrative; this includes being able to move beyond what has happened and to live in the present moment. In integration, different aspects of the trauma, including memory, body, emotions, and self-understanding are working together with enough harmony that one can feel regulated and present. In a training session decades ago, Yvonne Dolan described integration as she stated that the goal of treatment was to have the traumatic experience of gently walking by one's side without tripping on it or nipping at one's heels. This metaphor defines the goal of integration.

When trauma occurs, a *trauma vortex* is formed according to Levine (1997). The vortex includes the same repetitive experiences; these experiences are familiar and consist of recurrent nervous system states, body sensations, emotions, relational patterns, and/or core beliefs. Some of these experiences are the direct result of the traumatic situation (and the corresponding activation of the nervous system states of SNS and DVC), and some are more connected to the *trauma identity* (Cheryl Fidelman, Conscious Co-Dependence™ Conference, August, 2019) adaptations needed for surviving trauma. These experiences feel like "the same old, same old," as they do not change for the client. All of these elements of the trauma response are part of the trauma vortex. This vortex describes the nucleus of trauma work as it brings clients to therapy for the relief of these struggles held in the vortex. Clients come to treatment for help with symptoms of their nervous system states such as anxiety, anger, and depression. They also want help with the repercussions of trauma, as their life and relational patterns are often not giving them fulfillment. All of these issues are part of the trauma vortex (Levine, 1997) in which the client is stuck. Levine also underlines that in addition to the trauma vortex, a counter-vortex will also be formed, the healing vortex (Levine, 1997). In the Post-Traumatic Growth Chart (Figure 3.1), this is identified as the resilience vortex, which develops as positive states are embodied. In trauma work, this resilience vortex is not integrated into one's experience without intentionality and interventions, as it is usually not even in awareness.

Similarly, Siegel's "river of integration" (2010a) outlines that a system moving toward complexity is the cornerstone of well-being; chaos and/or rigidity are understood as the two banks of the river, which act as impairments to well-being that keep trauma states stuck. In simplifying these concepts, Siegel (2010a) describes chaos as "being out of control" and rigidity as "needing to control." The river of integration is where things flow, and ease and well-being are present. Chaos and rigidity are "the antithesis of the harmony of a more integrated flow" (Siegel, 2010a, p. 67), highlighting the representation of trauma states and stuckness, which is how clients often experience the aftermath of trauma. Integration is identified as the "principle underlying health at all levels of experience" (Siegel, 2010a, p. 68). In integration, experiences are part of one's life, supporting underlying health with flow and without the chaos and rigidity of stuckness. Moving more to complexity is at the crux of resilience and post-traumatic growth, as "a system that moves toward complexity is the most stable and adaptive . . . a clear definition of well-being" (Siegel, 2010a, p. 69). Well-being is the bedrock of the VVC and at the heart of growth or expansion in therapy.

These two frames of reference from Levine and Siegel are combined in Figure 3.1. The trauma state is identified as being both a vortex and having characteristics of chaos and rigidity. Siegel's chaos and rigidity and Levine's trauma vortex share a similar nervous system state dominance of SNS and/ or DVC, with minimal access to the VVC. In delving more deeply with this lens it is clear that the trauma vortex and chaos and rigidity are linked. Both models are focused on describing a type of stuckness. With Levine's model (1997), stuckness is the "eddy" of the trauma vortex, and in Siegel's model (2010a), the stuckness is the lack of integration stemming from the chaos and rigidity. Both are fitting metaphors for understanding how the nervous system remains anchored in trauma states, as trauma experiences become entrenched. The eddy with its chaos and rigidity hijacks one's focus, leaving out the bigger picture of life and limiting one's experiences; this keeps one out of the flow of life. Unlike other nontraumatic experiences, trauma-related experiences tend to either remain at the forefront of awareness in daily life or feel completely out of reach, as they do not seamlessly integrate into one's overall life narrative.

The lack of integration impacts general nervous system states as well as core beliefs and relational patterns. For the ANS, its responsibility is survival through safety; if safety is integrated, it can be responsive in the moment. If safety is not integrated, it remains in fixed states of SNS and DVC. As clients integrate safe experiences through embodiment, they have more access to the VVC. Likewise, a lack of integration is central to the effects of developmental wounding; when childhood experiences are suboptimal, they lead to limited core beliefs because necessary needs are not integrated. If feeling valued is not integrated as a result of childhood experiences, a client might adapt by trying to be successful and trying to prove themselves. If the client were to use embodiment to integrate a sense of feeling valued, there is no need for the adaptation of making efforts to constantly prove themself. The normal developmental need to feel a sense of worthiness and value is then integrated. In these instances, integration shifts the trauma vortex and alters the experience of chaos and rigidity. The client is no longer in the trauma vortex, which holds feelings and experiences of not feeling valued; instead, a sense of being valued shifts the chaos and rigidity associated with this adaptation as it becomes integrated into the resiliency vortex. The client isn't feeling out of control or the need to control. The lack of integration is the underpinning of trauma states; integrating both embodied safety and positive states will shift physiology to the VVC. Similarly, in relational patterning, as co-regulation is available and becomes embodied, it leads to more integration.

If you reflect on yourself or others for a moment, you can see that most people have the same patterns occurring as part of how they struggle. Their patterns may encompass various body sensations, emotions, and a core belief. All three experiences could be present, or only one or two might be part of an embodied pattern. Examples might be having a clenched stomach while feeling sad and alone, or perhaps it might be feeling mobilization in the body with tightened muscles coupled with feeling a fear of abandonment. Another example might be feeling anxiety with tension in the chest while having the thought of not belonging. Additionally, there could be bracing in the body while having self-critical thoughts. There are countless patterns, and they all lead to being in a trauma vortex. The patterns tend to be automatic; they keep the stuckness alive and are very familiar to the client.

THE NEGATIVITY BIAS

When in the trauma vortex, there are constrictions and limits in experience, and neutral or positive experiences are often unintegrated. These unintegrated experiences are often parts of the situation that would create some access to the VVC if they were integrated; they are the experiences that might feel good, as well as the neutral experiences that are not part of the trauma. The lack of integration can be attributed in part to the negativity bias. The negativity bias is designed for survival and is focused on what is wrong for the assurance of safety; instead, it reinforces the trauma state, keeping it more alive. Other aspects of the negativity bias are over-focusing on the negative, remembering the negative more, and not seeing the bigger picture of what else might be happening (Vaish et al., 2008).

With the power and influence of the negativity bias, it is important to focus on shifting the trauma vortex state to integrate other experiences, which can lead to having a foothold in the VVC. Strengthening the resiliency vortex through the embodiment of positive states is critical for the development of capacity, as it is foundational to accessing the VVC (Walker & Newcomer, 2025). As a portal into the VVC, the integration of positive states must be cultivated and installed; positive states become embodied using the "felt sense" (Gendlin, 1996). As has been established earlier, as positive states are embodied, the VVC is accessed more readily, and there is more fluidity in the ANS overall (Porges, 2022; see also Dana, 2018; Walker & Newcomer, 2025). Dana (2018) offers the concept of looking for "glimmers," defined as "cues of safety arising from the ventral vagal state" (p. 67), to support shifting to the VVC. Similarly, Hanson (2009) discusses "taking in the good" as the internalization of positive experiences (p. 68) for the promotion of general well-being. General well-being leads to internal harmony, which inherently promotes integration (Siegel & Hartzell, 2014). These practices are a way to remedy the influence of the negativity bias.

THE ROLE OF EMBODIMENT

To accomplish this endeavor of embodied positive states, it becomes essential for the clinician to become a detective, paying close attention to anything that is not part of the trauma state. Clients getting in touch with their strengths rather than their weaknesses is highly beneficial (Seligman, 2011) as it shifts their physiology. Any person, place, quality, or skill can be a part of the resiliency vortex, and it will need to be integrated to shift the nervous system. There are countless examples: noticing support after a difficult loss, parenting well while in the throes of a divorce, feeling satisfied after communicating a need, or taking a risk toward leadership at work. The list is endless as the focus is tracking what the client has not embodied; these aspects or details are obscured when one is in the trauma state. Through embodiment, these obscured experiences are integrated.

It is important to note that the embodiment of positive states is much more than simple resourcing used in trauma work. The difference is the required embodiment aspect, as well as the more pointed focus on noticing what is not part of the trauma state as it is occurring in sessions in the present moment. This becomes a means to deactivate the ANS in real time. This process focuses on the organic aspects occurring right in the session, making it very natural and not an applied process like in resourcing work.[14] Additionally, the embodiment of positive states is training the nervous system to change the focus of attention; attention is shifted to states that support being in the VVC rather than focusing only on potential threats. This management of attention toward what is positive or neutral is critical to being more fully present and out of trauma states.

Being more fully present includes being with the entirety of an experience. The trauma vortex and the lack of integration limit the inclusion of the full experience. Additionally, it is important to emphasize that the embodiment of positive states is not an attempt to deny reality with "toxic positivity" (Lukin, 2019) or "unrealistic optimism" (Shepperd et al., 2015).[15] Instead, it's accurately holding all aspects of an experience, difficult and supportive. The mindful and present attention, coupled with the embodiment of positive states, can change the physiological state of the ANS from threat states to VVC-green zone physiology.

Additionally, even the embodiment of neutral experiences can help change one's mental state. Neutrality is a valuable state in trauma work because it is not within the trauma vortex. Teaching clients to value neutrality can be supportive in developing resilience. Noticing neutrality might be as simple as noticing that it now feels okay to talk about their challenge, or it might be noticing at the moment that nothing feels bad in the body. Neutrality is a highly underappreciated state, and it is helpful to notice it when it is present. It is also a shift away from both chaos and rigidity, as it is more in what Siegel calls the "flow of the river" (2010a, p. 70). For some clients, it can be a way to begin movement toward integration of positive states, which is easier as this capacity is developed.

The embodiment experience leads to a strengthened capacity and a doorway to the VVC. As Hanson says, "Good feelings today increase the likelihood of good feelings tomorrow" (2009, p. 75). Simply put, experiencing good feelings leads to more good feelings. In applying this concept, it is essential to interrupt the eddy in the vortex to support integration. Slowing down the process by taking time to notice what else is present besides the trauma can lead to a change in one's state and provide access to the VVC. This intervention is a form of Hanson's "taking in the good" (2009, p. 75). Access to the VVC is enhanced by "savoring" or staying with positive sensations (Bryant & Veroff, 2006; Dana, 2018).

Examples of the integration of moments of "taking in the good" can include having support during an accident because a person standing by steps in to help. Other examples can be feeling someone is on one's side during a challenging interaction or maybe being believed after a sexual assault. The influence of the negativity bias steers clients to focus mostly on the trauma vortex, bypassing aspects of an experience that might feel good or at least neutral. After being overlooked, these other experiences often do not become part of the narrative, as they are typically unacknowledged. Because these aspects are unintentionally overlooked, the client misses the opportunity to integrate them. This lack of integration results in the client not benefiting from the experiences that can shift their nervous system state.

The steps to strengthen and integrate the resiliency vortex include stopping, slowing down, noticing any aspect of resilience or neutrality, and embodying it. This is quite profound since the process can downregulate the nervous system into deactivation. In a session, this could look like stopping the client and taking a moment to notice that they are supported and to feel that experience in their body. Or it might be commenting to the client that they are showing resilience by parenting well in a stressful situation and having them take time to embody this demonstrated strength. It's important to emphasize that focusing on unintegrated resources isn't about trying to put a positive spin on the difficulty. Instead, it's about taking an all-inclusive look at what's happening to support the integration of the entire experience. This repositioning into the resiliency vortex begins to fortify the capacity for embodying resilience.

As experience molds the nervous system, clinicians use embodiment to cultivate temporary desired *states* intentionally, supporting their transition into enduring *traits* (Hanson, 2009). If a client is exhibiting self-compassion, the clinician might first ask how they feel it in their body. When the client reports that their self-compassion is a warmth in their heart, the clinician might say, "Let yourself notice the warmth in your heart as you talk kindly to yourself." This embodiment practice, over time, is shaping the nervous system and providing access to the VVC, as well as amplifying a desired quality. According to Hanson (2009), the regular embodiment of positive states can transform the *state* of compassion into a *trait* of compassion; this occurs through positive neuroplasticity (Hanson, 2018). Repetition, time, and reminding oneself of the value of feeling a desired quality as a state can reshape the nervous system to internalize a quality as an accessible internal trait (Hanson, 2018; Hanson & Hanson, 2018). There are many obvious positive states for clinicians to be aware of that support resilience and post-traumatic growth: self-compassion, gratitude, curiosity, a sense of inner strength, and trust in the process. Many others show up in therapy: grit and determination, knowing one's needs, having clear boundaries, the ability to receive and ask for help, and strong interpersonal skills. The regular embodiment of any of these positive states, large or small, can transform the *state* into a *trait* (Hanson, 2018). The key is the embodiment process, which includes having Gendlin's "felt sense" (1996) of one's experiences with awareness of the body.

For some clients, the embodiment process will bring up struggles with positive affect tolerance. Positive affect tolerance is the ability to hold positive feelings in the body. Positive affect tolerance often occurs after long-term childhood abuse or neglect; positive affect becomes hard to hold in the nervous system as a result of early life experiences. This manifests in trauma work as the client having trouble feeling positive sensations easily, or for extended periods, or at all. Addressing this limitation might need to become a treatment goal to better support the client in tolerating positive feelings as a critical step toward resilience. In offering psychoeducation to the client describing the trauma state versus the resilient state, I might say directly to the client, "I am noticing how hard it is to stay with positive feelings. I am guessing this is connected to the struggles in your childhood. Because strengthening positive affect tolerance is such an important aspect of trauma recovery, I would like to work directly with you on strengthening your ability to hold positive feelings in our sessions. I am wondering if you are up for that?" Clients are generally interested in this, and it seems to make sense to them. Buy-in from the client makes it easier for them to feel committed to the process and less likely to move out of these states too quickly. The client gains a sense of the map you are using and why it is important.

The work of growing positive affect tolerance needs scaffolding, as positive sensations can quickly turn into negative or disturbing sensations. Frequently, starting with general interoception work can be useful (covered in Chapter 4), if building body connection is part of the obstacle. It can also help to support the client in embodying neutrality. Again, neutrality is an underappreciated and undernoticed state. When neutrality occurs, clients often say that nothing is happening. Differentiating neutrality can be a building block to developing resilience and positive emotions, making it easier to transition to positive states over time.

To facilitate scaffolding of positive sensations, it is necessary to spend time both building up positive state tolerance and interrupting the positive-to-negative loop that occurs as clients integrate positive affect. To accomplish this, the clinician can have the client briefly notice the sensation in their body for only a few seconds and then use social engagement or lead the client to orient to the environment by noticing their surroundings. (Orientation will be discussed fully in Chapter 4.) Like social engagement, orientation can support lengthening the experience of holding positive sensations a client has before the sensation changes. As both social engagement and orientation to the environment can be more neutral for some clients, they can interrupt the usual pattern. On their own, social engagement and orientation often lead to regulation and ease which can be safer avenues for shifting states than directly embodying positive sensations. Utilizing social engagement and orientation as an interruption also brings the client out of the trauma vortex and into the flow. This process can help the nervous system calibrate to embody the more neutral sensations without immediately returning to the trauma vortex. Gradually, the neutral experiences can expand to more direct embodiment of positive sensations; this can progress to having increased positive affect tolerance over time. This supports the potential for deeper integration. (It should be noted that many clients will find social engagement and orientation to be pleasant immediately, making both interventions for the embodiment of positive sensations.)

There are lasting influences in embracing the development of capacity through the embodiment of resilient states. Not only do clients feel better and have more agency, but also they are creating the cornerstone for resilience in other situations. Additionally, they are accessing the VVC as the neural platform for resilience and potential post-traumatic growth. As an ongoing trauma technique, the ANS is learning to be primed to notice more often what is going well, rather than all that is wrong. This is a shift out of the threat state and an entry into more consistent access to the VVC. This creates shifts from the eddy of the trauma vortex and back into the flow of more integration.

> *Practice Tip:* Clients might try to change a sensation on their own when you have them notice a positive sensation that occurs after a difficult sensation. They might feel a lightness in their chest after body tension in their torso. Without your direction, they will begin to work internally to move the lightness to the tension in the rest of their torso. As it is more effort, it will get in the way of the process of the embodiment of positive states. It is essential to have the client simply notice *without* the goal of trying to broaden the positive sensations. When they stop the effort, the positive sensation often changes on its own and expands to the rest of the body. If it does not, there are other deactivation pathways that might support the change.

Occasionally, clients might feel you are not hearing them when working with the embodiment of positive states. When attention is focused this way, the therapy does become less about the story because the therapy focuses on shifting states to create more capacity. If a client reports that you are not hearing them, it is necessary to attune to this request. Often, they were never heard, making it important that the clinician makes room to hear the story. Along with that, the clinician would also want to offer the embodiment of that positive state: "Can you take a moment to feel in your body that I really hear you?" This supports the client in integrating this experience of being heard. This is both reparative and supportive of embodying positive experiences. At other times, clients might need psychoeducation to understand the value of integration of the embodiment of positive states; learning the value of developing capacity is useful.

> *Practice Tip:* If clients are set on telling the story and it is clear that they will get dysregulated as they do so, consider a contract with the client to support their nervous system: "I know being heard is important, and I truly want this for you. Because I also want to be in service of your nervous system and for you to be able to integrate what you have been through, I would like permission to stop you occasionally. When we stop, I will be trying to support your nervous system in some way so that you can be in some regulation. Would this be okay with you?" Getting this agreement with the client supports the clinician in being more effective while also fostering the client's autonomy as they are making a choice. It also supports the client's ability to keep some access to the green zone of the VVC.

Additionally, the embodiment of positive states is best applied after every deactivation pathway intervention. This reinforces access to the green zone, and it strengthens the VVC. Deactivation pathways lead to feeling better in some way; reinforcing the change with embodiment lengthens the amount of time a client is in deactivation. This is important because clients have often been in the yellow and red zones for long periods of time. Strengthening their "felt sense" (Gendlin, 1996) of deactivation provides the template for the entry to the VVC, as well as assisting the clinician in knowing that this is occurring if it is not visible.

Embodying Positive State Example 1

In a session, the client begins talking about a difficult interaction at work and showing visible dysregulation. In an offhand way, the client mentions that another employee came up later and told them they heard about what happened and agreed with them; the client might also add that the same colleague hoped to talk to the department head about the situation. The client goes on to the next part of the story, not integrating the fact that support and validation were offered. This is significant as this more positive interaction is also part of the whole picture, and yet, it is not part of the client's narrative. Instead of taking in and embodying both the validation and the support, the client continues with the story, which interferes with integrating what might feel good. The client, stuck in the trauma vortex, has a limited ability to integrate other aspects of a situation that are also important. This requires a therapeutic intervention to support the process. This includes stopping the client, slowing down, noticing, and embodying to support shifting the nervous system to the VVC.

To facilitate this integration, the clinician would likely need to interrupt the client. The clinician could say, "Let's slow down if that is okay, as this feels important. What is it like to hear your colleague support you by speaking out for you?" The client might notice that it feels good to have support. This comment is an entrance into the resiliency vortex, moving back into the flow of the whole narrative. Often, the physiology changes with a deeper breath, a lightening on their face, and less body tension. The clinician would go further and say, "Can we stay longer in being with this experience of having someone be on your side? What sensations go with this now in your body?" The client might say, "It feels pretty good to hear this. I had no idea she was going to speak out for our team about this. I do not feel as tense." The clinician then slows down more, stating, "Can we just stay with this for now, noticing less tension?" This builds even more positive affect capacity as it extends the time of embodiment. As this occurs, the client becomes truly present as they take in the whole picture of what happened, which is more integration. Indeed, the boss did not handle the situation the way they hoped, yet it is equally true that a colleague validated their concern and offered support. This integration of the positive or neutral aspects that were not part of the client's felt experience because of the trauma state can now support regulation. This creates more integration, as the whole story is present, and it is moving the client from deactivation to the VVC.

Embodying Positive State Example 2

A client with a history of being ignored and disrespected in their family reports that their sibling called to ask their opinion on a situation. They casually mention this interaction and begin to go on to a new topic. Because the clinician has a history with the client, they recognize this as an unintegrated aspect that could shift into the resilience vortex. With that in mind, the clinician might say, "Can we take a minute here to check in? I wonder what it is like for you to have your brother ask your opinion. That seems like that is what you have been wishing for in your relationship." The client, who is bypassing all of this with the negativity bias, says, "Yes, can you believe it? He never does that with me. He always puts down my point of view." With this response, the client has not changed states. The negativity bias is compelling, so the clinician needs to challenge the client and say, "Yes, I know—and what is it like that it was different in this phone call?" This is when the client can embody being responded to differently and move into the resiliency vortex. The client might say, "Yeah, I am surprised, but it does feel good." To reinforce this new state, the clinician asks more questions about the situation, trying to strengthen the body's sensations of feeling valued. Even questions about this unintegrated experience create access to the resilient state as they tap into the state, in a similar way that questions about trauma tap into the trauma state. In this vein, the clinician could ask questions about what opinion the client offered, what it felt like to be asked, or anything that supported this new experience, extending the positive experience that occurred with their brother. Additionally, the clinician would want to encourage the client to savor how it feels, supporting more VVC access and regulation. In this case, the client can be back in the flow of integration again.

SUMMARY

The embodiment of positive states, despite being simple in many ways, should not be underestimated in its impact. It shifts the nervous system out of the trauma vortex that is holding the chaos and rigidity. Through the integration that occurs with the embodiment of positive states, clients' nervous systems deactivate. Additionally, this embodiment provides a priming to notice positive aspects of life, which is a reset of the nervous system; this reduces the impact of the negativity bias while strengthening the resiliency vortex. It is crucial to apply this pathway generally in sessions as well as after downregulation of each deactivation pathway. This strengthening leads to increased capacity overall through more well-being as part of the VVC access.

EXERCISE FOR EMBODIMENT OF POSITIVE STATES

Take a moment right now to turn toward yourself in any way that works for you, perhaps noticing your breath, a certain place in your body that feels okay, or maybe just noticing yourself seated. As you do this, let yourself reflect on a quality in yourself that got you through a difficult situation. Name this quality to yourself and notice what this is like in your body now. As you do this, allow yourself to say to yourself, "I am . . ." naming this aspect of your resilience. You might get an image, or you might feel a shift in your body. Allow yourself notice this and take in a sense of an aspect of your resiliency, really feeling it in your body.

CHAPTER 4

Being Present in the Here and Now

Trauma is a disorder of being in the here and now.

—Bessel van der Kolk, MD

There is a lot of discussion these days about mindfulness and truly being present. Now viewed as a key aspect of trauma treatment, learning to be present through mindfulness is the foundation of trauma work (van der Kolk, 2014). The beauty of applying this concept in therapy is that the benefits extend way beyond the therapy room. Mindfulness, underlying *being present in the here and now*, results in more engagement in life, bringing a sense of aliveness. This chapter will delve further into this concept.

As part of mindfulness, being present in the here and now is a crucial step in trauma recovery. If a client truly stays in the present moment, they no longer are in the vortex of their trauma symptoms. Trauma symptoms are centered on what might happen and what did happen, not here and now.

> *Reflection:* I have shared the Bessel van der Kolk epigraph that begins this chapter with many of my clients, as it is one of my favorite trauma quotes. Every time, they report that they feel complete resonance with those words. It truly captures the experience of being hijacked into the past or being caught worrying about the future. Not being able to be present in the here and now is the experience of anyone with trauma. Sharing this concept also normalizes this behavior.

Being present in the here and now as a deactivation pathway includes being in both the environment and one's body. Being present in the environment through the senses is *orientation*. Being present with access to the body is *interoception*. Both are necessary components and can signal safety to the nervous system; both are part of mindfulness, defined as the "state of being aware." When a client is fully in the present moment, trauma symptoms are absent. Therefore, assisting clients toward being present in the here and now through mindfulness is paramount in treatment.

Mindfulness is key to trauma recovery as it can soften experiences, helping them to integrate (Siegel, 2010a). Additionally, as it supports being grounded and focused on the present moment, it can help in processing intrusive memories (rooted in the SNS) of previous traumas and mitigate emotional numbing symptoms (as part of the DVC) (van der Kolk, 2014).

Mindfulness also fosters the development of distress tolerance, which is the ability to manage challenging emotions without being overwhelmed (Linehan, 1993). This encompasses being able to be with the sensations that accompany difficult emotions, which is a key aspect of emotional regulation. Through small mindfulness practices, even for seconds at a time, the client strengthens the psychological and physiological capacity to hold their own challenging emotions. Distressing experiences lose their grip, resulting in more regulated responses, which is at the base of being present in the here and now.

When both orientation and interoception are online as a type of mindfulness, the nervous system is present and not diverted into a trauma state of yellow or red zone physiology. Building a sense of being present in the here and now supports safety and access to the VVC and is often the first step in working with clients. Applying this pathway from the beginning of treatment provides a foundation for trauma therapy, and *it is the therapy*. Learning to be present in the here and now is the antidote to more ease and even alleviates the challenging sensations that are part of the SNS and DVC physiology; the client builds the muscle of tolerating sensations, which changes their experience. Being present in the here and now becomes the cure over time.

Additionally, this process of being present in the here and now teaches the management of attention. As noted, there is a tendency to focus on whatever has happened (the past) or to fear what might happen (anticipating the future); both are examples of not being able to manage attention (van der Kolk, 2014). Besides making one less present, trauma keeps one not in control of where one's attention is going. To paraphrase Porges, self-regulation includes having the ability to put our attention where we want it to be and manage emotional arousal (Porges, 2011, 2021). This management of attention offers a contrast to the trauma state and underlies the importance of moving toward the embodiment of being present in the here and now.

ORIENTATION AS BEING PRESENT IN THE HERE AND NOW

Orientation is a neural exercise and is one of the first places to start with clients. Even with challenging nervous system states of SNS and DVC, it is often accessible. Using the senses, orientation starts guiding the nervous system toward being in the present moment. Levine (1997) defines the orientation response as a biological process of responding to novelty in the environment to assess safety. There are two types of orienting: *defensive orienting* and *exploratory orienting* (Levine, 2010). When defensively orienting, one is actively trying to detect the danger and locate the threat. This is often linked with the SNS and mobilization. In exploratory orienting, one is simply noticing the environment without a focus on threats; this naturally deactivates the nervous system (Ogden et al., 2006). Registering the sense of safety with exploratory orienting is regulating, because when safety is registered, VVC is on board. In general, the orientation response utilizes the head, neck, and shoulders, which are connected to the VVC architecture, supporting the green zone (Walker & Newcomer, 2025).

You can see from Figure 4.1 that if there is novelty in the environment, we will orient to it as a potential threat. If the nervous system deems that it is safe, we can return to exploratory orienting. If the novelty appears dangerous or life-threatening, and we can take necessary protective actions, we can also move back to exploratory orienting. If we cannot complete the protective actions for safety, we tend to get stuck in defensive orienting (SNS) or not orienting (DVC). With this impact on physiological state, utilizing exploratory orientation as a deactivation pathway in sessions supports access to the VVC.

To introduce orientation, clinicians could say to the client, "Let your eyes go where they want" (Somatic Experiencing®, personal communication, 2009–2011). Clients might need to be encouraged to pay attention to what they enjoy in the environment or at least what is neutral to them. Sometimes the negativity bias leads a client to focus on something that bothers them, rather than something neutral or pleasant. They might notice the cars outside the window rather than the trees they enjoy, or they might focus on a pile of dirty laundry during a video call rather than on a picture they love. For this reason, offering more structure about orienting might be necessary.

An example of a more structured approach is: "What else do you notice?" or "What do you find yourself drawn to look at?" When a client orients toward things they do not like, there is a need for more leading: "Is there something else you might enjoy looking at?" This can be a way to shift from the negativity bias. The goal is to get the client in the environment without the associations of memories, as memories do not occur in the present moment. Orientation is about being exactly where one is in the environment. This orientation toward the present moment assists the client's physiology in building the neural pathways for not being stuck in the trauma. This repetition over time builds more connection to self as well as achieving the goal of being and living in the here and now of the present moment.

Clients often experience a shift in their physiology that is both supporting the neural pathways of being in the here and now, and also regulating and connecting to the green zone of VVC. This can be done repetitively in a session with clients. Bookending strong experiences with exploratory orienting is often useful. This supports deeper settling in the nervous system, since the nervous system benefits from spaciousness and time after strong experiences.

Based on the dominant nervous system state, clients need different types of coaching to orient. In DVC dominance, it can be challenging to be in the environment, as there is often an inward focus. For these clients you might need to add more direction: "Can you name three blue items you see?" In SNS dominance, they might feel impatient or want to just get to the next thing, and they will hurry with the process. This hurrying through the neural exercise is an indicator that they are not actually orienting. The clinician will need to add more guidance to do the orientation to get the client into presence. Asking questions about what they named can help: "You mentioned you like the flowers in the vase, and I am wondering which flower you like most?" Although this might challenge the client initially, it becomes a way to regulate over time. It shifts the SNS from urgency ("What is next?") to the ease of the VVC (being present in the here and now).

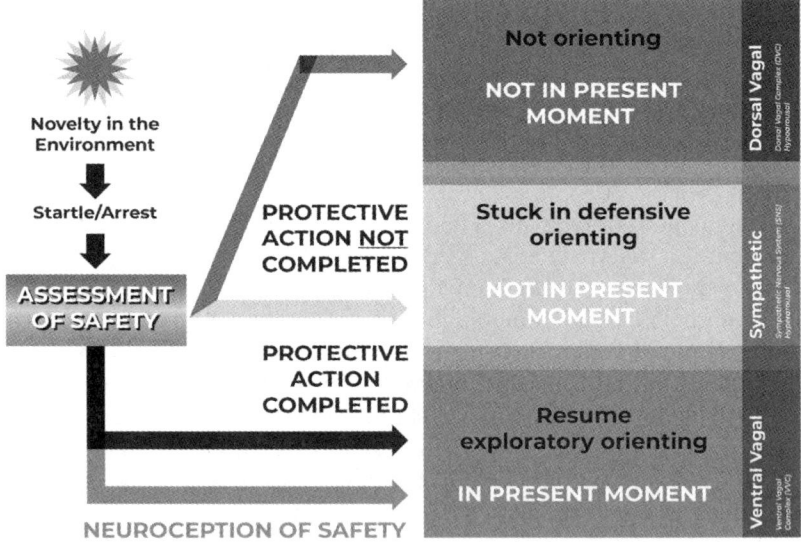

FIGURE 4.1:   Orientation Response   Credit: Ruby Jo Walker with concepts from Peter Levine, Somatic Experiencing®, and Stephen Porges; graphic by Cindy Miller Atchison Design & Art

Over time, clients will begin to orient on their own; this can be an indication of regulation in the nervous system. Orientation can be given for homework as a neural exercise to support nervous system regulation, as it results in being in the present moment. For most clients, this is a very nervous system–friendly intervention and quickly becomes useful; it is also easy to integrate into sessions and into their lives.

INTEROCEPTION AS BEING PRESENT
IN THE HERE AND NOW

Interoception is another aspect of being present in the here and now through the awareness of internal states. Interoception is being in our body. Van der Kolk (2014, p. 96) names three important functions of interoception:

1. to draw out the sensory information that is blocked by frozen trauma;
2. to help patients befriend (rather than suppress) the energies released by that experience;
3. to help complete the actions that were thwarted when they were trapped, restrained, or immobilized by terror.

Interoception can be defined as the sense that "allows us to feel our internal organs and skin and gives information regarding the internal state or condition of our body" (Mahler, 2017, p. 1). When the client can feel their body, they more accurately get the cues that will support being regulated and in the present moment. This regulation includes basic comfort activities like eating or drinking when needed or putting on a warm coat in the cold. Strengthening interoception awareness restores the body-based cues that provide the signaling that leads to actions that support regulation. These actions include the appropriate use of protective behaviors to ensure safety such as social engagement, mobilization, and immobilization. Interoception signals extend beyond basic safety to also include signals that promote making choices for life satisfaction. Such choices could be everything from finding meaningful work to experiencing satisfying activities and engaging in reciprocal and supportive connections. Interoception supports embodiment, which lends itself to green zone physiology, but it often needs to be built over time.

Body sensations for both SNS and DVC can be difficult. SNS dominance can flood the nervous system by feeling too much, or in DVC dominance, body sensations might be inaccessible. With SNS dominance, learning to be with strong sensations is challenging because they often hold more intensity. That intensity can be mediated by staying with mindfulness as one learns to be with and tolerate experiences. Being with strong sensations is supported by starting with positive and neutral situations, as were outlined in the last chapter. Embodying first what feels good or neutral in the body supports safety in being in the body. This safety creates both the capacity for holding sensations and access to the VVC. More challenging sensations can be added as the client progresses in their ability to hold positive sensations. Using mindfulness through orientation as well as focusing first on positive sensations supports the under-pinnings of regulation.

In DVC dominance, body sensations can often be inaccessible. This lack of awareness directly impacts client's ability to notice their painful internal experiences; this includes their distressing emotions, including how they are impacted by others. Even if they are not aware of these cues, their nervous system can be affected because a threat state is evoked. General life satisfaction is highly influenced and often harder to attain when DVC is dominant, as cues for the right action to support oneself are not procurable for the client; the client often cannot feel the body signals in DVC dominance as described in Chapter 1. Missing these cues brings about missing the actions that might support more regulation in the nervous system.

Building interoception is particularly important for DVC dominance. This can be challenging in somatic work as clients often do not have an answer when clinicians try to check in, asking "How do you notice this in your body?" or "What do you feel in your body now?" Oftentimes, clinicians start by asking these types of somatically focused questions. Clients can get very frustrated with somatic questions because they cannot answer them. Not being able to answer the sensation questions can lead clients to feel something is wrong with them and it inhibits a sense of agency. When there is more awareness through interoception, "the greater our potential to control our lives" (van der Kolk, p. 95), a key aspect of agency and trauma recovery. Somatic questions can only be answered if interoceptive awareness is fully online and available. There is often little body differentiation in sensations, and that differentiation needs to be developed. It is a process that can occur in stages and over time (Mahler, 2017). Normalizing that interoceptive awareness skills take time to develop is important; providing education that difficulty with interoception is connected to the red zone physiology helps. Clients need the normalization of their therapeutic process and an understanding of the importance of having interoception.

Mahler divides interoceptive feelings into two categories:

1. Body states. These involve the basic functions or physical conditions of the body. Body states include hunger, thirst, needing to go to the bathroom, pain, sexual arousal, itch, tickle, temperature (e.g., hot/cold), nausea, headache, illness, [and] muscle tension.
2. Emotion states. These involve our moods or emotional states of the body. Emotion states include anger, embarrassment, happiness, anxiety, excitement, sadness, [and] fear (2017, p. 7).

Practice Tip: Helping clients understand the importance of interoception is supported by tying it to their therapeutic goal and/or nervous system regulation in general. I often tell clients that restoring body sensations provides information for their needs and boundaries and helps support more clarity and connection in relationships. I also let them know that interoception is key to developing optimal skills for regulation in general, as it helps in knowing what would bring them back to the green zone. I also note that interoception becomes a way to bring in self-attunement, a lifelong need for finding one's path in life and relationships. When clients understand that interoception has a major role in their comfort in life, they are interested in developing it.

One of the first ways to build interoception is for you to note things you are seeing that the client is not able to recognize yet: "I noticed you just took a deeper breath, and I wonder if you feel that change?" or "It looks like your shoulders just dropped—can you feel that difference?" This kind of observation or statement can teach the client to start feeling changes. It will often feel indiscernible to the client initially. They might comment, "I think so," as they are not sure. Letting that kind of response be enough can support clients in building interoceptive skills. In the early learning of interoception, clients' awareness will often initially be tentative, and that is normal, so looking to the client for a definitive "I feel this" is not likely to happen in the initial stages. The clinician can just encourage this growing sense of embodiment by responding, "See if it is okay to just notice this shift."

> *Practice Tip:* For clients who feel challenged by being in their body, I often, again, use a contract. After the psychoeducation, I ask, "Would it be okay for us to have some focus on embodiment as part of our sessions?" If they are agreeable, I ask, "Could we try to set aside a few minutes each session and build up to 10 minutes or so?" This agreement helps both the clinician and the client. With the contract, the clinician has permission to stretch a client as there is an agreement to work on the issue; it also helps the client make the commitment to work with their challenge.

It additionally helps to let clients know that developing interoception can feel clunky; then, this alleviates their concerns about their limited awareness. As noted, they often are not able to identify their sensations. Educating the client about the learning curve of the process can help make the connection easier with practice. Also important is underlining for clients when their ability to access interoception is shifting even when it does change minimally. The clinician could say, "I am noticing that it was easier today for you to feel your body as you talked about your feelings. Did you notice that?" Because the interoceptive process is about self-connection, sensing, and feeling, they need external validation that it is happening for them. They often won't notice the change otherwise.

When clients have less access to interoception, it can also be helpful to feel the edges of their bodies. When regular sensations in the body are not clear, the edges of the body are often easier to feel. You can say, "See if it is okay to notice where your body is making contact with surfaces," or "As your body is sitting on the couch now, I wonder what edges of your body are easiest to notice?" Noticing can grow over time and become a measure of starting their interoception process. Even asking what is easiest to notice in the body can be useful, as there is often a more accessible part of the body for the client.

Another building block is having the client feel contrasts in their body. You can have the client notice if more is happening in the upper body or lower body, the right or left side, or the front and back of the body. Contrasting experiences can make it clearer to the client that they do feel something. Because sensations are generally undifferentiated, clients often feel that nothing is happening. Conveying that there are differences between body parts helps clients realize they can feel something, even if it is subtle at first or not very clear. This reinforces their sense of "I can." Again, external validation helps strengthen their connection with their experience. When it is noticeable, the clinician could say, "Yes, I see your upper body does look looser than your lower body" to assist in validating their experience.

The next building block in developing interoception is to offer choices (Mahler, 2017). "I wonder if your shoulders feel tight, loose, or somewhere in between?" or "Is the tension across your chest, on the surface, or deeper in your body?" or "As you talk about your family, do you notice your chest or belly more right now?" Giving choices starts building a repertoire they can use to get closer to describing on their own and assists with the ability to differentiate sensations.

Having sensation word lists (Figure 4.2) available to clients can give them a range of options that lead to sensations becoming clearer over time. As stated earlier, a question like "What do you notice in your body?" is a common question, but it can take time to build that awareness for the client (Mahler, 2017). Clients with DVC dominance will need more interventions and a scaffolding process to develop interoception to answer that question. Creating embodiment is the focus of trauma work. It is both the antidote and the cure to be embodied and to tolerate the sensations of experience.

> *Reflection:* If this feels available to you, let yourself bring into awareness what kinds of sensations you tend to notice. Temperature? Muscular? Skin? Ease or constriction? Upper body? Lower body? Whole body? Without judgment, see if it is possible to notice another kind of sensation. If your skin is easy to notice, can you also notice temperature? If muscle constriction is the easiest to notice, can you also notice some ease? If you tend to always notice your upper body, can you bring awareness to your lower body? Interoceptive awareness can be developed with practice.

One caveat is that increased awareness in the nervous system, particularly interoception, can lead to having more access to internal sensations. If a client is moving from DVC into SNS, there is a lower level of activation in the nervous

SENSATION WORDS

cold	calm	heavy
relaxed	waves	blocked
prickly	opening	goosebumps
tender	fluid	trembly
hot	tensed	throbbing
fidgety	releasing	twitching
burning	intense	pins-and-needles
contracted	heavy	neutral
light	soft	clenched
moving	dry	hollow
knotted	electric	tightening
achy	full	suffocating/hard to breathe
nervy	clammy	stuck
flowing	solid	tight
preparing	nauseated	damp
compressed	vibrating	flushed
shaky	floating	dull
connected	pulsing	jumpy
bracing	itchy	full
thick	shivery	numb
trembling	flaccid	wobbly
airy	disconnected	tense
spinning	smooth	cool
spacious	open	easy
constricted	sweaty	energized
comforted	icy	burning
expansive	gurgling	puffy
sore	draining	cramping
sharp	congested	supported
tight	wiggly	closed
hard	empty	
warm	buzzing	

FIGURE 4.2: Sensation Words

system; this deactivation is downregulation. However, it also means clients will feel and notice *more* challenging sensations as they move from DVC states to SNS states. Since sensations feel stronger in SNS, it can be helpful to educate clients, as they might think they are getting worse rather than getting more in touch with themselves. It is essential that clients know that symptoms might feel heightened in the yellow zone, even though the nervous system is in a more downregulated state than the red zone. The assurance that they are getting better is indispensable information. This psychoeducation can help them understand and tolerate the changes easier. Even asking the question, "Is this tolerable?" as they report a challenging sensation can support their awareness that *they can* tolerate the sensation as they are building their capacity. It can be helpful to remind clients that they often can now also feel more positive sensations as that develops.

Interoception is linked to following the "internal gut feeling" (Mahler, 2017) and to actions that support more regulation. Additionally, interoception is fundamental to restoring accurate neuroception signaling. Remember that neuroception is our body's radar system; it is always detecting safety, danger, or life threats. Interoception feeds into neuroception. As interoceptive signals can be less available in nervous system dysregulation, particularly in DVC dominance, it is important to reconnect these needed signals to support accurate neuroception. As a key principle in trauma recovery, interoception and neuroception work together. Van der Kolk discusses resetting the physiology when clients have inaccurate neuroception; he states, "This means helping them to respond appropriately to danger is important, but also helping clients recover safety, relaxation, and true reciprocity" (2014, p. 80). Van der Kolk is describing both sides of inaccurate neuroception; overseeing danger means cues of safety and connection might be missed, and underseeing danger means potential risks are overlooked. Interoception skills help clients with the process of developing accurate neuroception for more emotional well-being.

ORIENTATION TO LIFE AS BEING IN THE HERE AND NOW

Because orientation encompasses being present in the here and now, extending orientation toward all aspects of life is also important. It leads to truly being present in life. Without it, parts of life remain unavailable or frozen off, contributing to dysregulation. Orientation to life means truly being present to things happening in all aspects of one's life is important; this includes work, finances, home and family, relationships, and health. Part of trauma's legacy can be to turn away from things that are difficult as part of the flight response. Turning toward all parts of life *is being oriented to life*. This engagement is critical for ongoing nervous system regulation. When a part of life is not being attended to because of its challenge, the threat state remains, sending signals to the nervous system. This is occurring even if the client is avoiding the situation. In ignoring nervous system signals, the client cannot take the necessary action that would support the nervous system back into regulation. These necessary actions often first require a courage to be present to face these situations.

Many times, fear and shame can stop clients from addressing the reality of something occurring. Examples can be anything from concerns about a loved one's addiction, shame about not doing parts of their job, to worries about finances. Both fear and shame make it hard to confront a painful aspect of one's life. It takes courage to face what is, and doing so is part of being present in the here and now. Not engaging with what is happening in life can lead to dysregulation. Any challenges that the client is not oriented toward will keep the nervous system signaling threat and activation, creating dysregulation. When clients learn to be present in the here and now of their environment, it can set them up to learn to be present toward other issues in life. This can lead to more regulation overall and settling of the ANS.

As stated in the last chapter, it is important to embody the positive state of deactivation after utilizing this deactivation pathway. Embodiment of resilient states includes reinforcing the green zone by strengthening the positive states as the client moves more into being present in the here and now.

SUMMARY

Being present in the here and now is one of the most important pathways for the nervous system because of the power of truly being present. As an antidote to the trauma state, it can be cultivated and strengthened, which is always the objective of trauma work. Being present in the here and now includes both orientation, which is being in the environment, and interoception, which includes being present through connection with the body. Although both can be challenging for clients, interoception is particularly hard in DVC dominance. When clients can hold the experiences of what is occurring both in the experience of their life and in their body, they are no longer in a trauma state; their experience is then manageable. This manageable state is often an entry into agency and the VVC. Like many nervous system interventions, it will take time and repetition to strengthen. Over time, this pathway can become a way of being, even leading to searching more for safety in the environment. As a deactivation pathway, this can also be strengthened and developed.

EXERCISE FOR CULTIVATING BEING PRESENT IN THE HERE AND NOW

Take a moment to simply notice your surroundings, letting your eyes go wherever they want, seeing where your eyes are drawn, and going toward whatever might feel pleasant or neutral. Notice what you like about what you are looking at, anything from the color, movement, or texture, naming it to yourself. Allow yourself to take in the details of what you are drawn to. Take your time with this as you take in your surroundings, following any impulse to curiously look at whatever draws you. After you make contact with the environment with your eyes, turn toward your body and notice how you are doing. Bring awareness to any shifts you can feel now. This can be applied to any of the senses. (This is adapted from Somatic Experiencing®, 2009–2011.)

CHAPTER 5

Co-Regulation

Our biological imperative is that our lives are meant to be intertwined with the lives of others.

—Stephen Porges

One of the beauties of learning about co-regulation in therapy is that it offers a term for what we are already doing with clients. It provides the needed foundation for safety, connection, and regulation (Porges, 2011, 2021, 2023), an integral aspect of all our work with clients. It also underlines the reciprocal relationship that gives clinicians nourishment from our work. The more we are in a co-regulated state, the less likely we are to get burned out or overwhelmed. This chapter will focus on a deeper understanding of this inherently mammalian feature of relationships.

Co-regulation defines the interactive process of regulatory support of another human being (Porges, 2011, 2021, 2022). Because of the nature of trauma work, co-regulation is a natural deactivation pathway for downregulation in therapeutic settings. "In our biological quest for safety, we have an implicit biological imperative to connect and co-regulate our physiological state with another" (Porges, 2021, p. 236). Because this is an intrinsic part of survival wiring, co-regulation through social engagement and connection is often a way trauma is mediated and integrated; through this process, co-regulation becomes part of the narrative. The narrative then includes both the trauma and the co-regulation experience; together, they often support integration.

The imperative need for connection is the primary need for a baby upon entering the world. Unable to care for itself, a baby needs both its physical and emotional needs met. Babies naturally turn to a caregiver for co-regulation. The process of the baby moving into dysregulation when a need arises, followed by a response to that need, strengthens the co-regulation capacity. The baby can have normal distress arise from a need, creating yellow or red zone activation in the ANS, and the attuned response deactivates the baby's nervous system back to the green zone. "Associating intense sensations with safety, comfort, and mastery is the foundation of self-regulation, self-soothing, and self-mastery" (van der Kolk, 2014, p. 113). A sense of safety is further developed as each attuned interaction shifts the autonomic state to VVC as the baby's needs are satisfied.

The attunement process was discussed earlier for clinicians and clients, and it is similar for other relationships including a caregiver and a baby, where co-regulation is learned (see Figure 5.1). In optimal caregiving, the caregiver starts with attending fully to the baby (presence) and noticing a need (tracking). Attuned caregiving then interprets the baby's needs (perception) and responds (response). These accurate responses, over time, provide an experience of co-regulation for the baby. The blueprint of co-regulation lays down its tracks as the baby experiences distress, followed by the need being met, resulting in deactivation of the nervous system back to the VVC. Over time, these experiences teach the ANS the pattern of co-regulation. Through effective attunement of the caregiver, this co-regulatory pattern is strengthened with these countless ongoing interactions. Not only does this attunement process of presence, tracking, perception, and response create the template for co-regulation, but it also provides a future map for self-regulation for the developing child (see Figure 5.2).

Co-regulation capacity and self-regulation are deeply intertwined. Co-regulation creates the bedrock and template for the development of self-regulation capacity later in life. Even as self-regulation skills are learned, we are

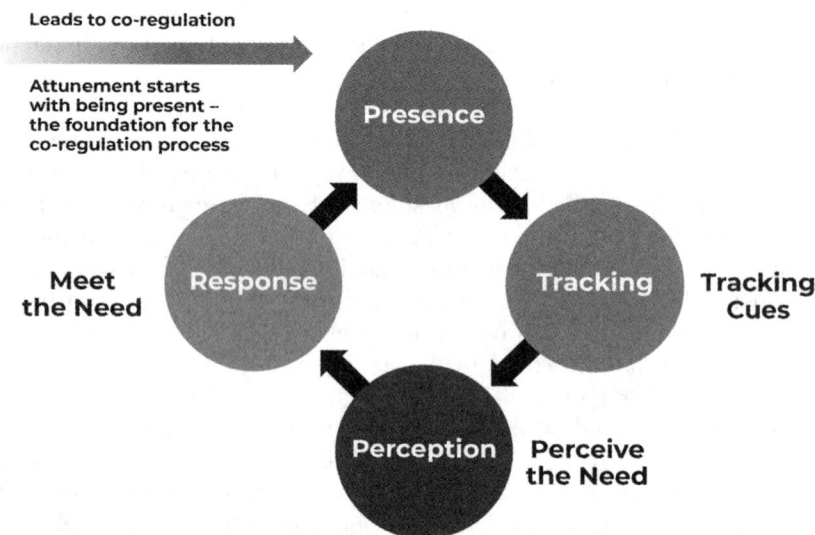

FIGURE 5.1:   Attunement to the Child   Credit: Ruby Jo Walker with concepts from Dr. Margaret Blaustein; graphic by Cindy Miller Atchison Design & Art

wired to need co-regulation throughout our lifetime. Until the day we die, we long for safe and reliable connections (Dana, 2021). For children, all self-regulation starts with co-regulation. Depending on experiences and temperament, there is a range of when self-regulation is possible, but it is not a need that a child will outgrow. Instead, this lifelong quest for co-regulation will change over time. In babies and toddlers, only co-regulation is possible and generally comes from caregivers. In the teen years, co-regulation will more often occur through peer relationships and often less from parents. For optimal well-being, we need both co-regulation capacity and self-regulation skills. Self-regulation is measured by autonomic flexibility; the key to autonomic flexibility is being able to deactivate into the VVC with ease. As the nervous system experiences deactivation into the VVC with co-regulation, it teaches autonomic flexibility.

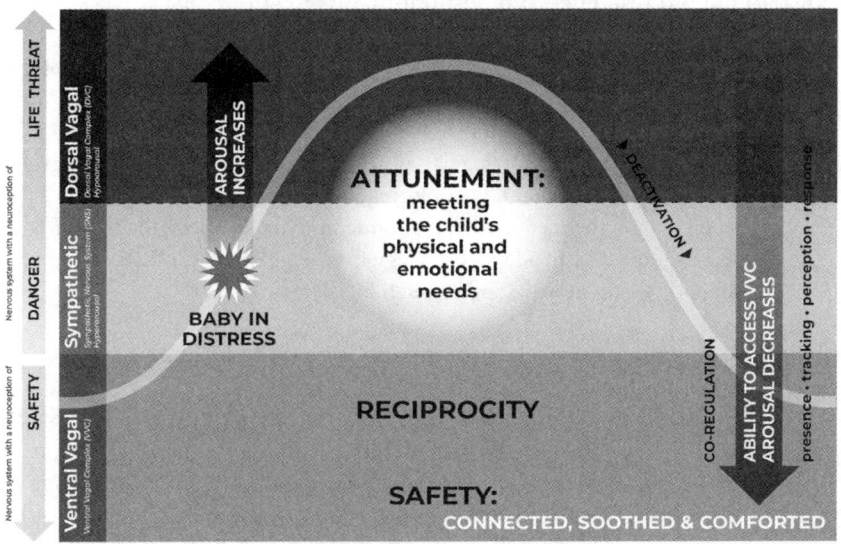

FIGURE 5.2:   Co-regulation and the Nervous System   Credit: Ruby Jo Walker based on concepts from Stephen Porges; graphic by Cindy Miller Atchison Design & Art

Even though some adults can utilize self-regulation more easily than children at times, co-regulation for adults engages in a similar process. Through attunement, an adult caring relationship offers presence, tracking, perception, and response; it is easy to feel met and co-regulated by another when these elements are present. If you are having a hard day, and a friend says, "Are you okay? You seem upset today," they might offer a hug or ask if you need to talk. This interaction includes all four elements of the attunement cycle and offers co-regulation while supporting the deactivation of the nervous system.

Rewarding relationships are linked to positive physical and mental health. Co-regulation capacity supports many aspects of life:

- emotional regulation
- individuation
- development of a sense of self
- embodiment
- personal power
- comfort and protection strategies
- healthy intimacy (Rahman, 2016)

Working toward more co-regulation in relationships is a critical step for thriving. Positive social connections and meaningful relationships are aspects inherently part of both resilience and post-traumatic growth.

> Resilience is a complex construct that appears to embody the successful integration of several skills and underlying neurophysiological mechanisms to recover from severe survival-related challenges . . . . Resilience and feelings of safety share a common neurophysiological substrate. On its most foundational level, resilience reflects behavioral, physiological, emotional, and social processes that are dependent on the recovery of autonomic function to a state that supports social engagement as an adaptive strategy to co-regulate with others and to mutually support health, growth, and restoration. (Porges, 2022)

The power of connected relationships cannot be underestimated, as they profoundly impact resilience and post-traumatic growth.

It is recognized in trauma work that how trauma is responded to is often more impactful than the actual event. This is understandably connected to our need to be co-regulated as we experience distressing situations that dysregulate the nervous system. Clients often report being upset because of how they are responded to concerning events that happen to them. Most people have some experience of having a challenging or traumatic situation, and someone makes a misattuned statement, which indicates the other person just does not get it. If someone is sexually assaulted and they are then questioned about what they were wearing or if they were drinking, that interaction will often become a significant trauma for the client, as it evokes a sense of being blamed. Oppositely, someone might say, "No one has a right to hurt you that way, no matter what you wear or whether or not you were drinking." That kind of statement will often set a trajectory of healing for a victim/survivor. The response aspect of the attunement cycle is powerful during a trauma, as we expect to be comforted by another. If the co-regulation does not happen, the lack of that experience will often become a very painful focus, leading to nervous system dysregulation.

Grief and loss situations often highlight the need for co-regulation when there are misattuned responses. Misattuned responses seem to have a significant effect on clients because of the high need for co-regulation during times of loss. Many grieving people report frustration with others' responses. At such a tender and vulnerable time, the biological expectation is co-regulation from another; the grieving person has a need of soothing from another. Therefore, a misattuned response will dysregulate the nervous system. When in the throes of struggling with a loss, well-meaning statements, like "I guess it was just his time to go," "It was God's will," or "She is better off now," will feel painful and be dysregulating. We are wired to need co-regulation in the form of comfort and understanding during our struggles. It becomes very challenging and even dysregulating if the expected support does not happen.

This need for co-regulation after strong experiences connects to the embedded wiring to look for support and regulation from another. Downregulation through co-regulation can include different elements of connection such as simple social engagement and/or offering responses that support the shifting of the dysregulated state back into regulation. An example of a response that could shift the dysregulation could be, "I am so sorry for your loss." This is very different from the statements listed above. Clients want to hear words that validate their experience or convey understanding. Other examples for other situations might be, "What happened sounds so unfair to you" or "I can't imagine how that feels" when someone has a difficult experience. Additionally, hearing things that offer direct support is also useful for co-regulation. "I want to support you. Can I take your kids once a week or bring you dinner this week to give you some time?" "I am here to listen to you." "You do not need to 'be fine' for me; I can handle hearing how you are really doing." Co-regulating responses will depend on the situation, and they require attunement to what might be most comforting and supportive to the person to calm their nervous system. It is important to note that co-regulation will not always be words. The connection of a loving presence, a warm embrace, and careful touch can all be part of co-regulation.

As part of a deactivation pathway, co-regulation is an inborn part of responding to trauma. Humans are wired to have other humans offer comforting responses that soothe their nervous system; these responses are essential in therapy, close relationships, and skillful parenting. The main parts of co-regulation are social engagement and soothing through witnessing and comforting. These aspects of co-regulation tend to happen both interpersonally for clients and also in therapeutic settings.

> *Reflection:* The clinician is always responsible for initiating and supporting the co-regulation of the client. Clinicians tend to be naturally skilled at offering this to clients. Integrating therapeutic presence as part of co-regulation is key for deactivation in this pathway. Without judgment, allow yourself to notice which

clients are easy to work with and which ones bring a challenge. Consider this another place to apply skills to support presence.

Comforting another through soothing offers co-regulation. *Soothing* is defined as having a gently calming effect and reducing pain or discomfort. From birth, caretakers provide soothing through physical comfort and emotional presence. Soothing throughout the lifespan offers a calming effect on another person and creates access to the VVC. Soothing is a resonant response that acknowledges another's pain, fostering regulation and co-regulation by activating the VVC. Comforting interactions help shift the nervous system into the green zone, allowing a person to feel seen, supported, and less alone. Simple sounds of intonation ("hmm," "ohh") can also convey presence and attunement; as calming vocalizations, they offer soothing. Validating statements offer a sense of soothing; for example, "I am so sorry this happened to you" or "I fully support you." These co-regulating interactions can deactivate the nervous system, as the person feels less alone and more supported.

Grounded in compassion, witnessing starts with deep listening; it leads to another person having a different experience of their struggle than they could have on their own. Witnessing is simply being with the client and letting them know that you understand what is happening. The process of knowing someone gets it creates resonance, which is inherently regulating. When witnessing another, presence is at the forefront, sending signals of safety and letting the client know you are with them. As a critical therapeutic experience, being witnessed is important when one has gone through a challenging situation. Witnessing includes supporting their experiences and not judging, which allows the client to feel the attunement of another. Even though the clinician does not have the same experiences as the client, they can show that they understand and are with the client; this is demonstrated through bearing witness to clients' challenges through their presence. As part of witnessing, presence includes "being grounded, immersed, and spacious with the intention of being there for the other" (Geller & Porges, 2014). As stated before, this kind of presence is inherently regulating, and it will often shift a client into the VVC as part of the interaction of mirror neurons (Cozolino, 2006). The sense of being witnessed through presence is one of the most basic co-regulatory offerings that a clinician can offer their clients.

Being witnessed creates a sense that one matters and helps one not feel alone, which also supports the VVC. Being fully seen by another, the client can often see themselves differently. This results in clients having more self-compassion, being able to identify their strengths, or even accepting the reality of what they have survived. Being witnessed can include the client having a new experience of themselves as they share their experience, or it might simply be feeling seen by another. Clients will often say, "It feels good to just tell someone about this," referring to a struggle or traumatic experience. Being witnessed supports the development of coherency, a sense of being in connection with one's story (Siegel, 1999). This will be discussed later in this book in the coherent narrative section of Chapter 11, and it is a critical aspect of trauma integration and healing.

Some challenges with technology have more recently affected connection capacity. Our social interactions are far fewer than our hunter-gatherer ancestors, who had a ratio of four adults to every child under 6 years old. Perry discusses that we are not living in a way that connects to our biological origins anymore (Winfrey & Perry, 2021), leading to more dysregulation. This adds an extra challenge as the connection gets more remote through devices with texting and emails and there is less in-person connection. Many educators report that the emphasis on technology is changing the topography of mental health in schools. Anxiety and depression seem to be on the rise for young people, and there is some evidence that this is connected to the increase in the use of technology (Winfrey & Perry, 2021). The increase in technology shifts our biological experience for being together in co-regulatory spaces. Co-regulation remains a primary aspect of the treatment of trauma and may even be more important with current social impacts.

With this connection to the regulation of the nervous system at stake, strengthening clients' capacity for co-regulation provides access to the VVC, the neural platform for more resilience and potential post-traumatic growth. "Being able to feel safe with other people is probably the single most important aspect of mental health; safe connections are fundamental to meaningful and satisfying lives" (van der Kolk, 2014, p. 79). The power of this statement underlines how important it is to strengthen co-regulation capacity in ourselves and our clients. Not only does it support feeling more satisfied in life, but co-regulation capacity is also necessary for physical well-being (Porges, 2011, 2024). To examine co-regulation capacity further, it is important to explore the typical patterns in relationships.

AUTOREGULATION AND EXTERNAL REGULATION

Intimacy needs vary, but most of us want support, belonging, trust, and reciprocity in relationships. Without these qualities, relationships would not be so important and valued. With the role of the nervous system, we are primarily in either *protection* mode (red or yellow zone) or in *connection* mode (green zone) (Porges, 2011, 2021, 2024). As discussed earlier, these states can limit us and impact our emotions, behaviors, and relational capacity. We can certainly learn to have a foothold in the green zone when in the red and yellow zones. This requires both awareness and regulation skills, like slowing down, breathing, and not taking things personally. Tracking whether we are in protection or connection states is useful for clients as it supports the potential for shifting the interaction. It is important to ask the question, "Am I defending against, or am I available for connecting?"

Clients will have limits in their co-regulatory capacity that will be based on their life experiences. Tatkin (2023) discusses the tendency for clients to either adaptively autoregulate or externally regulate.[16] The concept of autoregulation involves the need to regulate oneself primarily through solitude. By contrast, external regulation is associated with difficulty in self-regulation, as it involves relying more on someone else to provide regulation. Because both autoregulation and external regulation are also normal responses, these descriptions are referring to the patterned and more fixed responses connected to adaptations. Co-regulation might feel welcome in some situations, and at other times, it might feel intrusive (*autoregulation*) or desperately needed (*external regulation*). Both adaptations affect and limit self-regulation and co-regulation capacity (Tatkin, 2023). As adults, we need the ability to co-regulate with another as well as self-regulate. Having the capacity to do both is another indicator of a regulated and flexible nervous system.

Attachment patterns are a very popular topic and are often discussed in terms of being fixed relational patterns. In Polyvagal Theory, with the recognition of physiological state in attachment, these adaptations can be seen as less locked in and more dependent on physiological state, the specific relationship, as well as on early and current experiences. Rather than fully exploring attachment styles by examining secure, insecure, or disorganized attachments, we will focus on these processes through the lens of co-regulation capacity. Applying this perspective, we are examining co-regulation with the understanding that VVC can be strengthened and developed through positive relational experiences. Therapy itself can help to shift this capacity as co-regulation is an embedded part of sessions, particularly when the focus is on supporting the development of co-regulation capacity.

If the terms were to be cross-referenced, there is a correlation between autoregulation as an indicator of avoidant attachment patterning (red zone dominant) and external regulation as an indicator of anxious-ambivalent attachment patterning (yellow zone dominant). Included here is a list of common attributes seen with each tendency.

General behavioral and emotional indicators of autoregulation:
- Values autonomy
- Fears enmeshment and loss of self
- Task-focused
- Avoids vulnerability
- Intellectual, avoiding emotions
- Direct communication in conflict
- Tends to withdraw or shut down in struggles (Poole Heller, 2019; Marriott & Kelley, 2024)

General behavioral and emotional indicators of external regulation:
- Values relationship and connection
- Fears abandonment and loss of relationship
- Emotional and expressive focus
- Trusts others more than self
- High awareness of others
- Fearful in conflict
- Tends to communicate more in struggles (Poole Heller, 2019; Marriott & Kelley, 2024)

These patterns are interwoven with co-regulation capacity. They are both one-person regulatory systems, not two-person co-regulatory systems, which is our biological wiring need. In autoregulation, the regulation is occurring autonomously, which is a one-person system. In external regulation, the regulation comes from another person, also as a one-person system (Tatkin, 2023). To support co-regulation capacity, the goal is to shift it to two-person co-regulatory patterning. This expansion of co-regulation capacity is dependent on finding enough safety to attain a two-person system of regulation.

Shifting co-regulation capacity can have challenges because, in both adaptations, others become automatized (Tatkin, 2015). Automatizing others feels similar to a trance in which implicit biases take control. Prior beliefs such as thinking someone is not safe, assuming they won't be there, or perceiving them as intrusive and smothering, can negatively impact relational and co-regulation capacities. Automatization of another comes from the brain's need for efficiency and managing its energy; however, the process of automatizing in relationships hinders the connection since it is based on past experiences and the current nervous system state. Lanius (2023) says dysregulation of our nervous system can alter perception by distorting reality, therefore, limiting the ability to connect. The client's co-regulation capacity may improve by addressing these misinterpretations toward others that have been influenced by their emotional and physiological states.

For clients, this might require gently challenging their statements that assume someone's availability for deeper connection in a relationship. "I wonder if we could slow down to talk about this. It sounds like you might be assuming here, and I wonder if you might want to check that out." Or "I hear something different when you talk about your partner and the conversation you had—I wonder if it would help to talk further about this." Clients automatizing others and being in childhood patterns skews what they see in others; this goes across all realms of relationships and is seen every day in therapy offices regarding partners, friends, and coworkers. This is transference, similar to what happens between the client and clinician, but applied to other relationships. This limitation means clients will not have the experience of the necessary co-regulation that could support them when it is available.

Intimacy is a dance between autonomy and dependency. With autoregulation tendencies, the client will stay in the pattern of doing it alone and also hold a fear that they will be smothered. This fear reinforces the autoregulation tendency. In external regulation tendencies, the client wants the other to provide regulation to them, with restricted access to self-regulation; this behavior is grounded in a fear of abandonment. With an underdeveloped ability to self-regulate, clients can set themselves up for abandonment as they reach out often when in distress. Others might feel pressured or overwhelmed by the expectation and pull back from the relationship, which in turn, reinforces the need to stay in constant connection. Again, neither of these patterns is a two-person system. Co-regulation wiring is meant to be both a two-person system and reciprocal; clients need support in stretching to attain this balance. The good news is that with neuroplasticity, co-regulation capacity can grow and evolve as it is a part of our natural wiring, Shifting from earlier conditioning and adaptations can restore co-regulation and bolster self-regulation capacity. It is important to remember that neither tendency is better or more evolved, as both are simply adaptations from life experiences and ANS states. For autoregulation, there is typically red zone dominance. As noted earlier in this book, DVC, as part of conservation physiology, is a not a relational state. Because clients may have often experienced being dismissed and/or deemed unimportant, helping the client learn to integrate the offer of support through embodiment can be very important to strengthening co-regulation capacity. In sessions, helping the client bring awareness to the clinician's interest and willingness to be in connection with them in a nourishing way can be underlined and explored; the co-regulation that is part of the client–clinician relationship can be its own reparative experience. Along with that, as disconnection can be part of this pattern, embodiment practices in general can be supportive. Embodiment practices can shift red zone physiology over time; they support biological signals being more easily read. This deeper connection to self and access to interoception can help clients express their needs and emotions. It gives them the needed signal to feel the necessary self-connection to identify their needs and emotions. Clients also might need to be encouraged to ask for help and to reach out to others. Additionally, sometimes the fear of engulfment drives autoregulation. The fear of engulfment has its origins in threat physiology and automatization from these previously mentioned experiences. Clients may need assistance to separate reality from fear to combat automatization, since automatization can lead to misreading cues. The client with this tendency needs to find balance in healthy boundaries that honor solitude needs and connection to support their co-regulation capacity. Therapeutic work to foster true co-regulation will need to include embodiment, healthy boundaries, skills for reaching out to others, and solutions to transference issues that are based on projections.

For external regulation, yellow zone physiology is often dominant. There is more fear and anxiety in general as part of this underlying physiology. It is certainly normal to want to be regulated by another, but threat physiology makes it difficult to absorb and feel satisfied with the connection, leading to a lack of embodied co-regulation. Instead, the nervous system state stays in activation—feeling one can't do it alone and that one will be abandoned; this makes true co-regulation difficult. The client is often not integrating their positive relational experiences or embodying the support of another; often times, they are not even registering that it is occurring. They need help both seeing it, and having it embedded in a real experience. They often need to be supported and guided to have the embodied experience of being able to integrate the care of another. This integration of someone reliably being there is often at the core of external regulation tendencies and is often something that childhood did not provide. In addition to needing to integrate how others are really there for them, clients also often need help using mindfulness to hold strong emotions and to learn to tolerate distressing states. Strengthening personal agency also is useful for this adaptation. This combination of embodying others support and presence, developing affect tolerance, and accessing a sense of personal agency supports the development of co-regulation; ultimately, this leads to more self-regulation capacity as well.

As with applying all interventions, to shift these co-regulation adaptations, it is first necessary to make sure this is what the client wants for themself. With interest from the client, this can be worked on directly. Other deactivation pathways can also support the return to access of the VVC, which is generally going to support the unfolding into co-regulation. For both adaptations, the clients will benefit from using the intervention of the deactivation pathway of reparative experiences. (This is covered in depth in Chapter 7.) This will assist the client in shifting the underlying beliefs of "I will be abandoned" (external regulation tendency) or "I will be engulfed" (autoregulation tendency) that come from their childhood experiences. Reparative experiences can create a new experience and new belief that open the client to having different experiences in relationships (Kurtz, 1990). It is important to remember that we are designed for co-regulation and that it is part of our Essence; therefore, the pathway for this deactivation process is inherently available.

Since many of these experiences have corresponding body sensations, approaching the co-regulation tendency somatically can provide the attachment map that might be activated in relationships. This could be directing the client to notice their body after imagining being in connection. In autoregulation, wanting to get away, bracing, and/or feeling intruded on is a common report. In external regulation, imagining being in connection might bring up anxiousness, lack of satiety in the connection, and maybe a sense of wanting more from the other. Feeling any of these impulses in the body and the association of their earlier experience (even if it is only a feeling memory in the body without an image) and contrasting that "felt sense" (Gendlin, 1996) experience with current relationships can be useful in helping the client differentiate this early experience from the current time. Having the client work with an embodied practice of this exercise is critical, as these patterns run deep in the body.

> *Practice Tip:* The client can also benefit from bringing in memories or live experiences of known safe relationships. Applying the embodiment of positive states, focusing on the particular person, pet, or spiritual entity that symbolizes safety, can be useful. The clinician could offer, "Take a moment to bring in the image of _____ and notice what it feels like in your body as you remember the sense of safety you have had with this being." When clients are working on strengthening their relational capacity, it is very useful to utilize a relationship, past or present, that has offered safety.

For increased relational capacity, another important therapeutic intervention includes top-down support, not automatizing others through projections. This requires helping them understand that their perceptions might not be accurate. Addressing these perceptions needs a gentle type of feedback from the clinician. There is a sensitive combination of attuning to hearing the clients' struggles in relationships while helping them consider another possibility of what might be occurring in their relationships. Often, I remind clients that in relationships, we look for what we think is true as part of our confirmation bias. If a client always feels they will be abandoned, they will be looking for signs of abandonment as part of their confirmation and negativity biases. Likewise, if the client always assumes they will be engulfed, they will be looking for indicators that will confirm their fears. Addressing this directly with clients is necessary to support their movement toward co-regulation capacity.

EXERCISE FOR EXPANDING CO-REGULATION CAPACITY

Without judgment, let yourself bring into awareness what you see as your own tendency in the dance of intimacy, the fear of abandonment, or the fear of engulfment. Placing your heartfelt attention on your heart with your hand if that feels right, take in the humanness of this adaptation in yourself. Bring gentle awareness that this tendency was a well-earned adaptation, even if you are not fully clear on how it developed. As you might lovingly hold another's feelings and experience, let yourself be with the sense that you are okay as you are right now, keeping attention on your heart area. Breathe into your heart, offering any loving words that might feel good such as "You are safe now," "You get time to learn about this," "You are okay as you are," or anything that feels nourishing to hear. Let these words wash over you, taking all the time you need.

Co-Regulation Capacity: Autoregulation Examples

A client struggling with autoregulation often comes into the office upset about a painful incident with their partner, having never talked to their partner about their feelings. They frequently have a pattern of not bringing issues up in their relationship. In this situation, the client needs encouragement and support to turn toward their partner. To gently guide toward being more relational, the clinician might say, "I wonder what it would be like to reach out and let your partner know you were hurt when that incident happened at the party." The therapeutic intervention is to guide the client toward a more relational way of interacting rather than dealing with it in the habituated autoregulated pattern. The therapy that would follow would be to work with the barriers that arise if they imagine connecting more intimately with their partner. The client might not have even considered it because they are not used to talking about their feelings, or they might report a fear. These fears could include voicing their needs, not feeling skilled enough to communicate, or their partner's reaction to communication. As these concerns are shared, they become the therapeutic focus so the client can examine their tendency and find ways to build more co-regulation capacity. Any fear will have a deactivation pathway that can support this reworking of the habituated response in the direction toward co-regulation.

It is also important to use embodiment when a client has an experience that does not fit their expectation of being smothered or engulfed. A client might report that their partner gave them space and support to do something important for themselves. Like many things that occur in therapy sessions, the client might mention this and go on to the next topic. It would be important to have the client take time to reflect and notice this desired behavior from their partner. Noticing includes bringing awareness to how it feels to have their partner support them in this particular way and to embody the experience of "I am supported in having the space I need" or another important belief. As stated before, the client might not even notice that their partner is giving them exactly what they most want from them. Integrating the desired experience can alleviate the underlying fears of engulfment. As with other applications of the embodiment of resilient states, clients need to have it reinforced to shift the pattern.

Co-Regulation Capacity: External Regulation Examples

A client tending toward external regulation often comes into the office describing a situation in which they are assuming being abandoned by their partner. In this example, when their partner is late coming home, the fear of abandonment surfaces. The client might have the awareness that they are overreacting but still feel upset and in the yellow zone from their fear of being abandoned. Similar to the example of working with autoregulation, clinicians also need to underline things the client has said in the session such as their partner letting them know they are important, and the partner is committed to them. The client will need to embody and truly take in these messages; often the client struggles with absorbing and feeling the satisfaction from the positive experience they are desiring. There might be some exploration focused on helping the client differentiate on the somatic level the past experience versus the current one with their partner.

In general, it would be helpful to have the clinician guide the client to take in those experiences when their partner has conveyed their care and commitment. When dealing with the strong fear of abandonment, taking in the holding and care from another is a critical step toward getting out of the pattern. This needs to be built through experiences with repetition, like other aspects of the resiliency vortex. Over time, the client can learn to be more trusting of relationships as reliable while they integrate experiences that they might not notice currently. Because external regulation is associated with a lack of being truly nourished and able to take in care from another, I often suggest that the clients take time each day to notice how someone is there for them and to embody this experience. Having this focus on their partner, friends, and work relationships helps the client to prime their nervous system to take in relational support. Helping the client feel satisfaction when emptiness and abandonment has been their experience is crucial, as satisfaction is often unintegrated. Focusing on registering and embodying the nourishing presence and availability of another person is key to developing the ability to co-regulate. In this example, the integration of their co-regulation is important for the development of self-regulation.

SUMMARY

Stretching co-regulation capacity ensures clients can benefit from the potential regulation relationships can offer. Close and connected relationships are linked to better health and well-being. Limits in this capacity are directly linked to relational experiences and adaptations; they lead to the tendency to automatize relationships. Nervous system interventions can support clients in shifting their co-regulation capacity. This includes working with the core beliefs and nervous system states that are underlying the patterns. It is also important to help the client embody nourishing offerings from their relationships that dispel their fears of abandonment and engulfment. Clinicians are also charged with delicately holding the clients' feelings about their perceptions as well as assisting the clients in a deeper examination of their relationships and their patterning. This deeper examination supports working with their negativity and confirmation biases to shift toward more co-regulation capacity by broadening their awareness and decreasing their tendencies to automatize another.

EXERCISE FOR INTEGRATING THE SKIN BOUNDARY TO SUPPORT CO-REGULATION CAPACITY

Take a moment to connect to yourself, noticing how it is to move your attention to being with yourself. As you notice this, allow yourself to feel your skin boundary, tracing the edges of your body with your aware-ness. Notice how your skin is an actual barrier to protect your inner self. It supports you at both holding what you receive from others as well as creating the space that you need from others. Allow yourself to feel the safety of this boundary as it offers you most what you need, noticing it now in your body.

Let yourself bring up a real or imagined person, pet, spiritual being, or place that represents relational safety for you. Take a moment to be with the image and invite yourself to feel the ease and comfort that it offers, noting your skin boundary's protection as much as you need, while also allowing yourself to feel the connection to another. Allow yourself to relish in this experience of safe connection with the bound-aries that feel right to you, and allow yourself to stay with this embod-iment practice as long as it feels good to do so. This can be practiced often to support co-regulation capacity.

CHAPTER 6

Reparative Experiences, Part 1: Broad Applications of Reparative Experiences

The wish for repair after misattunement never goes away.
We stay hungry for painful misattunements being made right
through repair.

Being able to repair relationships allows our imperfections to be a normal aspect of interaction while also offering us a call to make it right for another. The process of tending to our impact on another supports the fullest version of being present and holding the value of the relationship. Our most integrated selves value connection more than being right. This is a way to live in the VVC, honoring connection and holding the intention to find the way back to safety with another. This chapter will explore how important this pathway is in restoring regulation.

As we discuss reparative experiences, you will notice that they are inherently co-regulating, as there is a definitive crossover between these two concepts. A reparative experience will always offer co-regulation, but it extends beyond typical aspects of co-regulation, requiring its own focus as a deactivation pathway.

Reparative experiences play a crucial role in deactivating the nervous system in therapy after childhood abuse, developmental wounding, and other forms of misattunement. This chapter will explore the general applications of rupture and repair for deactivation. The next chapter will focus on developmental wounding and childhood trauma, specifically addressing how reparative experiences can help shift inaccurate core beliefs at a nervous system level. While reparative experiences for developmental wounding and trauma will incorporate concepts from this chapter, they will also require additional interventions to change core beliefs to fully shift the physiology of the ANS.

RUPTURE AND REPAIR

Underlying relational struggles, developmental wounding and trauma are ruptures. Ruptures are defined as "a break in an optimal way of relating to others"
(Siegel, 2012b, p. 24). Relational disconnection from ruptures is a continuum
including everything from misattunement to unmet needs and trauma. This
disconnect requires repair to reestablish the connection. Without the necessary
repair, the nervous system moves to threat states of yellow and red. As part of
rupture and repair, repair is what Siegel (2012b, p. 24) calls an active effort to
restore the connection through an attuned response, resulting in the deactivation of the nervous system. Occurring in the context of relationships, repair
requires relational experiences to heal.

Ruptures and repairs are a normal part of human interactions and relationships. In the natural act of relating to others, there are misattunements from
misunderstandings and communication errors. This happens in any interpersonal dynamic, including parenting, therapy, and everyday relationships.
Although ruptures are normal, they still require repair to reinstate safety. In
healthy, connected relationships, repair occurs with mindful and intentional
communication and actions. It involves acknowledging the break in connection, recognizing its impact, and reestablishing safety through renewed connection. In personal relationships, repair may involve:

- validating feelings
- taking responsibility
- sincerely apologizing
- creating agreements regarding the negotiation of needs
- defining desired ways of interacting

In this chapter, we explore the situations in which repair from rupture has not
occurred, and how the deactivation pathway of reparative experiences is utilized to support access back to the green zone of the VVC.

As stated above, the most important aspect of rupture and repair is that
the repair *does* happen. Rooted in the evolutionary need for co-regulation,
reparative experiences help regulate the nervous system. When misattunement occurs, it triggers a physiological threat response (yellow and red zones),
especially in close relationships, which are vital for survival. Providing repair
restores a sense of safety in connection and access to the green zone again
(see Figure 6.1).

Reparative experiences are a key part of therapeutic interventions and are essential for healing from many types of trauma. Because co-regulation helps restore
access to the VVC after distressing events, attuned relational interactions are critical
for recovery. Most forms of trauma benefit from reparative experiences: accidents,
medical crises, natural disasters, interpersonal violence, oppression, marginal-

ization, and bullying. These experiences offer support and may include being in the soothing presence of another, feeling witnessed, and/or receiving a validating response.

How one is responded to after trauma plays a significant role in how trauma is integrated. When responses are attuned, they offer an experience of co-regulation (Siegel, 2007), supporting deactivation. Because the nervous system has a neural expectation (Porges, 2011, 2021, 2024) for co-regulation, the pain of disrupted relational cues keeps the nervous system in dysregulation. Misattuned responses are often the most painful aspect of these experiences. Such responses tend to be the aspects of memory that hold the most charge for the client. Biologically, humans are wired to need repair when ruptures occur in a relationship. Many clients often do not know they need repair in developmental trauma, particularly when knowing how they are/were impacted is part of the trauma adaptation. Part of healing often includes bringing back the awareness of even wanting repair, as the importance of reestablishing safety is recognized. When the recognition and acknowledgment of pain caused is followed by regret, it will often help to settle another's nervous system.

Reparative experiences start with attunement being restored, as misattunement is at the core of any kind of rupture. In contrast to attunement, misattunement leads one to not feel understood and met with emotional awareness.

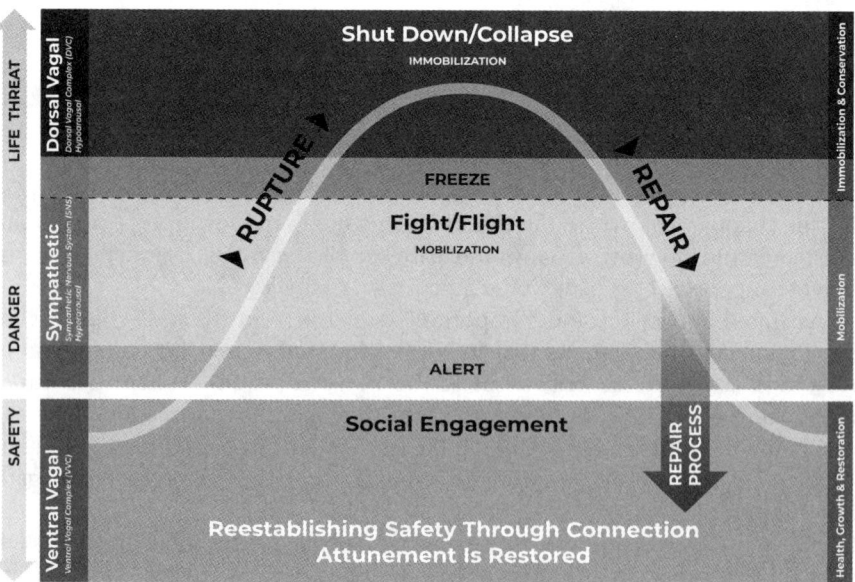

FIGURE 6.1:   Rupture and Repair   Credit: Ruby Jo Walker based on concepts from Stephen Porges; graphic by Cindy Miller Atchison Design & Art

Experiencing misattunement or mistreatment leads to nervous system dysregulation. As previously discussed, we naturally seek regulation from others, especially when we are distressed. A threat state is evoked when this regulation is absent or when responses are misattuned. Because we long to "feel 'felt'" (Siegel, 2010b, p. 55) by another, misattunement can sometimes feel as bad or worse than no response. Misattuned experiences lead one not to feel seen or heard in some way. When misattunement is not repaired, the nervous system remains in threat physiology (Wood, 2024), especially in significant relationships.

> *Reflection:* Bring up a time you offered repair to another that felt good because it was received well and even strengthened the relationship. Maybe you were edgy or grumpy with a partner, child, or friend, and you apologized to them. Feel what it is like in your body to take in the renewed connection and your ability to make the necessary repair. Notice if there is a shift in your state. If you moved more into the VVC, take time to feel that in your body, noticing the sensations.

Let's look at an example of misattunement and possible repair scenarios. Misattunement happens when someone loses their job and a friend says, "Lucky you, you get unemployment now, and you do not have to work." This kind of comment negates the possible experience of the person's sadness and potential anxiety about finding a new job. The repair could come from the friend simply acknowledging their mistake. It also might occur in therapy or with another friend who might offer, "That sounds hurtful and insensitive," when the first comment is shared. Feeling seen and heard again through validation is the repair that creates a return to the green zone.

Repair is most effective when initiated by the person who caused the misattunement; relationships are negatively affected if repair is not made in the context of that relationship. Nevertheless, even in these situations, some settling of the nervous system can happen simply by being understood by another person, even if they are not the one who originally caused the breach in connection. This frequently happens in therapeutic settings when clinicians provide restored attunement through understanding. In restored attunement, the individual feels seen, heard, and understood; this leads to nervous system regulation again. This process is further enhanced if the reparative experience occurs with the person involved in the original misattunement, but repair acknowledging the rupture can be helpful. True repair will shift physiology, which is the goal.

The steps in general repair in the therapeutic setting are:
1. Acknowledgment of what happened
2. Validation of feelings
3. Reeducation when necessary

These steps tend to blend, and some aspects are more important for certain clients, depending on the situation. Acknowledgment of what happened includes naming the rupture. Clients often need to hear comments such as, "That is bullying," "That sounds like a mean thing to say," "That prejudice you are describing is unacceptable," or "That was not sex, that was an assault." In the last statement, reeducation is also part of the acknowledgment.

Validation reflects the impact of an experience. Examples include, "Of course, you felt hurt by such a cruel response," "It sounds really painful," or "It is normal to feel confused and betrayed when you are sexually assaulted by someone you thought was a friend." Validation sends the message of safety as it bridges the loneliness one can feel after trauma and challenging experiences. Feeling that someone understands a challenging experience provides a sense of being less alone in it.

Reeducation can offer the needed piece of information to assist the client's understanding of the situation. "How your dad behaved toward you is not an okay way to treat a child," "Kids are not supposed to have to take care of their parents because of their drinking," "Sometimes, bodies respond to a sexual assault, and it does not mean they wanted to have sex," or "Being different does not make you less than others." The goal of reeducation is to promote the clients' better understanding of themselves or to offer a new perspective to support something they might be judging. (You can see that reeducation could begin to move into the area of inaccurate or limiting core beliefs, which is covered in the next chapter.)

After reparative experiences, clients report feeling better because they got the relief they were longing for, without always knowing they were longing for it. An indicator that a reparative experience has led to deactivation occurs when the client's nervous system settles and they are no longer stuck. At times, they make changes in their life informed by the integration of a reparative experience. This includes restoring any kind of impulse that has underlying agency and choice. These emerging impulses often have a sense of vitality or aliveness as opposed to just adjusting to how it is. When realizing that a boss's behavior is unkind and crosses the line of acceptable workplace behavior, the client could decide to speak up to their human resources department, or they might decide to quit. As a byproduct of any deactivation pathway, clients have a stronger connection to themselves as Essence is restored. (Essence has been defined earlier as our true self, without the limits of nervous system functioning including our co-regulation capacity and core beliefs, where choice and agency are available.) Back in regulation, the client can make the best decisions for themselves, unencumbered by conditioning, self-blame, and unrealistic expectations. Instead, the reparative experiences support empowerment to move forward. Their choice is connected to their Essence and to what will ultimately support them in their regulation.

EXERCISE FOR INTEGRATING REPAIR

As a way to look at the power of repair, let yourself now bring to mind a situation with someone you wish had offered repair to you after an experience of misattunement that led to hurt for you. For this exercise, have the experience be a 3–5 on a scale of 1–10. Notice how it feels in your body. As you bring this up, imagine the person saying these words to you: "I am so sorry. I was so wrong in my response to you, and I truly regret my behavior. You matter to me, and I want you to know that I want to work on being more skillful with you." Take a moment to just let this in; allow yourself to embody these words. As you feel it in your body, notice what happens.

Generally, it is reported that more ease comes into the body, which is the pathway of the VVC. This is the power of repair.

> *Reflection:* I have noticed that the wish for repair never seems to go away. Clients remain hungry to have a painful situation "made right" by another in some way. The need for reparative experiences seems to evoke a primal longing that is usually meaningful whenever it happens. Knowing how deep this need is helps clients understand why they often wonder, "Why am I still wishing this could happen?" I often relay this to them as it supports their acceptance of this need.

SUMMARY

Rupture and repair are a normal part of all relationships and an integral part of therapeutic relationships. This includes validation, soothing, and witnessing, all which offer a template for shifting physiology to VVC. Going beyond general co-regulation, they are intentional interventions to support nervous system settling, touching on the deeper human needs to be fully understood and supported. Evoking the VVC, these interventions shift the client from the trauma vortex and back into the flow of integration. Clients generally report feeling relieved and more peaceful as a result of this profound form of co-regulation.

CHAPTER 7

Reparative Experiences, Part 2: Developmental Wounding

All patterns make sense in the context of the impact of challenging experiences.

One of the most profound lessons I've learned in my work is how core beliefs take hold and shape a person's trauma identity, often unconsciously. It's been eye-opening to see how these beliefs can limit a person's life, yet when we look at them in the context of past experiences, they begin to make sense. This understanding brings both clarity and compassion—it's no wonder people develop patterns of protection. But what's even more powerful is witnessing clients reconnect with their true selves, their Essence (see Figure 7.1). Watching that transformation unfold is one of the most rewarding parts of therapy. In this chapter, we will discuss how to apply these interventions to help clients break free from limiting beliefs and step into their Essence, accessing their vitality and agency.

The previous chapter outlined how general reparative experiences are required to deactivate the nervous system. This chapter will focus on specific reparative experiences for developmental wounding. The nervous system imprint of unresolved earlier relational traumas is a powerful variable in nervous system dysregulation. Childhood trauma often lays the groundwork for internalizing inaccurate and limiting core beliefs, requiring an in-depth intervention. These limiting core beliefs from developmental wounding are the basis of trauma identity, which will be further discussed in this chapter. Offering reparative experiences can address changing the limiting core beliefs to recover one's Essence, often leading to more resilience and post-traumatic growth.

FIGURE 7.1: Essence Qualities   Credit: Ruby Jo Walker; graphic by Cindy Miller Atchison Design & Art

DEVELOPMENTAL WOUNDING

Developmental wounding refers to the emotional and relational injuries that occur during crucial stages of childhood development due to unmet needs, misattunement, neglect, or harmful relational experiences. They encompass both the painful interactions that do occur and the needed nurturing experiences that do not occur. These suboptimal relational interactions lead to dysregulated physiology, and they affect one's sense of self and relational patterns. In childhood, these subpar experiences can result in difficulty with social engagement, emotional regulation, and overall well-being (Porges, 2021). The heightened state of perceived danger after these experiences, even in safe experiences, is at the root of this shift in physiology. Simply put, these powerful experiences of abuse, unmet needs, and inadequate co-regulatory experiences lead the nervous system to become stuck in SNS or DVC. The stuckness is part of the vortex and the chaos and rigidity pattern and often includes the internalization of limiting core beliefs, all of which create a barrier to resilience and traumatic growth.

LIMITING CORE BELIEFS

While *limiting core beliefs* can create significant distress, they also offer an opportunity for transformation through intentional healing. Transforming them becomes a way to promote personal expansion. These inaccurate beliefs lead to many life difficulties and are often the foundation of many mental health issues (Beck, 1979).

> Beginning in childhood, people develop certain ideas about themselves, other people, and their world. Their most central core beliefs are enduring understandings that are so fundamental and deep that they often do not articulate them, even to themselves. The person regards these ideas as the absolute truths—just the way things 'are.'" (Beck & Beck, 2011, p. 37)

These beliefs arise as a means to make sense of one's experiences; formed in protection, they support survival. Being regarded as Beck and Beck's (2011) "absolute truths" keeps these beliefs alive.

After trauma, clients either move into depreciation or post-traumatic growth (O'Connor et al., 2022). Depreciation can be likened to Levine and Siegel's analogies of stuckness, described earlier, of the stuck "vortex" (Levine, 1997) or "chaos and rigidity" (Siegel, 2010a). This depreciation occurs when negative core beliefs are confirmed, rather than becoming an avenue for expansion (O'Connor et al., 2022).

In childhood abuse situations, clients often feel unworthy or unlovable; this core belief is formed from the childhood challenges of not feeling loved and valued. As an example of how depreciation after trauma manifests, consider the client who experienced abuse, which formed a limiting and inaccurate belief of unlovability. Even with their adaptation, they might have navigated their life through their adaptations. Years later, they experience company reorganization at their workplace. Being the only person laid off, the old belief of unlovability and lack of worthiness reemerges despite their understanding of the company's need to cut their job. As these beliefs surface, it becomes hard to move forward. In addition to the grief of a job loss, the client becomes stuck in the trauma vortex again, experiencing the chaos and rigidity of a lack of integration of their value and lovability. This is depreciation, when negative core beliefs become confirmed. In this case, the client is not able to recognize that they were laid off because of their position, not their inherent worth. The client's early belief of unlovability moves to the foreground of their experience. The deterioration process, rather than potential expansion, limits the client; the early core belief is undeniably in the way, causing deep pain.

In contrast, post-traumatic growth involves facing these early childhood beliefs and transforming the newly uncovered harmful ones. In this same example, the clinician would help the client integrate a sense of self-worth and lovability despite being the only person to lose their job. Through the integration of new experience, what was once a source of loss now becomes an opportunity for deeper self-connection, allowing the client to release the limitations imposed by this inaccurate core belief. In this way, metamorphosizing limiting

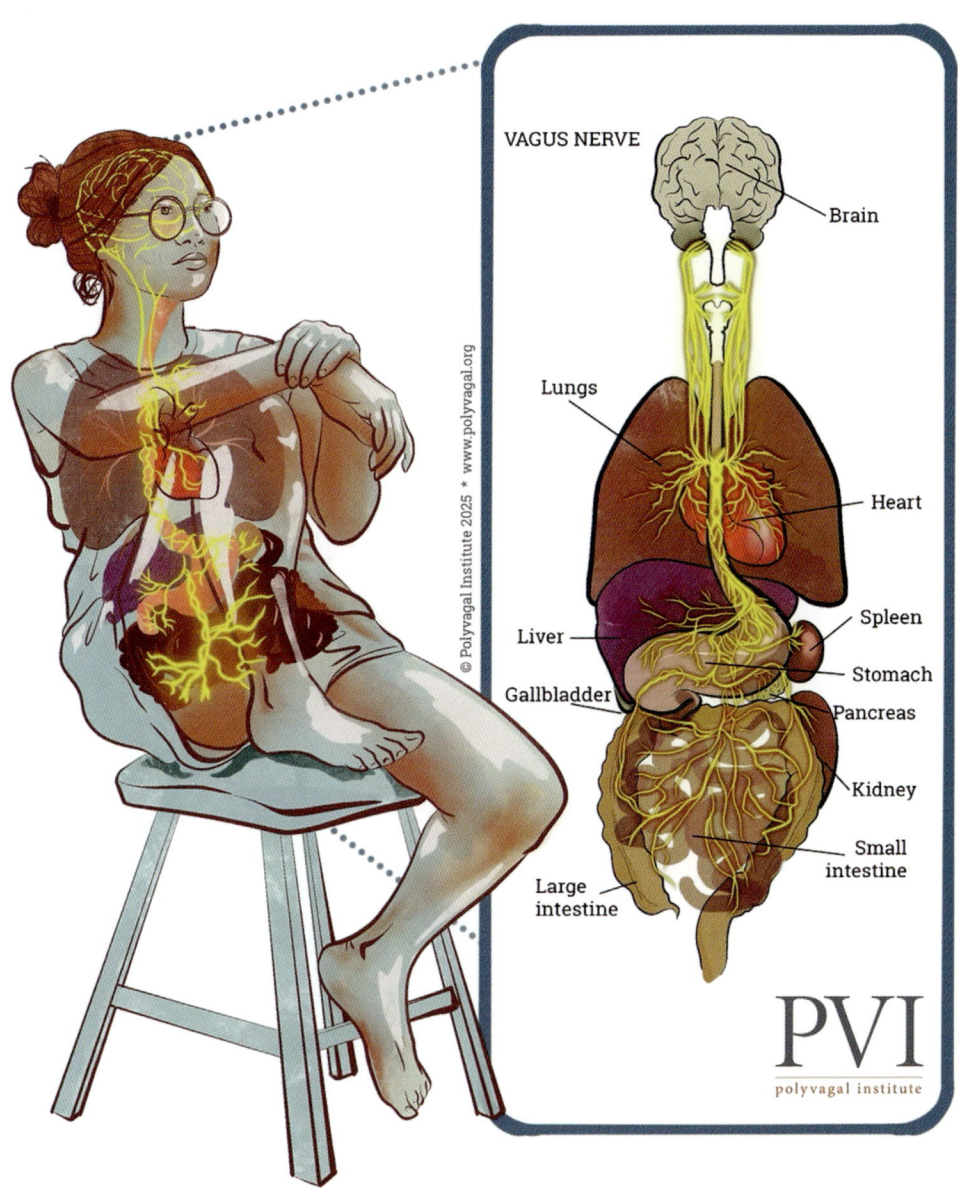

VAGUS NERVE

Brain

Lungs

Heart

Liver

Spleen

Gallbladder

Stomach

Pancreas

Kidney

Small
intestine

Large
intestine

© Polyvagal Institute 2025 * www.polyvagal.org

PVI
polyvagal institute

FIGURE 1.2: Vagus Nerve   Credit: Illustration by Alexis Cruz Gómez, "Anatomy of the Vagus Nerve," Polyvagal Institute

Parasympathetic Nervous System
Dorsal Vagal Complex (DVC)

▲ INCREASES
Fuel Storage and Insulin Activity
Immobilization Behavior (with fear)
Endorphins to Numb/Raise Pain Threshold
Conservation of Metabolic Resources

▼ DECREASES
Heart Rate · Blood Pressure
Temperature · Muscle Tone
Facial Expressions and Eye Contact
Depth of Breath · Social Behavior
Attunement to Human Voice
Sexual Responses · Immune Response

Sympathetic Nervous System
(SNS)

▲ INCREASES
Blood Pressure · Heart Rate · Fuel Availability
Adrenaline · Oxygen Circulation to Vital Organs
Blood Clotting · Pupil Size · Dilation of Bronchi
Defensive Responses

▼ DECREASES
Fuel Storage · Insulin Activity
Digestion · Salivation · Relational Ability
Immune Response

Parasympathetic Nervous System
Ventral Vagal Complex (VVC)

▲ INCREASES
Digestion · Intestinal Motility
Resistance to Infection · Immune Response
Rest and Recuperation · Health and Vitality
Circulation to Non-Vital Organs (skin, extremities)
Oxytocin (neuromodulator involved in social bonds that allows immobility without fear)
Ability to Relate and Connect
Movement in Eyes and Head Turning
Prosody in Voice · Breath

▼ DECREASES
Defensive Responses

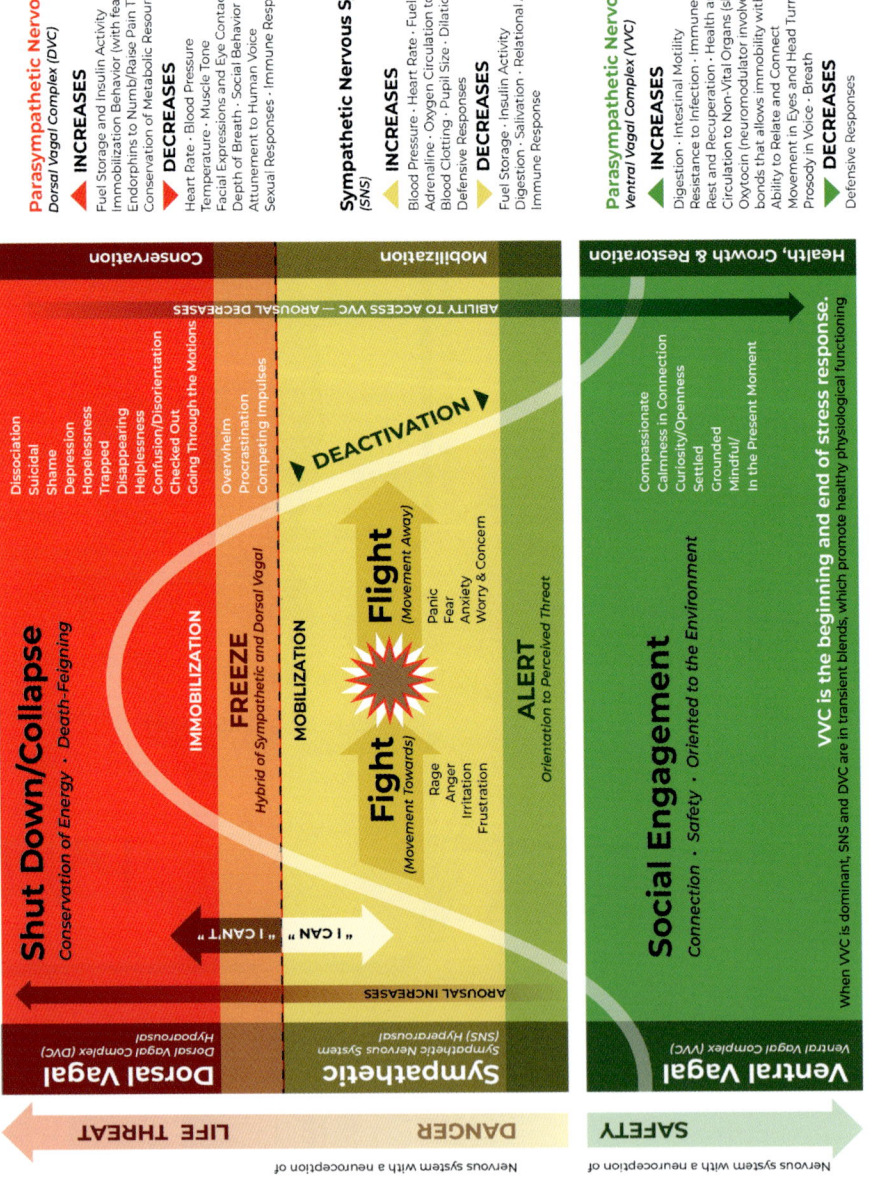

FIGURE 1.3: Polyvagal Theory Chart of Trauma Response   Credit: Ruby Jo Walker adapted from Cheryl Sanders, with ideas from Peter Levine, Anthony "Twig" Wheeler, and Stephen Porges; graphic by Cindy Miller Atchison Design & Art

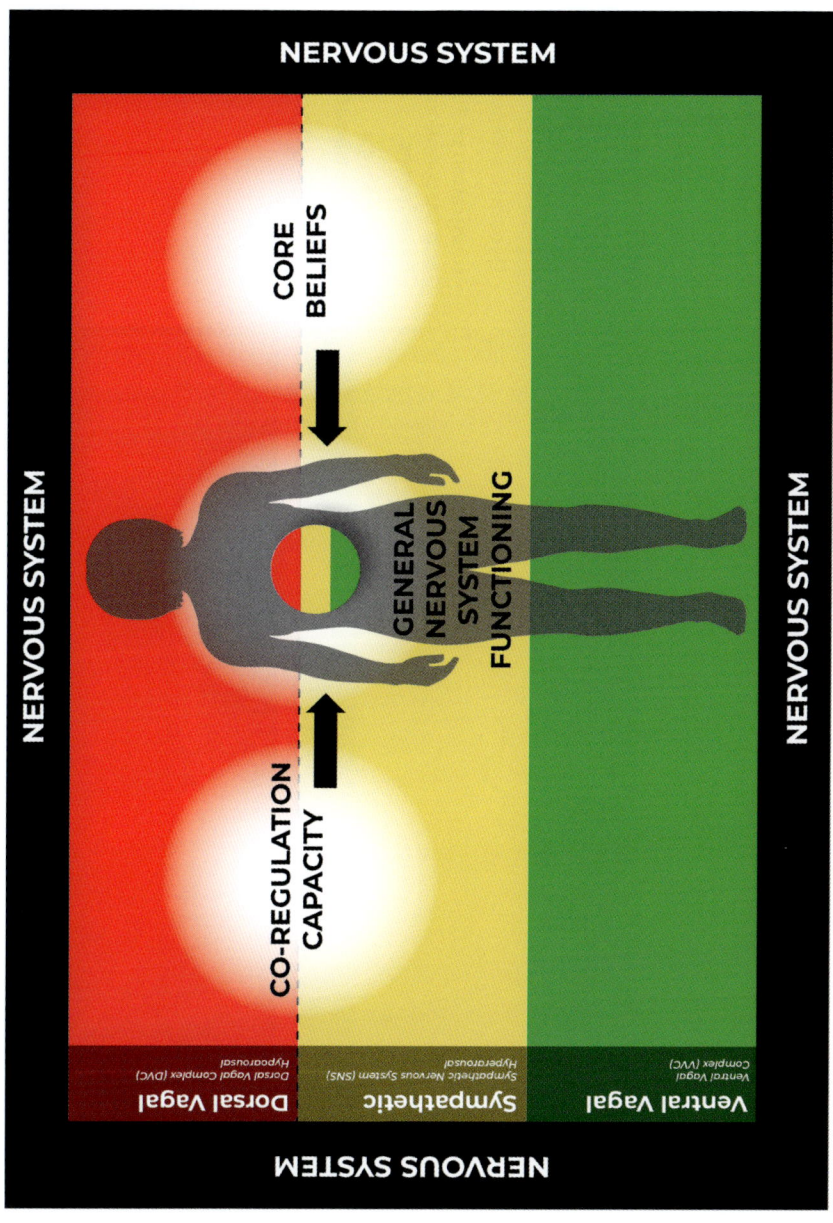

FIGURE 2.2:   Three Nervous System Maps for Treatment   Credit: Ruby Jo Walker; graphic by Cindy Miller Atchison Design & Art

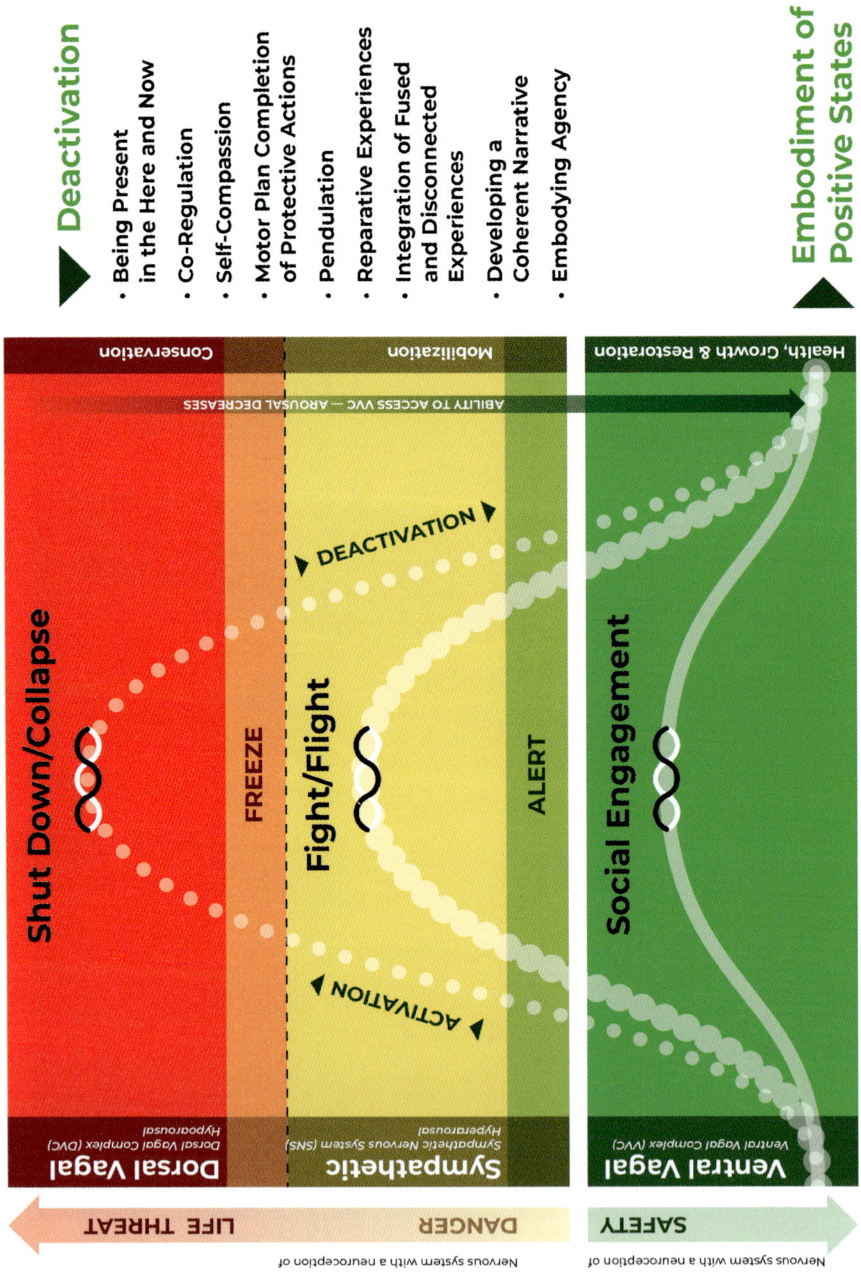

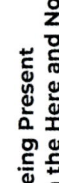

Deactivation

- Being Present in the Here and Now
- Co-Regulation
- Self-Compassion
- Motor Plan Completion of Protective Actions
- Pendulation
- Reparative Experiences
- Integration of Fused and Disconnected Experiences
- Developing a Coherent Narrative
- Embodying Agency

Embodiment of Positive States

Conservation · Mobilization · Health, Growth & Restoration

ABILITY TO ACCESS VVC — AROUSAL DECREASES

DEACTIVATION ▶

Shut Down/Collapse

FREEZE

Fight/Flight

ALERT

Social Engagement

◀ ACTIVATION ◀

Dorsal Vagal Complex (DVC)
Hyperarousal

Dorsal Vagal

Sympathetic Nervous System (SNS)
Hyperarousal

Sympathetic

Ventral Vagal Complex (VVC)

Ventral Vagal

LIFE THREAT · DANGER · SAFETY

Nervous system with a neuroception of · Nervous system with a neuroception of

FIGURE 2.3: Deactivation Pathways   Credit: Ruby Jo Walker with the general concept of activation and deactivation from Peter Levine and Somatic Experiencing ®; graphic by Cindy Miller Atchison Design & Art

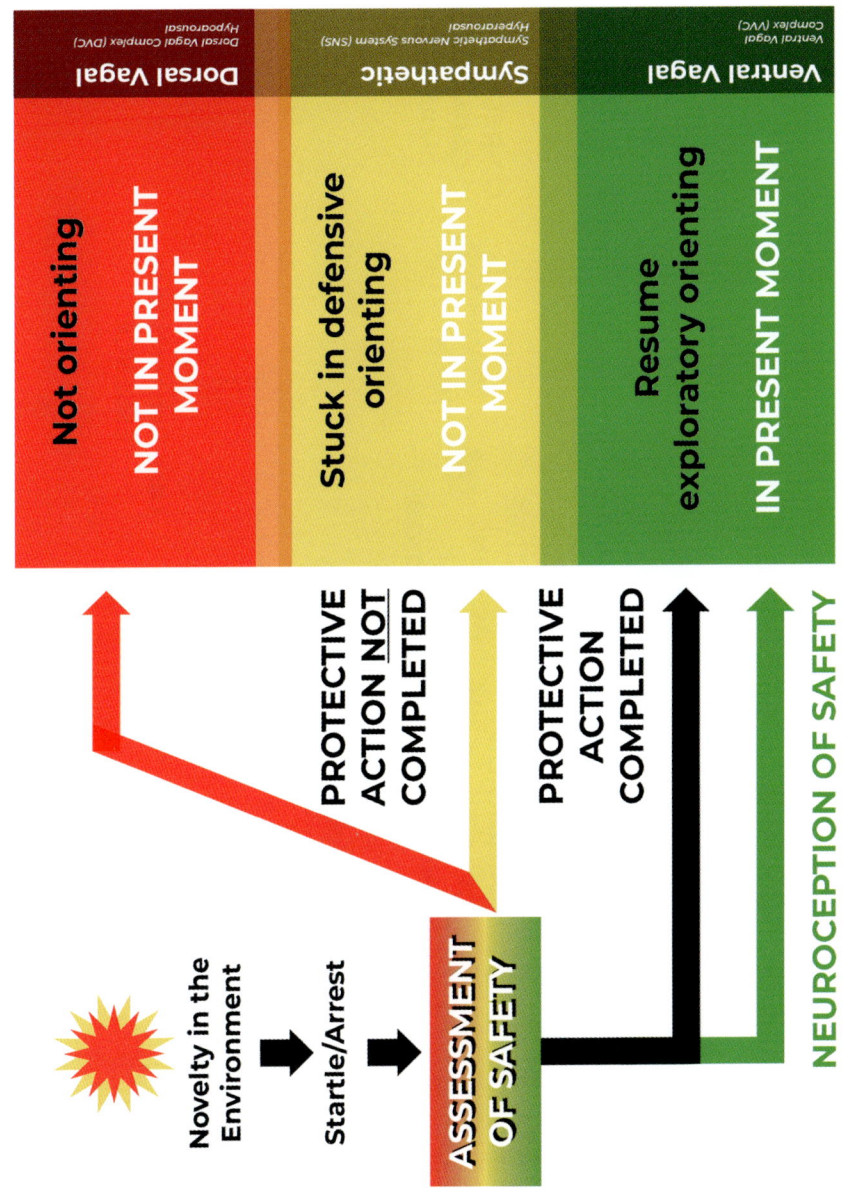

FIGURE 4.1: Orientation Response   Credit: Ruby Jo Walker with concepts from Peter Levine, Somatic Experiencing ®, and Stephen Porges; graphic by Cindy Miller Atchison Design & Art

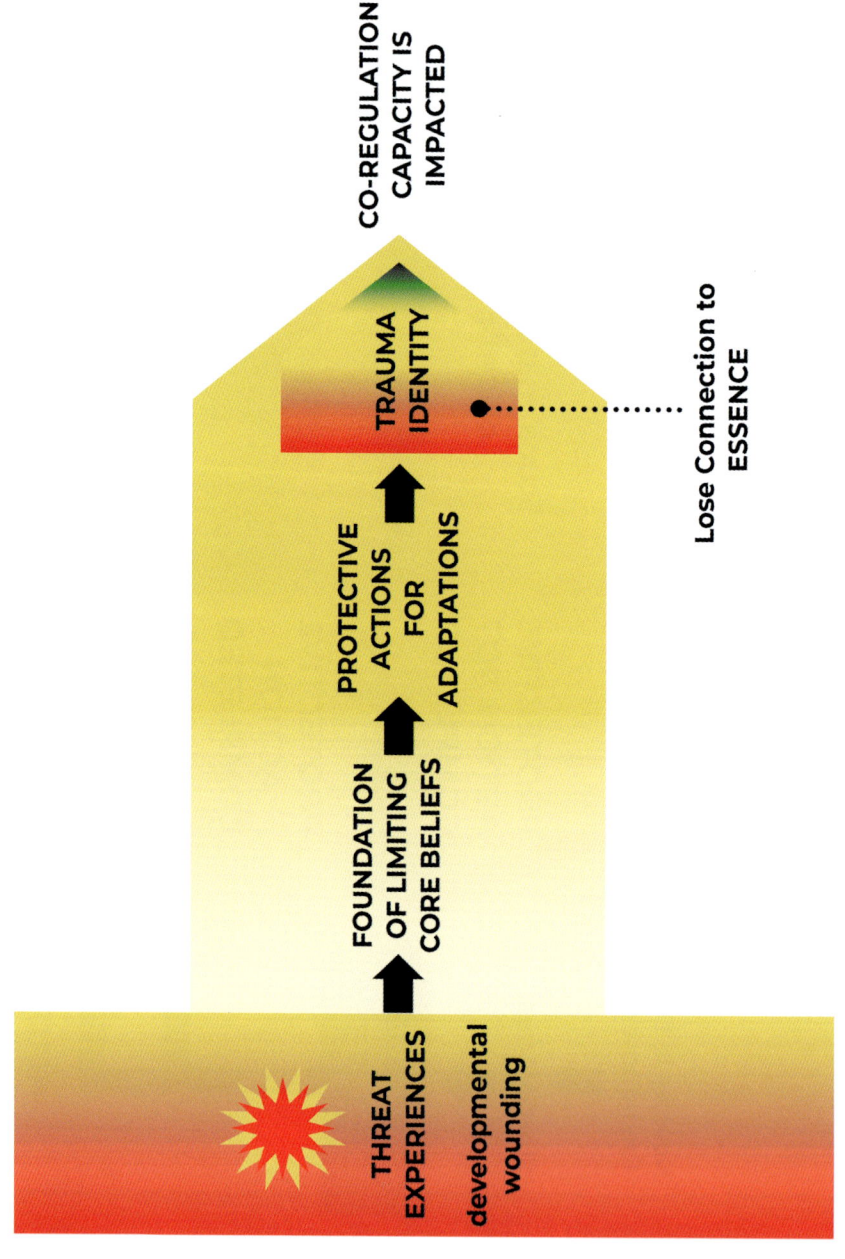

FIGURE 7.2: Trauma Identity Process   Credit: Ruby Jo Walker; graphic by Cindy Miller Atchison Design & Art

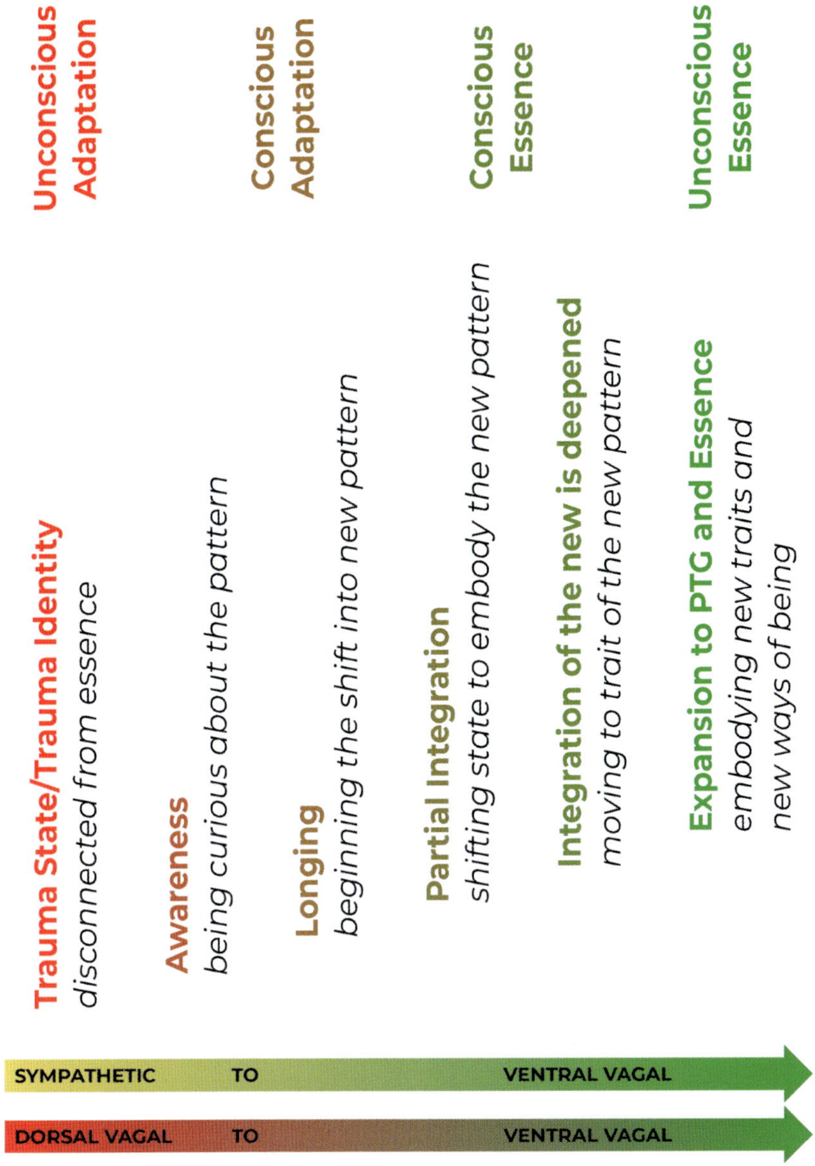

Unconscious Adaptation

Conscious Adaptation

Conscious Essence

Unconscious Essence

Trauma State/Trauma Identity
disconnected from essence

Awareness
being curious about the pattern

Longing
beginning the shift into new pattern

Partial Integration
shifting state to embody the new pattern

Integration of the new is deepened
moving to trait of the new pattern

Expansion to PTG and Essence
embodying new traits and new ways of being

SYMPATHETIC → TO → VENTRAL VAGAL

DORSAL VAGAL → TO → VENTRAL VAGAL

FIGURE 13.1: Continuum of Embodiment   Credit: Ruby Jo Walker with inspiration from Emily Newcomer; graphic by Cindy Miller Atchison Design & Art

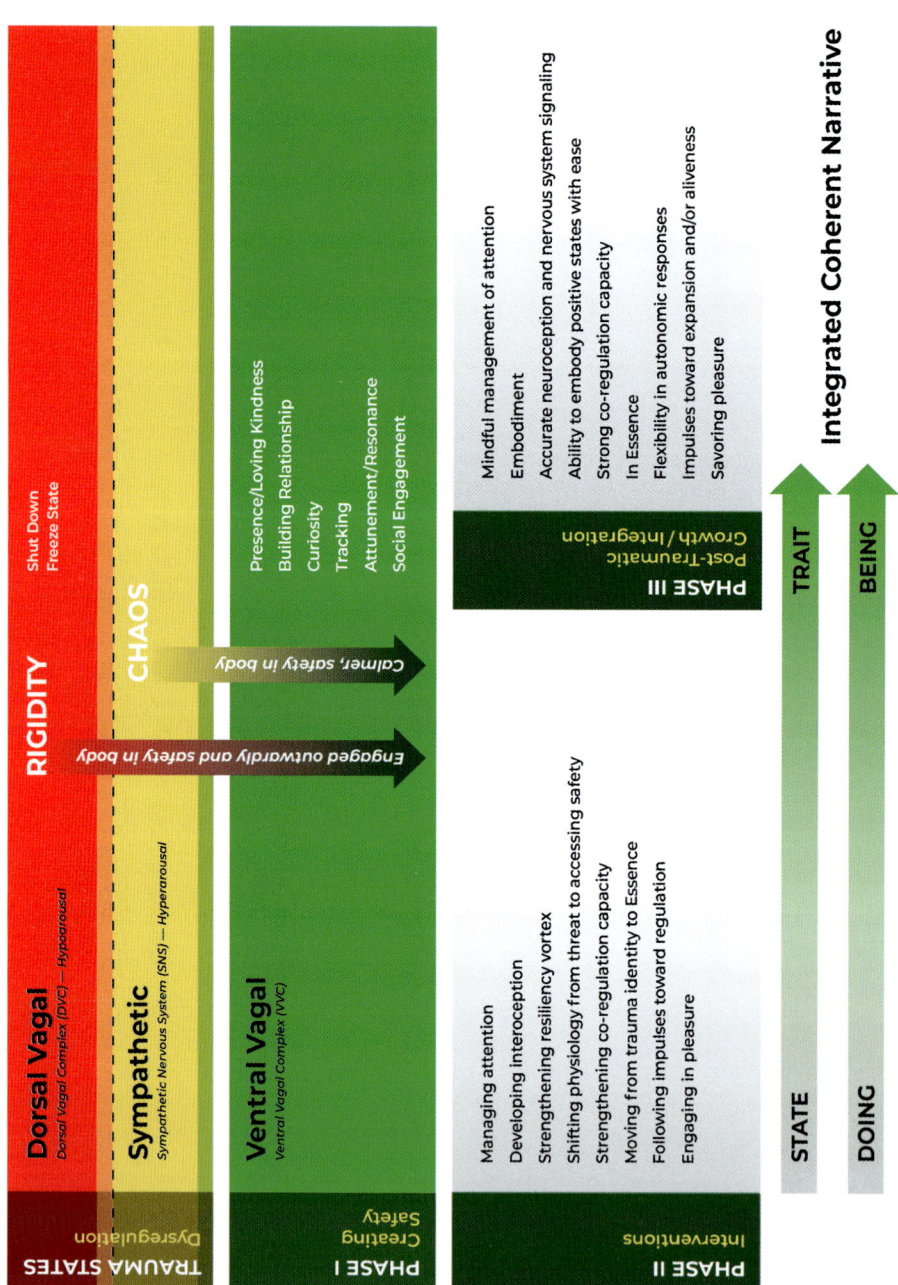

FIGURE 14.1:   Phases of Treatment   Credit: Ruby Jo Walker; graphic by Cindy Miller Atchison Design & Art

core beliefs to more accurate, positive, and/or realistic beliefs serves as a key pathway to post-traumatic growth.

The development of limiting core beliefs relates directly to needs being met. In Maslow's well-known hierarchy of needs, the primary needs for development are basic physiological needs of food and housing, safety, love and belonging, and self-esteem (Maslow, 1968). These needs are built on one another to derive the possibility of self-actualization, defined as the realization or fulfillment of one's potential. Realizing one's potential and post-traumatic growth are linked, as both are about reaching the highest version of oneself. If needs are met, more growth and expansion can happen.

In addition to needs not being met, abuse and neglect will also affect how one sees oneself, relationships, and the world (Beck, 1995; Kurtz, 1990; Reeds, 2015); from these experiences and their corresponding core beliefs, an adaptation occurs (Kurtz, 1990).[17] The core beliefs lead to protective actions to avoid the pain of an unmet need; this helps with survival. Stemming from the core beliefs, adaptations become the default way of experiencing life; the habituated and often unconscious adaptation is based on past experiences and is not inclusive of current reality (Kurtz, 1990). As life narrows with the necessary adoption of an adaptation, there is a wide range of ways these limiting core beliefs negatively impact clients' ability to thrive. Ultimately, they undermine personal volition and agency. Agency includes freely being in one's true self and not being hindered by an earlier adaptive pattern that inhibits one's needs.

The context for change encompasses honoring the adaptation, while also bringing awareness to how life circumstances are different now. It also often requires the intervention of a *deactivation pathway* of *offering a reparative experience* for it to change fully.

As an outcome of the adaptation, choices will be limited (Reeds, 2015). If someone's basic needs are not met in some way, the protective action might be to simply ignore those needs later in life. As another example, if there was a lot of anger growing up, an adaptation might be to please others to ward off the anger. Adaptations will be further discussed later in this chapter, but there are many variations, and they all connect to finding a way through a challenge as part of survival. Even though these adaptations result in aspects of self being frozen off, adaptations are useful in avoiding the more immediate pain of the unmet need. What gets a client through a challenge will almost always get in the way as adaptations carry both underdeveloped and overdeveloped aspects of self. They require reparative experiences to shift the physiological state, beliefs, feelings, and/or patterns.

> *Reflection:* The following quote from Stephen Porges is very relevant to how we want to view and approach all adaptations: "If we want individuals to feel safe, we do not accuse them of doing something wrong or bad. We explain to them . . .

how their responses were adaptive, how we need to appreciate this adaptive feature, and how the client needs to understand that this adaptive feature is flexible and can change in different contexts." (2012, p. 122)

TRAUMA IDENTITY

When these survival adaptations to shield oneself from unmet needs, abuse, or neglect become deeply ingrained, they form *trauma identity*. Trauma identity becomes a central part of how someone sees themselves, their relationships, and their place in the world. One's sense of self becomes organized around these adaptations from their experiences. Essence, which has been defined as our true self, without the limits of nervous system functioning including, our co-regulation capacity and limiting core beliefs, where choice and agency are restored, has a home in the VVC. Because trauma identity arises in response to threat, it anchors the nervous system in states of red and yellow zone physiology. The therapeutic goal is to return to Essence, which is rooted in green zone physiology.

Trauma identity has blended nervous system states. As SNS is the platform for taking action, it is recruited to take protective action for the necessary adaptation. It both minimizes pain and becomes the foundation of the trauma identity. Depending on the road map of action needed for protection from pain, the VVC will be affected. (See the Trauma Identity Process in Figure 7.2 in the text and on the color insert.)

The SNS uses its ability to mobilize in the face of a threat and takes actions driven by the developmental trauma. An example of this might be a client who has an early experience of not having anyone attend to them. This creates a belief, formed in a threat state, that "no one will be there for me." This mobilizes the action of trying to do it alone in life. The adaptation of approaching life alone helps shield the pain of feeling alone, as that pain is frozen off. These threat-based behavioral actions take on a life of their own over time. The action of doing it alone becomes habituated in the nervous system, often below awareness, deeply embedding trauma identity. These default responses, the foundation of the trauma identity, impede them from receiving what they never received as a child (Eisman, 2015; Reeds, 2015). Continuing the childhood pattern, trauma identity will also prevent one from receiving nourishment (Kurtz, 1990). Nourishment is the satisfaction received from relationships and enriching experiences. Trauma identity blocks being able to receive and absorb these positive experiences that bring fulfillment to life.

Trauma identity is reinforced by the negativity bias. The negativity bias will lead to a block in experiences that are not part of the pattern; instead, the pattern stays alive, not allowing needs to be fully met. Just like in adaptations in co-regulation, confirmation bias, defined as the tendency to interpret new evidence as confirmation of one's existing beliefs or theories, leads one to actively

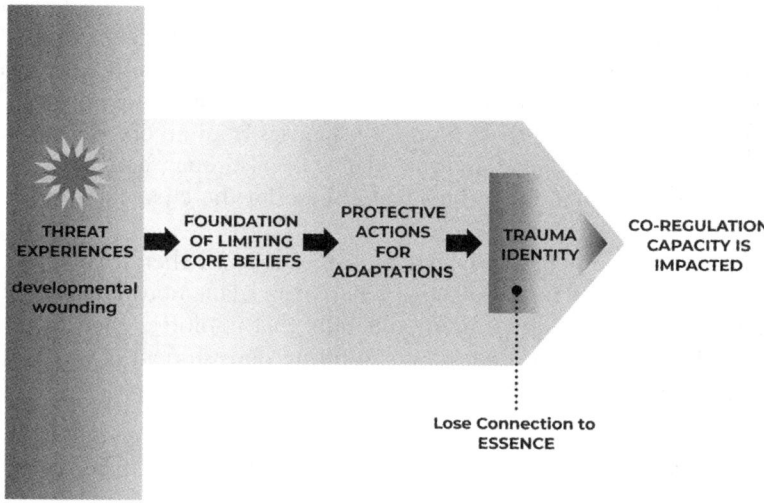

FIGURE 7.2:　Trauma Identity Process　　Credit: Ruby Jo Walker; graphic by Cindy Miller
Atchison Design & Art

look for how a core belief is true. These biases reinforce limiting core beliefs; potential positive intentions and actions that do not align with the beliefs are often not recognized.

Trauma identity keeps a client in the trauma vortex, where they are stuck in chaos and rigidity. Although trauma identity is designed to protect from the pain of unmet needs, the adaptation itself creates significant loss, with inherent limits as it becomes the default way of being in the world. This default pattern constricts perception and experiences, severely diminishing life satisfaction and agency.

If a client has the experience of not being allowed to have personal power in their life, they could develop a trauma identity of staying isolated from others, so they can stay in their personal power while not being impacted by others. Or they could turn over their personal power to others by never having opinions or preferences. Both trauma identities become the automatic way of being in the world and are a protective adaptation to their earlier experience. In the first trauma identity adaptation example, of limiting connection, they stay lonely through the adaptation to isolate. In the second trauma identity adaptation, the impulse for personal power and agency is not a part of their being, resulting in a life that might not feel truly aligned with their true nature. In both trauma identities, developmental wounding creates a core belief and a survival adaptation that becomes a pattern, limiting nourishment in life.

As another example, a client could have a coworker who wants to support them at work, and the client never notices their offer for help. They might have a friend who reaches out for connection with true interest and care; trauma identity prevents this from being received. Often, the trauma identity will lead to the person not noticing these kinds of responses from others; the confirmation bias reinforces the belief and the adaptation. Trauma identity becomes a blinder that inhibits noticing others being there for the client, narrowing the client's life.

In summary, the client's early experience leads to a belief; this belief leads the SNS to be recruited for a protective action of an adaptation. This habituated adaptation over time creates a trauma identity that reinforces their worldview and what they can receive from others, limiting nourishment. As part of this process, one loses access to Essence and life-enhancing choices.

APPLYING REPARATIVE EXPERIENCES

If a child has enough experiences of safety through co-regulation, they can develop into their Essence; they will have fewer limits from their nervous system functioning, co-regulation capacity, or limiting core beliefs. Having their needs met and a sense of belonging assist in the development of the belief of their inherent lovability. This supports authenticity, agency, and feelings of being valued; all of these experiences provide the neural platform for resilience, post-traumatic growth, and fullhearted living. When these experiences do not occur, inaccurate and limiting core beliefs form about oneself, others, or the world; these hamper personal expansion, as the nervous system becomes stuck in dysregulation. When reparative experiences address patterns that stifle life fulfillment due to erroneous core beliefs, expansion and growth can result (Walker & Newcomer, 2025).

Beyond reparative experiences of co-regulation, there are therapeutic interventions that provide reparative experiences to transform core beliefs. As a typical part of therapy, these interventions can include an offering from the clinician, creating for the client a new embodied experience of themselves, relationships, and the world; the experience provides a reeducation that alters their current belief. These new reparative experiences can change formerly adaptive patterns to create more options for getting needs met, thus deactivating the nervous system. These reparative experiences could be seen as "missing experiences" (Kurtz, 1990). Reparative experiences will always offer what needs to be integrated to shift the experience of the client to learning and embodying a new belief that opens up possibilities of flourishing (Kurtz, 1990; Reeds, 2015).

To support this transformation from trauma identity to Essence, it is necessary to understand basic needs and how the adaptation supports not having those needs met. As trauma identity shifts to Essence, the client can begin to move away from thwarted impulses that temporarily seemed offline; instead, they become able to access healing impulses that support deeper regulation, authenticity, and self-connection. These impulses can include a wide range of new behaviors and longings, including wanting to belong and connect, having their needs met, feeling reciprocity in relationships, feeling a sense of value, and feeling a desire for agency. As these impulses are restored; there is a return to wholeness and Essence.

The main themes for developmental wounding revolve around our most human needs:

- Safety-Belonging: Can I be safe? Do I feel a sense of belonging? Is it safe to be seen?
- Connection-Reciprocity: Am I met with attunement? Am I soothed and seen around my needs? Is there a balance of give-and-take with shared nourishment?
- Inherent Lovability-Value: Do I feel lovable and valued for my authentic self? Can I be my authentic self and in my true Essence? Can I have value just by being?
- Agency-Differentiation: Do I have a sense of personal power/agency? Can I access my sense of "I can" with choices? Can I be cared for even if I need to do things differently than others?

> *Practice Tip*: A client's longings often underlie the new healing impulses that are ready to be restored. Because developmental wounding thwarts natural impulses towards these developmental themes, a client's movement towards more wholeness will start with them knowing what they long for in their life. This includes wanting to belong and feel safe, to feel connection and reciprocity, to feel inherent lovability and value, and to be able to differentiate and have agency. Having the client focus in on their longing can restore the thwarted impulse that was necessary for survival. Longing will often be coupled with grief as the recognition of not having their needs met is present in their current adaptation. Working with the client's longing offers information of the needed reparative experience. (Longing and grief is covered more in Chapter 11 and working with longing is covered more in Chapter 13.)

These questions are only samples of the the backbone experiences that will affect one's core beliefs. They underline the four primary areas of limiting core beliefs: safety-belonging, connection-reciprocity, inherent lovability-value, and agency-differentiation. To bring in additional perspectives, Beck and Beck (2011) describe the categories of beliefs as helplessness, unlovability, and worthlessness. The Hakomi Method follows a child development model and the needs of safety/being/belonging, support/needs, authenticity/power, freedom, value/worth (Kurtz, 1990; Weiss et al., 2015).

Understanding core belief themes is essential in working with clients. Attuning closely to each client to identify the specific belief blocking their growth is critical. One key way to pinpoint this belief is by asking: "What does this nervous system need to integrate to live more fully?" It's important to recognize that experiences can shape related but distinct core beliefs beyond the categories already mentioned. Ultimately, clarifying the core belief requires attunement.

EXERCISE FOR TRAUMA IDENTITY AND GROWTH

What trauma identity jumps out at you as one you have worked on in your life and feels the most integrated? What does it feel like to acknowledge your growth in this area? Allow yourself to just embody the sense of growth in yourself.

INTEGRATION OF NEW BELIEFS
THROUGH EMBODIMENT

Psychotherapy is a type of learning. In this case, the learning is applied to provide integration of reparative experiences to shift the core beliefs; because of the state evoked when core beliefs are formed, this reeducation does not occur as cognitive education. The beliefs are held in the body and need a new embodied experience to transmute and change. Rewiring new beliefs requires that the client embody a new reality now using their "felt sense" (Gendlin, 1996); it often includes an understanding of what happened. The embodied layer of integration is designed to shift the underlying beliefs on the somatic level. Psychoeducation can also be beneficial in helping the client understand how their experiences have influenced the development of their core beliefs, serving to normalize their experience. Although this will be discussed later, let's illustrate this now. If someone experienced having their feelings shut down by caregivers who became easily overwhelmed by their own emotions; the client then believes, "I am too much." As an adaptation, the client learns to hide their feelings from others (and themselves) to protect against being too much for the caregiver. This protection pattern forms a trauma identity with an underlying protective action to suppress feelings. "I am too much when I express feelings" might be the core belief of that action and their way of being in the world.

A reparative experience can also be either a *personal-relational offering* from the clinician or a *general offering* of a new experience (Kurtz, 1990). In this same example of feeling they are too much, the offering might be, "Your feelings are not too much for me." The general offering might be, "You have a right to all of your feelings." The clinician decides through attunement which might be more effective for the client.

Questions to consider as you make clinical decisions:

Personal-relational versus general:
- Does this person need a personal-relational interaction to deepen their integration?
- Would having the personal-relational interaction increase the safety and intimacy of the therapeutic relationship?
- Is a relational interaction from me, as the clinician, going to feel too intimate, and then lose its effectiveness?
- Is this issue so broad that applying the integration generally will be more beneficial to the client?

Sometimes the client makes the belief relational toward the clinician, as occurs often in developmental wounding as part of normal transference; when this occurs, making a personal and relational offering can be more useful. This is demonstrated with this same belief, if the client expressed concern about tears, anger, or talkativeness in the session by saying to the clinician, "I hope I didn't overwhelm *you* with my problems," in that case, "Your feelings are not too much for me" is a more attuned response than the general statement, "You have a right to all of your feelings." This second statement does not bring in the same relational aspects that might be more potent for the client. Additionally, sometimes the clinician might decide that it is not the right time to directly deal with this belief, as another issue is more pressing. In that case, with intentionality and attunement, the clinician could simply encourage the expression of feelings as they occur in the session, which is also reparative.

When a new reparative experience is embodied, it lays the tracks for a new belief and a new way of being. Over time, this reparative experience can shift the core belief to "It is okay to express my feelings" or whatever belief is most helpful to the client. The clinician decides through attunement which might be more effective for the client to begin the process of connecting to their Essence.

These offerings, designed to elicit Essence, are the connection to wholeness. The invitation to access Essence is evoked by seeing how the new belief is present in any way by asking, "Where in your body is this true, *even if only slightly?*" The goal of this question is to start identifying and embodying any way the client can integrate a new experience to shift their core belief by harnessing the inner knowing of the client. When the client identifies where it feels true, *even partially*, it begins to create a somatic template for the new belief. This begins the deactivation process of the regulation of the green zone. Grief often comes up in this process of more access to Essence. The grief is connected to the losses that led to the adaptation earlier in life. The clinical choice that best supports deactivation is to focus on the regulation and work with the grief later (discussed in Chapter 11), when the client has more capacity for processing; the goal of this intervention is geared toward the integration of the new experience to transform the limiting belief.

The blueprint of the client's Essence is tapped into with the titration of breaking down the question to asking, "Where it is true, *even slightly?*" Generally, clients can only know this *slightly*, or they would not be in the struggle with the belief. There tends to be a place in their body where they are not taking in the new belief or where they might be holding an opposite belief. The invitation to notice the nourishing statement and the place in their body where they are taking it in is an important step. "Taking it in" creates the embodiment of this new belief and the step into Essence, using positive neuroplasticity (Hanson, 2009). The threat response is deactivated as the normalization of the need is restored with a new possibility. This critical step of noting where the new belief is true is different from many somatic therapies, as the goal is *to tap into Essence rather than the client's wounding*. This approach uses positive neuroplasticity (Hanson, 2009) to open the door to the client's inner wholeness.

ESSENCE EXERCISE

Allow yourself to bring to mind some aspect of yourself that feels truly *you* in an undeniable way, something that is easy to claim about yourself. It could be anything from a love of nature, a compassionate heart, a sense of integrity, or any quality that feels connected to your true self. As this quality arises, allow yourself to acknowledge this awareness is a sense of your Essence. As you name this quality to yourself, say "I am . . .", filling in the word that best connect to your Essence. Allow yourself to welcome the idea that you have a holistic blueprint inside of you that is connected to this aspect of yourself. Underneath any adaptations you might have needed, this quality is still part of you. Take time to notice how it feels good to connect with yourself, your true Essence.

With reparative experiences, the therapeutic work is focused on expanding the intrinsic wholeness of the client. This brings back the concept of the resilience vortex again, as it holds this wholeness or Essence of the client. With embodiment, the needed reparative experience begins to change the client's physiology and their lives as they open to new ways of being. This can be repeated in the session, and it will become stronger through brain neuroplasticity (Hanson, 2009; Siegel, 2012).

With the knowledge that limiting core beliefs are ingrained through strongly formed neural pathways, having the client do homework is useful. This encompasses having the client practice the embodiment of the new belief to reinforce the new patterning. Guiding the client to hold in awareness both the new belief and where it is held in the body supports the embodiment of a new pattern. The new embodiment of a belief reinforces the new neural pathways. Weiss (2015) notes, "It takes experiences to counteract learnings from previous experiences" (p. 232). Offering embodiment homework geared toward strengthening the embodiment of the new experiences promotes the transformation of the earlier experiences into a new way of being and bridging to one's Essence.

Sometimes, clients cannot embody the offering. In this case, the clinician then asks, "Where do you notice in your body that you would like this to be true?" Wanting this to be true is being on the path to integrating a new aspect of self, restoring Essence; it brings awareness to the new possibility. It evokes the movement toward wholeness that is always present underneath the adaptation. The client can still have a vague response, "I am not sure, maybe my stomach?" The clinician directs the client to feel their stomach and hold it with the statement, "I would like (naming the belief they are moving toward) to be true." Claiming this new direction often settles the nervous system as it accesses the core self, whose home is the VVC. This intervention starts the process of integration of Essence, as it is a gateway into the whole self. Connection with Essence starts unfolding wholeness and regulation. Just like the new belief, feeling the longing for the new pattern will often need to be repeated until it is more developed.

Practice tip: When the client is learning to embody a new belief, there is often a tentativeness to their responses. It helps to simply go with what they have named as it might stay tentative until it is further embodied. If it happens to be inaccurate, that will unfold. It is more important to underline where they think they sense it, even if they are hesitant and not fully sure. It will often become clearer as attention is given to it.

As stated earlier, these reparative experiences are offerings to initiate the integration of what did not occur, including acknowledgment of the harmful experiences that did happen; again, since both are significant, both are essential. These reparative experiences act as an overlay to these painful experiences, providing new information, context, and understanding, leading to an organic shift in core beliefs. In addition to the acknowledgment of what occurred or did not occur, they also include an honoring of the necessary survival adaptations. Reparative experiences will bring the client back into the present moment of how life is today. Most of what clients learned does not actually fit in with a current narrative of life now. It can help to explain to them the analogy that they are using an old operating system that needs a file update. The aspect of turning awareness toward their current life or the bird's-eye view of the situation now supports the development of a new possibility of having a different belief and a new way of being, thereby changing the pattern.

Offering developmental repair is always looking at what needs to be integrated for living life with more aliveness and options. The reparative statement to integrate is often the opposite belief that is held in trauma identity. The clinician's goal is to present a new belief that can transform the system into new possibilities and break free from automated patterns. This also embodies what is currently possible in life today. When the clinician has clarity on what needs to be integrated, a new belief is offered. As an example, in the connection/reciprocity category, for the core belief of "I can never ask for help," the clinician could go in a few different directions. They could say, "You deserve help," "It is okay to want help," "It is okay to ask for help," or "You can be strong and still need help." The clinician is attempting to offer the most potent variation of a new belief to support the necessary integration to shift the belief. With attunement, the statement often gets refined by the client's feedback. The client could say, "I know I deserve help, but if I were strong enough, I would not need it." That feedback offers the specificity of the place where the client is actually stuck. The clinician would need to attend to that specificity. The clinician would then state, "You can be strong and need help," as that statement might be a closer version of the needed integration.

It is important to note that when there is a negative sensation with either the embodiment of the words or the longing for the new pattern, it points to another layer of material; the negative sensation is an actual block to embodiment. To address this, the client could need more time or another type of intervention for the new pattern to take hold. Sometimes, after taking time for the integration to be solidified with embodiment, this block of taking in the reparative experience is simply gone. Other times, educating the client that a negative sensation indicates a block toward more nourishment is important; otherwise, they will report that they are taking it in, as they refer to their embodiment process of the reparative experience. The negative sensation is where their body is rejecting the new belief. This requires follow-up by asking again where else the words are even partially taken in. This keeps the client in the resilience vortex with more access to the VVC, helping them distinguish between taking it in and how it might be blocked. Holding the two experiences of both taking it in along with the block can begin the true integration of the new belief. (This is an example of pendulation.)

If the somatic deflection of new belief continues, it needs to unfold more; this includes attending to a different belief or the need to work with a child state. Integration of growth will always feel good, even though another aspect might come up. Let's look at a client who reports having a "tight belly" when they think of "using their voice to speak up." They might start wondering if others will still like them; this newly realized fear can keep the tightness present. If that concern stays present, it will need its own reparative experience, as there is an underlying belief in the camp of "needing to be liked." With that awareness, the focus of integration goes in a different direction as the shifting belief gets clearer. At that point, the clinician would ask the client to embody a different and precise statement: "Where in your body can you take in, 'I can be okay even if others do not like me when I voice my needs'?" This is a redirection to the new emerging pattern of Essence. This entire therapeutic experience keeps the client in the resilience vortex, which is the heart of regulation, as it keeps a foothold in the green zone. If this still feels blocked, working with the child part is often key to getting to the root of the block.

WORKING WITH THE CHILD PART[18]

Accessing the child part is utilized when providing the new core belief with these interventions is not effective; the ineffectiveness indicates a block on a deeper level that needs attention (Kurtz, 1990). It highlights the need to work where the belief is stuck, which is often directly with the child state. It is common to have a disconnect between adult parts (which are often cognitive) and child parts (which are often emotional and/or somatic).

Working directly with a child state can shift a limiting core belief (Kurtz, 1990). This entails directly talking to the child and the adult together. As a way to support not getting stuck in the trauma vortex (which is where the limiting core belief is often found), having the regulated adult self present supports regulation as the painful childhood experience is contacted.[19] Using the example above, the clinician could say, "I would like to talk to the child with the adult listening. I want you to know that I am so glad you found a way to hold back your voice growing up. It really helped you survive in your family, where speaking out was not accepted. I want you to know it is different now, and it is okay for you to speak up when you want to; you do not have to hold back your voice anymore." This is validating, honoring the adaptation, and underlining a new potential way of being; through this process, the belief can shift. Sometimes, there is another barrier that arises from the child state; this barrier is attended to in the same way. In this same example, the child part might add, "My mom gets so mad at me, and I am afraid she will be mad if I do speak up." With this new information, a new belief is identified, one that is less about the client using their voice and more about the fear of their mom's anger. The child state then needs help understanding that they are safe now from the anger, that they are not responsible for the anger, or whatever kind of integration is necessary. The clinician simply stays with the process with attunement until the necessary embodied belief can begin to be integrated.

Example

Let's look at one very common core belief from abuse and neglect. In early childhood trauma, the limiting core belief "I am the problem" occurs frequently. In addition the belief being tied to how they were treated, it is an adaptive way to have control when there is no control. In this trauma identity, the client looks for how things are their fault. This occurred to protect the child from feeling a sense of loss that might arise from acknowledging the caregiver's inability to provide adequate care. In abuse situations, taking on the belief of "I am the problem" and "it is my fault" is easier to feel. Even though it might seem paradoxical to do so, it is a way to survive. The client can keep trying rather than facing the grief of not having a caregiver who can adequately provide an emotional connection. The trauma identity of always being the problem becomes a way to avoid the pain.

Example

In this example, the clinician is directly engaging the adult and child states as a way to address a deeply held belief:

CLINICIAN: *I would like to talk to the child and have the adult listen in right now. I am so sorry that the way you were treated led you to feel you were the problem. Becoming "the problem" helped you get through your life as it was easier to be the problem than face what was happening in your family. It kept you from feeling hopeless as you kept trying to change in some way. I know this got you through, but it is okay now to know that you have never been the problem. You are not the problem now, and it is important for you to know this. What is this like to hear?* (The clinician is offering the reparative experience of a new possibility for the client as a way to change the trauma identity of "I am the problem.")

CLIENT: *I am not sure what to think. I have felt this way for so long.* (Shows some confusion.)

CLINICIAN: *I wonder what it is like to recognize that "being the problem" helped you survive, but it was never true.*

CLIENT: *I want this to be right. It is a little relieving to hear, as I am tired of feeling like I am the problem. Even though I feel relief, I also feel so sad about this.* (Begins to cry softly.)

CLINICIAN: *Where in your body do you feel a little of the relief at knowing you are not the problem?* (This is intentionally accessing the wholeness and Essence of the client and not the grief at this point; it is also bypassing the hesitancy, of "I want this to be right." New beliefs are generally held with hesitation in the change process.)

CLIENT: *My stomach lets go, and my shoulders come down.* (The body is integrating through embodiment as these are indicators of deactivation. This is likely more possible for the client as the longing for "wanting this to be right" is present even with the grief surfacing.)

CLINICIAN: *Can you take some time to feel that, noticing your stomach and shoulders and holding those sensations with those words, "I am not the problem"?* (The clinician is linking the new words with the physiological shift to support more neuroplasticity.)

CLIENT: (Takes a big breath, with more visible relaxation. This indicates more downregulation to the VVC.)

CLINICIAN: *Take your time here and feel this. Let's not hurry through this.* (The clinician is extending the VVC state.)

CLIENT: *It feels good. I have been waiting to hear this and I have wanted this to be true. I am not sure what to think now as I can see I quickly go into feeling like I am the problem at work and with my partner. It is a little scary also to start seeing myself as not the problem. I know that sounds weird, but I am not used to it.*

CLINICIAN: *Can you be with both how great it feels and the fear?* (Pendulation, which is discussed fully in Chapter 9, often works well with the two states that are naturally part of the change process—the old "scary" aspect noted by the client that created the adaptation and the new core belief.)

CLIENT: *It feels better as mostly, and I am glad to finally be feeling this. I feel less of a burden now in my whole body as I feel lighter.*

In sessions with reparative experiences, it is very important to help clients understand the importance of changing their trauma identity by applying daily neuroplasticity exercises. It is helpful to encourage the client to bring in the same words and physical sensations from the session. In this case, the client would link the new belief of "I am not the problem" with the more positive sensations in the shoulders and stomach; embodying this new pattern multiple times per day provides support to the new pattern. This reinforcement is critical as there are deep grooves with the adaptive trauma identity pattern. This supports the state-to-trait process discussed earlier (Hanson, 2009). The clinician would want to guide the client with homework focused on supporting change, including some discussion on how changing this pattern might affect other relationships. This could include directly asking, "What is it like now to think of trying out this belief in your relationships?" Additionally, helping the client understand that since others in their world have been used to the client being the problem, and the client might need to discuss ways to advocate for themselves.

SUMMARY OF CHANGING LIMITING CORE BELIEFS IN STEPS

Part 1: The steps for shifting core beliefs:
1. Identify the belief and offer it as a positive statement to integrate.
2. Ask, "Where can you take in this belief, even slightly?"
3. Have the client notice the sensations where the reparative belief can be embodied. Even if this is very small, focusing here helps. If the sensation is negative, the belief is not being integrated; instead, this is where the

client is *not* taking in the belief. Have the client note again where the new belief can be embodied, explaining that it would feel good.

4. As the belief is embodied, have the client stay with those sensations, holding them with the new core belief. (This will be the homework later for the client to reinforce positive neural pathways.)

This can be the new integration if it can be embodied. It can be completed with follow-up sessions as needed and as noted as client homework.

1. If this does not work to assist the client in the embodiment of the new belief, the next step is to ask the client, "Where in your body can you notice you would *like* to 'take in' this new belief?"
2. As they identify the area, have the client feel the sensations of "wanting this to be true."

This often starts the embodiment process of integration of a new belief. If this expands into taking in the new belief, integration is beginning, and the same reinforcement noted above is useful.

Part 2: If reparative experience remains blocked, it is useful then to work with the child state. There is often another layer needed for the client to integrate:

1. The clinician asks to talk to the child, with the adult present. (This is intentionally zeroing in on having a regulated state of the adult with the potentially dysregulated state of the child.)
2. The clinician then talks with the child, honoring how the child adapted and acknowledging how useful it was to get through their challenge, while noting things are different now, helping the child part understand that safety is different today.
3. As the child begins to take in the new belief with the new information, the embodiment process is again followed from above, supporting a new pattern.

Again, the client is encouraged to hold the new belief in an embodied adult place where it can be integrated.

SUMMARY

For developmental wounding, reparative experiences are a critical deactivation pathway in downregulating the nervous system and recovering the client's Essence. In reparative experiences, changing inaccurate core beliefs is key. These beliefs are in the substructure of any kind of adaptation and tend to be focused on safety-belonging, connection-reciprocity, lovability-worth, and agency-differentiation; they have a profound and often unconscious effect on how the client experiences themselves, others, and the world. The inaccurate beliefs and corresponding adaptations lead to dysregulated physiology of stuckness in the SNS and DVC physiology. These adaptations become a default way of being; when habituated, they lead to trauma identity, inhibiting one's authentic self. Reparative experiences are a primary way to support clients in returning to Essence.

REPARATIVE EXPERIENCE EXERCISE

Let yourself take some time to just connect with yourself. Allow yourself to notice what need stood out to you as you learned about developmental wounding—and whatever that need is—say to yourself now, "I have a right to . . ." naming what came up for you—"I have a right to be safe or belong." "I have a right to have reciprocity in my relationships." "I have a right to feel my inherent lovability and worth." "I have a right to agency and/or to differentiate from others." As you bring up what you might want to integrate, note where in your body you can take it in, even slightly. Feel this embodiment and notice how it feels good. If grief also comes up, let yourself have an awareness of the grief while also observing it as a separate sensation. Allow your attention to focus mostly on where you feel the statement is true. Take some time to notice this and be with this new belief that is connected to your Essence.

Doing this exercise regularly can support you in your integration of needs and move you more into your Essence. It also helps to start noticing where the new pattern is happening by asking yourself, "How is this new belief happening in my life now?" This question can support looking for where this might be true, combating the impact of the negativity bias, and seeing your experiences freshly and with openness.

CHAPTER 8

Self-Compassion

*When you are compassionate with yourself, you trust in your soul,
which you let guide your life. Your soul knows the geography of
your destiny better than you do.*

—John O'Donohue

Every time I bring in the concept of self-compassion to a client, I learn to hold myself more compassionately. It seems that the field of self-compassion spreads to me. In those moments, I feel the truth of how human we both are. It never ceases to amaze me how deeply moving it is to feel the unity of our shared humanity. I receive the benefit as it is also settling to my nervous system. This chapter explores using self-compassion in therapy as part of the deactivation process.

Self-compassion can be a very useful deactivating pathway for downregulation and supports the neural platforms for both resilience and post-traumatic growth. "Self-compassion is quite simply compassion for oneself, or a sensitivity to one's own suffering and a desire to alleviate that suffering" (Stevens & Woodruff, 2018). It includes being kind and understanding to oneself when we suffer, fail, or feel inadequate rather than being self-critical (Neff & Germer, 2018). It offers many benefits to general well-being. Some of the benefits include more happiness, increased self-confidence, better health, increased ability to face challenging emotions, and more ease in relationships. Self-compassion is particularly useful in shame presentations. Acting as an opposite, it offers a means to shift shame states. This will be covered more in this chapter. Self-compassion can serve all people, even those with psychiatric disorders and significant trauma histories (Neff & Germer, 2018).

Clients need to practice self-compassion when they make mistakes or feel imperfect. They also need self-compassion when they are too hard on themselves or have unrealistic expectations about how they handled a situation. When applied to making a mistake or from a pattern of self-criticism, practicing self-compassion helps clients feel more at ease with their experiences. This sense of ease with themselves calms the nervous system and allows access to VVC because the client is not resisting or judging what happened; instead, they are focusing on embracing the experience without judgment. This is a critical experience in any kind of trauma situation. Paul Gilbert says, "The more threat absorbed we are, the more difficult compassion can come to be" (2010, p. xxiii).

The goal of self-compassion is to help clients hold their experiences with kindness, accessing the VVC. Different than self-esteem, self-compassion "focuses on how we treat ourselves when things are going badly" (Gilbert, 2010, p. 330). Self-compassion tends to remove evaluation, as it is not about how well or poorly one is doing; it is about accepting oneself. Evaluation is SNS-driven, and self-compassion is VVC-driven (Walker & Newcomer, 2025); this makes self-compassion a powerful intervention to apply for clients as it shifts the physiology. Judgment for oneself and/or others is connected to the SNS threat state and can move to the DVC threat state as it accumulates. Because trauma often seems to evoke judgment, it is critical to apply self-compassion in session to support the deactivation to the VVC.

Additionally, applied self-compassion is an important life skill to acquire. As a way of relating to oneself, self-compassion's impact goes beyond just shifting the nervous system; it can profoundly affect how one holds one's own experiences. Holding one's experiences includes being able to experience painful and difficult feelings and not being overwhelmed by them. Instead, self-compassion creates an inner space where emotions can be processed with kindness and acceptance; this is not a small thing. This process of holding one's own emotions resembles effective parenting, where skillful parents assist their children in managing their emotions and experiences; this interaction forms the basis of co-regulation. The care and support from a parent conveys to the child that they are not alone in their struggles. The co-regulation experience that involves having someone share in the pain and hardship builds a template for learning to hold one's experiences, which is essential for self-regulation. Developing the ability to hold one's challenging experiences through self-compassion is a loving act of self-care, as it is a way of parenting oneself.

Self-compassion fosters self-regulation in general and also aids in downregulation. Downregulating the autonomic nervous system through self-compassion is facilitated by being fully present, accepting the struggle, and extending kindness to oneself, all of which are elements related to the VVC. With self-acceptance, there is a diminished identification with the struggle, as it becomes less prominent and less negatively charged. This shift from struggle and judgment also contributes to the deactivation of the nervous system.

> *Reflection:* Because of the power of self-compassion, I recommend it regularly to clients who are underparented or who have experienced developmental wounding. I see great results if they put this into practice, as it can offer a means of reparenting oneself.

BARRIERS TO SELF-COMPASSION

There are underlying barriers for clients in applying self-compassion. Looking at the framework in the last two chapters is useful because barriers are often connected to developmental wounding. Inaccurate core beliefs are at the root of self-compassion barriers; clients will question if they really should be doing it or if it is worth trying. Even when I describe what self-compassion is, most often clients think I am asking them to do an affirmation, saying a positive statement to themselves. Without some psychoeducation, they do not seem to understand that self-compassion is different. (In affirmations, the client might say, "I am a good person" when they make a mistake, which is different than self-compassion, which is learning to hold the imperfection.) They will oppose this idea because of inaccurate core beliefs related to naming anything positive about themselves; this lens is still utilizing an evaluative framework, which will bring up threat physiology and perpetuate the dysregulation. This misunderstanding is best addressed with a top-down intervention and more psychoeducation about the differences between affirmations and self-compassion. The other pushback from clients who say "I am not sure about this" is directly connected to the core beliefs discussed in the last chapter. The two most common beliefs are "I am not sure I deserve this" and "I should be perfect." Unlike offering psychoeducation that helps clear the confusion between affirmations and self-compassion, bottom-up interventions include further exploration of what might need to be integrated to shift the core belief that blocks a self-compassion process. Reparative experiences are often needed to address the underlying sense of not being deserving or the belief about needing to be perfect to develop self-compassion. Self-compassion can be a reparative experience on its own as it integrates a sense of deservingness, a letting go of perfection, and other potential barriers around limiting core beliefs. Integration of any new embodied belief that allows self-compassion to be integrated is often more necessary when there has been early developmental wounding or abuse.

Clients with histories of early childhood abuse or neglect will generally struggle with self-compassion; the barrier occurs as painful emotions surface. It is not unusual to see that offering loving-kindness toward difficult emotions and experiences can create *backdraft*, a term coined by Neff and Germer to describe the pain that can arise in response to a self-compassion practice (2018). In backdraft, distress and emotional comfort occur as self-kindness is introduced. As self-kindness has not been practiced, the opposing criticalness becomes amplified. Old wounds and a sense of unworthiness are often spotlighted as the client practices loving self-attention. This often requires building self-compassion over time and targeting the underlying beliefs with attuned reparative experiences.

The simplest step to take when clients are not ready for a whole self-compassion exercise is to break self-compassion down more. I sometimes have them simply put their hand on their heart and feel their breath move in their heart area. If that is possible, we sometimes add one word or phrase that is okay to take in, like "I try my best" or even going toward the longing discussed in Chapter 7, "I want to feel self-compassion." Using kind language toward oneself can help reduce self-criticism and its associated threat state. For some clients, adding in self-care actions and embodying them as loving care for the self is useful as a step toward integrating self-compassion. As a way to be kind to themselves, the client could get a massage or take themselves to lunch, or indulge in another self-care practice they enjoy. Some clients will benefit from somatically experiencing their compassion for others, noting the "felt sense" (Gendlin, 1996) experience they have when they offer it to another; this can also be a way to begin to develop the somatic road map of self-compassion. The process of applying a titrated version of self-compassion through heart breathing, self-care actions, or feeling it for others supports its integration more fully in time. With repetition and practice, self-compassion can be developed and grown.

The model developed by Neff and Germer (2018) is easy for clients to learn and apply.

They define three parts to self-compassion:

1. Mindfulness—awareness of personal suffering
2. Connection to common humanity—it is a human experience
3. Self-kindness—talking to oneself like one would talk to a friend

An in-session example in applying self-compassion is the client bringing up a poor parenting moment, an unskillful interaction with a friend, or a mistake they made.

1. Ask the client to bring heartfelt awareness to their heart area as they bring in the intention of self-compassion. With that awareness, ask them to be mindful of how it feels in their body to talk about the struggle and to bring attention to what they notice.
2. The next step would be to bring up that they are part of a common humanity who often makes mistakes or is unskilled in some way. Have the client feel the connection with others in their body. This will often begin shifting the physiology of the state toward deactivation to the VVC.
3. Lastly, ask the client to talk to themselves in the way they would talk to a friend (adapted from Neff & Germer, 2018).

SHAME AND SELF-COMPASSION

Shame often occurs in trauma and can be a barrier to trauma healing as it stops any kind of expansion and growth. With shame acting as a roadblock to both trauma recovery and post-traumatic growth, it is important to specifically address it. Because there is a direct connection between shame and self-compassion, it will be explored in this chapter as a special topic.

Shame is defined as a painful emotion caused by consciousness of guilt, shortcomings, or impropriety. There are two types of shame: *healthy* shame and *toxic* shame (Kain & Terrell, 2018). Healthy shame has an evolutionary function. As a community-oriented species, humans need to work together and get along. If someone breaks a norm that affects others in society, healthy shame helps them change their behavior to belong again to the community. In hunter-gatherer culture, if one person ate all the meat or did not contribute to the community, healthy shame assists the offending community member in changing behavior to belong and fit in again. This is the purpose of healthy shame, as it keeps individuals working together for the good of the whole community (Kain & Terrell, 2018). Toxic shame does not match the situation that triggered the shame; this includes feeling shame because of being abused or another situation in which the person has no control. This toxic shame is often associated with what has happened to the person rather than their actions; this is different from healthy shame, which is connected to one's actions.

Healthy shame is a blended state nervous system that includes all three nervous system states. It begins as a DVC threat state, with the SNS recruited quickly to help take action for reconnecting to the community, accessing the portal of the VVC. The sense of belonging, as part of the VVC, is restored by taking actions that remedy the situation. Unlike toxic shame, there is not a stuckness. Humans need healthy shame to support a working community. Toxic shame, on the other hand, is very different in that it becomes self-punishing. It creates a hijack in the nervous system, as there is a desire not to be seen and to disappear (DVC) or to take actions (SNS) to avoid the pain of shame.

Toxic shame is demonstrated in various ways and will keep clients in the trauma vortex. This kind of shame is not useful and begins to create its own problems. Many times, the presentation of shame is very obvious, as in a client who reports feeling shame because they were abused. In this case, the client did nothing wrong but carries their shame as part of the pain of the trauma. In these kinds of instances, shame is clearly stated and known. Other times, shame appears to be more underground; it will be hidden as the SNS leads to protective actions to mask the shame, making it hard to recognize. This masking is adaptive for survival because of how deeply painful the shame state is. This masking with protective actions can be so deeply habituated that the toxic shame stays hidden from both the client and others around them.

When the SNS is recruited for adaptive protective action plans to protect from toxic shame, the adaptations become compelling and automatic, as well as unconscious (see Figure 8.1). Some of these protective adaptations are:

- To be perfect
- To never make mistakes

- To appease or fawn (placate)
- To focus on others
- To always be good by doing the right thing
- To externalize by blaming others

Some of these adaptations are closely related but have slightly different presentations. For example, being perfect can be different than never making mistakes and can mean being "good" by doing the "right thing." These nuances are connected to the precise core belief that is connected to the adaptation.

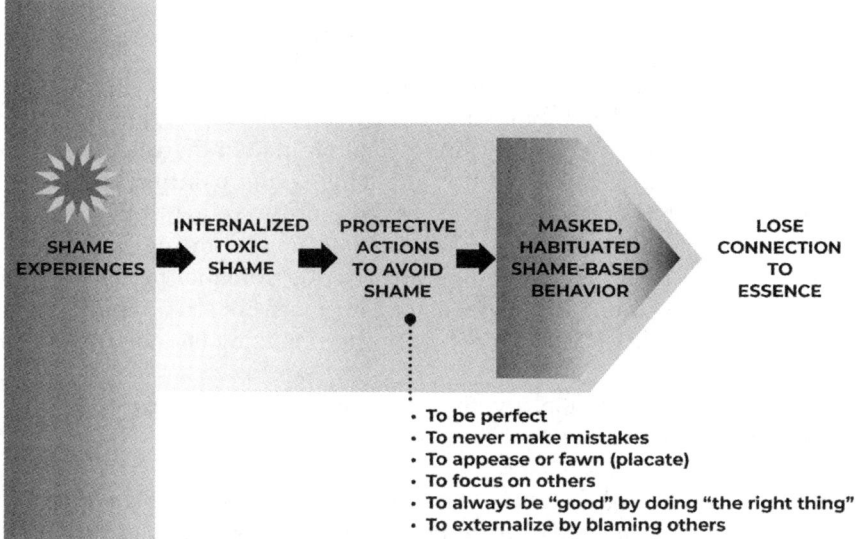

FIGURE 8.1:   Toxic Shame   Credit: Ruby Jo Walker with concepts from Kathy Kain and Stephen Terrell; graphic by Cindy Miller Atchison Design & Art

Because healthy shame turns itself around by taking action that alleviates the shame, it is toxic shame that is mediated by self-compassion. Toxic shame is often rooted in inaccurate core beliefs, creating stuckness in the nervous system. Similar to adaptations covered in Chapter 7, reparative experiences are also helpful to apply in addition to self-compassion. Self-compassion's effectiveness with shame appears to be that they are opposites (Neff & Germer, 2018).

Self-compassion versus shame:
- Mindful versus rumination (not mindful)
- Connected to humanity versus being alone
- Offering kindness versus being hard on oneself

The differences between these opposing views highlight the importance of self-compassion as a remedy for shame (Neff & Germer, 2018).

When a client is being self-critical about a mistake, it is an excellent opportunity to intervene with a self-compassion process. This can shift the client into having some movement toward the green zone of VVC by softening their judgment. Clients need self-compassion around making mistakes. Other times, they need self-compassion because they are hard on themselves or unrealistic about how they coped at times or even how they got through a situation. The practice of self-compassion starts supporting the client in being able to hold their experiences more easily with increased kindness toward themselves.

Self-Compassion Example

The client is a parent of two small children, and she has recently been experiencing some difficulty with her partner. As a couple, they are struggling with overcoming a recently disclosed affair in their marriage. They are working through the issues, but it is challenging and painful. The client's nervous system has been in a threat response of the yellow zone since the discovery of the affair. She comes into the session reporting that she has been edgy with their kids. In addition to offering potential parenting strategies to keep the parent in the green zone for more effective parenting, the clinician notices clearly that her self-criticism is making her nervous system more dysregulated.

This is an example of applying the integration of the reparative experiences model with self-compassion:

> CLIENT: *I feel horrible about the other night. I grew up with a lot of yelling, and I can't believe I am yelling at my kids. I never thought I would do this. When I say this, I literally feel sick to my stomach.*
>
> CLINICIAN: *I hear you are feeling really bad that you are not as skillful as you would like to be right now. I wonder what it would be like to take a moment to appreciate that you want to be more skillful, while also offering yourself some self-compassion.*
>
> CLIENT: *I do not think I deserve it. I can't believe I am acting just like the rest of my family. I am so upset with myself.*
>
> CLINICIAN: *I know this feels really hard right now. Could we start by noticing you would like to be different from your family?* (This question shifts the focus off of the trauma vortex.)
>
> CLIENT: *I guess so.* (Sounding sad and teary.)
>
> CLINICIAN: *What is it like to notice this?*
>
> CLIENT: *I feel sad that I was so off track with my kids.*
>
> CLINICIAN: *As you feel this sadness, I am wondering if you can now bring any self-compassion to how challenging it is to try to change family patterns.*

CLIENT: *It feels really hard. I am so upset with myself.* (This is a part of the trauma vortex and hard to shift for the client.)

CLINICIAN: *I wonder if you could notice that you would* like *to be more self-compassionate to yourself, taking in how you are trying to change.*

CLIENT: *I do wish I could, but it is tough to do.*

CLINICIAN: *As you feel this desire, what do you notice?* (The focus on the longing for more self-compassion and paying less attention to the trauma vortex of it being "tough.")

CLIENT: *I feel sad that I am so hard on myself.*

CLINICIAN: *Besides the sadness, where do you feel the longing to be different?* (The clinician is going toward the new pattern and less with the grief in applying this intervention.)

CLIENT: *It is in my heart. I feel how much I want to do better than my parents did with me. I do not want to affect my kids negatively like I was affected. I still feel sad about it, but I do feel I am really trying.*

CLINICIAN: *What is it like to recognize how much you are trying?* (The clinician brings attention to the embodiment of a positive state as there is a small shift happening now.)

CLIENT: *I actually feel a little better because I know I am trying to be different. I wish my parents had tried more to work with their anger.* (The client takes a big breath, which is an indicator of moving into downregulation.)

CLINICIAN: *Can you take a moment to just take in how important it is that you have this commitment?* (The clinician is trying to deepen this downregulation through embodiment of positive states with space and attention.)

CLIENT: *I am still sad, and I wish I had done things differently. But also, I feel good when I think of how hard I have worked. I was really out of line with my kids. I did apologize, and my parents never did that. I am also working every day to make sure I stay as much as I can in the green zone with my kids. I have been doing breathing exercises and other things we have talked about ever since that happened.* (Client is now having more eye contact with the clinician, indicating more movement into the VVC as well as less shame.)

CLINICIAN: *When you feel good at how hard you have worked, where do you notice feeling good in your body?* (The clinician is helping the client embody a positive state for more access to the VVC and supporting resiliency.)

CLIENT: *I feel some lightness in my heart. My stomach is still clenched, though, as I think of my yelling.*

CLINICIAN: *Can you notice the lightness while also bringing in some self-compassion that you have been in a challenging time lately?* (The clinician is paying less attention to the negative vortex state, intentionally supporting integration and movement from chaos and rigidity, supporting access to the VVC.)

CLIENT: *I really have been in a pretty tough place. Yes, I can bring in some self-compassion as I think of how hard it has been in my relationship.* (The client takes another deep breath, indicating more movement to deactivation.)

CLINICIAN: *And as you do this, are there some kind words that come up?*

CLIENT: *It is okay not to be perfect.*

CLINICIAN: *What is that like to say?*

CLIENT: *I soften more. My heart feels warmer and lighter. My stomach is not clenched now. I still think I need to apologize again to my kids and I need to let them know that I am going to work on staying calmer. But I do feel more okay, not so critical of myself.*

CLINICIAN: *Can we take some more time to feel this in your body, noticing the warmth and lightness in your heart and more ease in your body?* (This is the integration of the new belief "It is okay not to be perfect" that is allowing more connection to Essence.) *Allow attention to those sensations while also holding the awareness that you are taking accountability, as you will apologize again and talk to your kids about this. Let yourself bring in the sense of how different this was from your past experience and how important this is for you.*

CLIENT: *I feel so much better.*

In this example, the client does need to examine their behavior, because a real mistake was made. Using the integration of reparative experience, self-compassion is more possible for the client. By applying self-compassion, the client's nervous system can move to the green zone and stay in regulation. They might need to practice this exercise many times. As with all deactivation pathways, this example also underlines the importance of embodying the positive states as they present in the process.

> *Practice tip:* I usually see that clients are interested in feeling self-compassion, even if it is not available to them at the moment. They seem to know it is inherently going to be good for them. If the client rejects the process, there could be a blocking early childhood belief that needs addressing first. I often work directly with that belief using reparative experiences. Occasionally, I have also said to a client, "You needed a different childhood for this to be any different." Bringing awareness to that reality often stops clients immediately as they take it in; that statement reflects their earlier experiences and nervous system states make certain skills and actions difficult to access.

SUMMARY

Self-compassion is a powerful intervention for most clients. Rooted in the VVC, it shifts physiology to the green zone. The practice of self-compassion can lead to a version of self-parenting that supports deeper regulation; it becomes a tool for reparenting oneself. There can be a learning curve in integrating self-compassion, particularly with histories of early childhood abuse. The most important thing is to encourage clients not to give up, as self-compassion can need time to be fortified and strengthened. Other forms of self-compassion, such as heart breathing, saying kind words, or doing loving self-care activities, can be starting places for integrating this important pathway. Regularly utilizing self-compassion is a practice for general well-being. As Chris Germer says, "A moment of self-compassion can change your entire day. A string of such moments can change the course of your life" (2009, p. 2).

SELF-COMPASSION EXERCISE

Turn toward your heart with the intention to offer heartfelt attention to yourself with self-compassion. Allow yourself to feel your breath in your heart area. And if it feels right, you could place your hand on your heart as you notice the breath. As you feel the support of your hand or your heartfelt attention on your heart, allow yourself to pay attention to any settling in your body. Take time to be with the settling, noticing it and feeling the sensations of more ease or grounding. Bring up a self-judgment struggle, naming it to yourself, "I am judging . . ." As you bring up the judgment, also gently bring in the awareness that "No one is perfect. It is human to be imperfect." Allow your body to take in these words, noticing any place you can embody them, even slightly. Feel that place of embodiment, with awareness of staying with the sensations that feel good. If it feels okay, allow yourself to bring in the words "it is human to be imperfect" to be with those sensations.

CHAPTER 9

Pendulation

Neuroscience research shows that the only way we can change the way we feel is by becoming aware of our inner experience and learning to befriend what is going on inside ourselves.

—Bessel van der Kolk

Rhythmic pendulation is inherent in regulation. The flexible nervous system is not static and is dynamically moving in and out of different states. The body naturally has rhythms and contrasting experiences as part of everyday life. Restoring these rhythms is part of trauma recovery as it moves the nervous system from fixed states. This chapter will explore the concept of pendulation as a means of downregulating the nervous system.

Pendulation, as a deactivation pathway, is attributed to Peter Levine. "While trauma is about being frozen or stuck, pendulation is about the innate organismic rhythm of contraction and expansion" (2010, p. 78). Pendulation refers to the oscillation of back-and-forth movement; it is the natural state of the nervous system (Levine, 2010). Breath, heartbeat, digestion, and sleep cycles are natural rhythms in the body. This is evidenced through inhales and exhales, heartbeat movements, cycles of digestion and elimination, and sleep and wakefulness, which are all part of rhythmic pendulation in the body. These rhythms often get disturbed as the body's pendulation experiences are interrupted, a byproduct of trauma physiology. Clients can exhibit shifts in their breath with unconscious patterns of holding their breath or very slow respiratory functioning (DVC) or shallow breathing (SNS). Heartbeats can be quick (SNS) or slowed down in conservation physiology (DVC). Digestive and elimination functioning can also lose its natural cycle (SNS and DVC). Sleep issues, which also include not having restful sleep (SNS) or sleeping too much (DVC), are often reported trauma symptoms. Bodily rhythms that can be restored can support deactivation into VVC (Dana, 2020). A goal of trauma treatment is for body rhythms to be returned to their natural state (van der Kolk, 2014), which makes a pendulation process effective.

Pendulation is used in many therapeutic modalities, including EMDR, Somatic Experiencing®, Sensorimotor psychotherapy, and Hakomi mindfulness-centered somatic psychotherapy. Levine (2010, p. 79) describes pendulation as "one of the most important reconnections to the body's innate wisdom." Pendulation can assist in metabolizing trauma in the body. According to Paulsen & Lanius (2014, p. 374), pendulation is "fundamental to intrinsic healing processes, as the body comes into coherency, spontaneous oscillation often occurs." Pendulation is a natural pulsation between expansion and contraction, and it is often present during the change process as something new is emerging. In a change process, most people are familiar with the experience of a back-and-forth movement, as clients shift between the old and new patterns. This oscillation of old and new patterning is a very normal part of the healing trajectory. Pendulation can also manifest body sensations, states or feelings, images, or beliefs; this spontaneous presentation of these experiences can indicate the new pattern or way of being is ready to integrate. The intervention of applying pendulation can lead to the more desirable sensation, state, image, or belief becoming more dominant, creating this transformation (Somatic Experiencing®, personal communication, 2009–2011). "It is the holding together of these polarities that facilitates deep integration and often an 'alchemical' transformation" (Levine, 2015, p. 71).

As the clinician applies pendulation as a deactivation pathway to any experience, they direct the client to notice that there are two different states. The clinician would then have the client describe the "felt sense" (Gendlin, 1996), of filling out both experiences sensation-wise, noticing the nuances of each state. After both states are fully described, the client is then guided to pendulate. As the more desirable state becomes dominant, the client is encouraged to notice this newly integrated state through the embodiment of positive states, which supports the neuroplasticity of change.

As an example of how to apply pendulation with sensations, when the client notices tightness as they talk, the clinician can ask, "What is the least tight part of your body right now?" This question initiates the pendulation. As the client names the place in their body that is least tight, the clinician suggests, "Let yourself notice both the tightness you feel in (naming that part of the body) and (the place in the body holding less tightness). Allow yourself to go back and forth between the two sensations. Let's see what happens." Sometimes, the client reports two different states. They might report "I feel a spark of interest and I also notice how my body clamps down as I consider finding an activity that nourishes me." In both of these examples, as the client oscillates these contrasting experiences in the body, there is often a resolution of the tightness.

As a deactivation pathway, pendulation is described as the oscillation experience of putting attention on two different experiences; for our purposes, it can also include holding two experiences at once or focusing only on the more desirable experience. Although these last two options are not technically a pendulation experience, they can be used interchangeably for a similar effect, still using two separate and generally opposite or at least different experiences. The clinician can invite the client to shift attention to the other options if pendulation alone not shifting the physiology.

> *Practice Tip:* I often invite clients to lengthen their embodied experience in the more desired or positive state while doing pendulation. It seems to prime the nervous system more toward that state, but pendulation can work well without adding this guidance.

An example of pendulation is, "Can you notice the tension and the ease that is happening and just go back and forth a few times with each sensation, staying a little longer in the ease?" Or, to focus on one part of both experiences, the clinician can have the client pay attention to the more regulating experience; this is the one that feels better and is creating more VVC access. The clinician could say, "As you notice the ease in your shoulders, can you put your attention there, while allowing the tension to also be present?" The clinician could also have the client hold the preferred state in the foreground of their awareness, saying, "See if it is okay to just put your attention on the ease." Pendulation and these variations often move the more desired state to the foreground of awareness rather than the more familiar and more challenging experience. All three interventions support shifting the nervous system to downregulation to green zone physiology.

In working with all three versions of pendulation, let's look at another example of applying this to the sensation of a clenched stomach:

- Direct pendulation: "Notice where in your body has the least amount of clenching. Feel the clenched stomach while holding how your legs do not feel clenched and go back and forth a few times."
- Holding two parts together: "Notice the clench in your stomach while also noticing your legs do not feel clenched."
- Holding the preferred sensation: "See if you can put most of your attention on your legs not feeling clenched."

Although pendulation is useful in applying to all channels of experience, it is often most effective with sensations. Whenever two contrasting experiences arise in a session, it's useful to try pendulation since the experiences are already there. Any indication that the less desirable sensation, belief, image, or emotion is diminishing suggests continuing with pendulation. Clients typically need to repeat it three to five times initially to notice a change. If improvement continues but the more negative sensation is still present, the practice should continue to resolution of downregulation.

PENDULATION EXAMPLE FOR SENSATION

The client reports tension in their jaw as they process talking to their partner after a fight. As they name awareness of the jaw tension, the clinician leads pendulation by gently directing the client, "I am wondering if you can notice where in the body you feel the least amount of tension." The client names that their arms feel "pretty loose." The clinician says, "Can you let your attention go back and forth between this looseness in your arms and the tension in your jaw? Just take your time, staying a little longer in the looseness in your arms." The client does a few rounds independently and reports that their jaw now feels less tense. Because this leads to a positive state, the clinician guides the client in *embodiment of the positive state* to strengthen the deactivation and access to the VVC.

PENDULATION EXAMPLE FOR IMAGE

In this example, the client is talking about something they are worried about in their family. When asked what they feel in their body, they bring up the image in their belly of "something dark." In this case, using the image channel, the clinician could offer, "Where in your body do you notice it being lighter?" The client names their feet. The clinician then suggests that the client move back and forth between the light and the dark images. As this happens, the client reports that the darkness softens. They say that there is still some worry, but it is less. As the image changes, so does the physiology, supporting the client back into the VVC. In using the image channel of experience, simply asking if there is "an opposite image anywhere in the body" also helps with this pendulation process.

PENDULATION EXAMPLE FOR BELIEFS

The client brings up the struggle that they feel that their needs do not matter after bringing up a desire to ask for more emotional connection. Similar to the integration of reparative experiences and core beliefs, the clinician then asks, "Where in your body do you know your needs matter, even slightly? Even if you do not fully know, bring into awareness even a 'little bit' of knowing." After some hesitation, the client says, "I know it is just a little in my heart, but my stomach seems to be saying that my needs do not matter." The clinician has the client pendulate between "knowing in the heart" and "not believing in the stomach." "Let your attention go between this knowing in your heart and the not believing in your stomach, focusing a little longer on your heart as you do this. Take some time to be with this." The client pendulates the experiences and then reports that there is more of a sense of belief in having their needs met. Because this is now a positive state, it is followed with the *embodiment of the positive state*, "Can you stay with feeling in your heart area that your needs matter?" This supports the deactivation of the VVC. Shifting limiting core beliefs can require more interventions as discussed in Chapter 7.

PENDULATION EXAMPLE FOR EMOTIONS

A client reports feeling some grief around their career. Having decided to be a caretaker to their ill parent, they report missing the career leadership opportunities that come with the decision. In exploring it more, the client also reports feeling fulfilled in the role of caretaking. The clinician then suggests filling the sensations out for both emotional experiences. The client notes grief as "a heavy feeling in the chest" and the fulfillment as "a warmth in the heart." The client is then encouraged to allow both to be there and to pendulate the experiences: the grief with the heavy feeling and the sense of being fulfilled that is felt in the warm heart. As the client feels both, they oscillate between both sets of emotions. After this, they report that they have a sense of calm "from trusting their choice." They also state they are "feeling peaceful." This pendulation between the two experiences becomes integrated into a peaceful choice. The clinician supports this important shift by having the client embody those new words, feeling the empowerment that it is their choice. There may or may not be grief to still integrate, but it might feel more manageable as it is balanced by integrating their trust of the choice.

SUMMARY

Pendulation, as the natural oscillation of the nervous system, is often effective in shifting physiological states. This deactivation pathway can be applied to other body sensations, emotions, images, or beliefs as needed. These elements of experience can occur spontaneously from the client or can be evoked by asking about an opposite. Because it is so natural for the body to pendulate, this often can resolve symptoms with some ease, resulting in downregulation of the nervous system.

PENDULATION EXERCISE

Let yourself bring up a place in your body that has the most ease at this moment. Even if it might not feel fully comfortable, notice that it is holding more ease than other parts of your body. Let yourself just bring it into awareness with your attention. Take some time to notice this. If it feels okay, bring your attention to an uncomfortable place in your body that has some pain or tension. Let your attention be with this discomfort. Allow yourself to shift your attention back and forth between both places, taking time to stay a little longer in the place in your body that has less tension. As you go back and forth a few times, let yourself notice any changes and possible ease in your body now.

CHAPTER 10

Motor Plan Completion of Protective Actions

Long after the actual event has passed, the brain keeps sending signals to the body to escape a threat that no longer exists.

—Bessel van der Kolk

Merging the sciences of human psychology and mammalogy has shown us that animals have much to teach us about healing. The shift from traditional talk therapy, where clients simply sit or lie on a couch, to incorporating movement and body awareness has been transformative. In my own practice, transitioning to a polyvagal-informed approach has deepened my understanding of the body's innate impulses for healing and resolution. Learning to recognize and support these natural signals for regulation in real time has been a groundbreaking discovery. In this chapter, I'll explore how tapping into the body's wisdom can be a powerful tool for reducing trauma physiology and supporting nervous system regulation.

Because trauma memory is held in the senses, including the muscles and emotions, the healing process must include the body directly (van der Kolk, 2014). "When an overwhelming experience is insufficiently processed, the body still has the survival reactions to the traumatic moment ready. . . . This becomes apparent in muscle tension and movement impulses as well as dysregulated arousal" (Kalisvaart & Ogden, 2025). This is understood most readily by the work of Peter Levine.

Peter Levine's study of animals in the wild led him to realize that although they had constant threats, they were not demonstrating trauma symptoms (Levine, 1997). As he studied the animals, he was struck with the awareness that, unlike humans, animals followed the survival impulses in their bodies. They were able to utilize their protective survival actions when necessary and did not exhibit trauma symptoms, even though threats remained in their environment. This was a profound realization. His work brought awareness to the concept that animals in the wild were able to complete their motor plans of protective action. This led to their ability to not be stuck in trauma symptoms, unlike humans, who were not able to complete these actions. He understood that the lack of completion was the root of trauma physiology. Through his study of animal physiology, he originated the Somatic Experiencing® method to teach practitioners ways to create trauma completion.

> *Reflection*: You might note that I am using the term "impulses" in this section, and as noted before, there is a correlation between this concept and "restoring thwarted impulses" discussed earlier. In my Somatic Experiencing® Training, I learned about working with impulses in the body to facilitate the completion of protective motor plans, the focus of this chapter. It is important to note that completing motor plans of protective actions does involve working to restore thwarted impulses in the body. The outcome of applying any of the deactivation pathways discussed also results in awareness of other thwarted impulses that will promote even more regulation and personal expansion.
>
> When the motor plans of protective action are completed, restoring thwarted impulses follows. This often manifests as clients having more access to their protective fight or flight behaviors and being able to attend to themselves in important ways. This can include healing impulses for attaining personal power to set boundaries, speak out, and leave situations when necessary. Agency is recovered as this important deactivation pathway is utilized.

This frame of reference toward observing motor plans in the body remains an effective deactivation pathway for nervous system downregulation (Berceli et al., 2014; Dion, 2018; Levine, 1997, 2010; Ogden et al., 2006). These protective motor plans of action include fleeing or fighting when necessary for survival. Likewise, he also brought awareness to the protective survival response of the freeze and shutdown responses. As noted in the first chapter, freeze and shutdown terms are often used interchangeably, even though they are different responses. Ogden also differentiated these states as "tonic immobility" and "immobility" (Ogden et al., 2006) to reflect a similar view. To review, freeze (orange state) (see Polyvagal Theory Chart of Trauma Response, Figure 1.3 in the text and on the color insert) is a hybrid state with both SNS and DVC physiology; freeze often holds the physiology of the SNS, while also being immobilized (DVC). Shutdown has the physiological underpinnings of DVC. Both states have some crossover as immobility underlies both states. He recognized that animals moved into immobilization as part of survival; after some time and a physiological discharge, they would then rebound. Levine's work brought awareness to the idea that motor plans of protective action stay alive in the body because they do not get resolution as do animals in the wild.

Motor plan completion of protective actions is key deactivation pathway to downregulating the nervous system. They are the survival-oriented actions that are evoked in the body as a result of a threat experience (Levine, 1997, 2010; Ogden et al., 2006). As protective actions of fight/flight/freeze/shutdown, they encompass movements related to the associated actions of those states: fighting, fleeing, avoiding, bracing, freezing, and shutdown survival patterns. These states are the focus of the work in trauma completion and are observable in clients' bodies as movements during sessions.

Traumatic experiences seem to be single-trial learning, meaning that a single event or experience can create a survival plan in the body, reinforcing a motor plan of action (Scaer, 2005; van der Kolk, 2014). An example of single-trial learning occurs in food poisoning; people rarely want to eat that food again after that experience. Although most learning requires repetition, single-trial learning requires only one exposure. In trauma, this implies that the action memory is imprinted, leading to unconscious and automatic responses. "The patterns of muscles and tendons used in the act of defense during the threat become part of procedural memory" (Scaer, 2005, p. 42). Stored in procedural memory, similar to not forgetting how to ride a bike, these actions stay in the body's memory as a survival action plan. Both single-trial learning and trauma memory being stored in procedural memory might be at the heart of why these biological impulses for motor plans are so compelling to the nervous system, keeping it in a fixed state of trauma (Scaer, 2005; van der Kolk, 2014) with red and yellow zone physiology.

There is less disrupted physiology when the client can have agency to take and complete successful action (Levine, 1997, 2010; Ogden et al., 2006; van der Kolk, 2014). Similarly, if the client is not able to take the defensive or protective action, physiology will stay primed in the body to take that action (Levine, 1997; Ogden et al., 2006). Many trauma symptoms are connected to the incompletion of the motor plans of fight/flight/freeze/shutdown that were elicited in traumatic events (Somatic Experiencing Training®, personal communication, 2009–2011). These protective actions are often not completed because of further safety concerns. When the nervous system mobilizes to act, like running away or fighting back, these impulses stay alive in the body if they are interrupted and/or are not completed. These survival responses actively signal the body for protective action, even when the event is over (Dion, 2018; Levine, 1997, 2010; Ogden et al., 2006). They are often the origin and basis of trauma symptoms because they create yellow and red zone physiology.

The physiology of the yellow or red zones stays fixed, priming the body to take some action for completion. The impulse for those actions remains in the body. These impulses show up as involuntary movements exhibited by the client. These movements can present in any part of the body and will reflect the nervous system states of SNS and DVC, and they will be an indicator of an impulse for protective action (Levine, 1997, 2010; Ogden et al., 2006). These actions include fighting off, pushing away, kicking off, turning away, getting away, or any kind of action a person would take to protect themselves. These movements often occur after any kind of trauma, including sexual and domestic violence, wartime experiences, natural disasters, childhood abuse, accidents, and marginalization experiences (Somatic Experiencing Training®, personal communication, 2009–2011).

These observable involuntary movements in session can show up in various ways in the body, including tensing (SNS) and bracing (freeze) or lack of movement, getting still, and/or shutting down (DVC). The movements can be big or small and can be exhibited at any time. They may or may not be connected to the content of the session. As Scaer (2005) underlined, these motor plans are running in the background as signals for protective action; this leads them to be noticeable in the current time. They could be observed in a safe situation, like having dinner with a friend or in a session when talking about the trauma situation itself. They generally appear in the body as movements and/or somatic patterns, indicating an impulse in the physiology for completion.

This will be discussed in more detail, but these motions can show up dramatically as big movements in the body's extremities or very subtly as a small head tilt. The movements that are occurring are gestures that look to be part of everyday conversations and might not be noticeable if one were not studying this information. If one were to go into a coffee shop and observe people, there would likely be movements in almost everyone sitting and conversing. Clients will often not have awareness of these body patterns until they are identified in sessions.

SNS/MOBILIZATION: FIGHT-OR-FLIGHT

Mobilization includes the fight-or-flight movements, which are the foundation of anger and anxiety issues (see Figure 1.3 in the text and on the color insert). There are many ways motor plans are displayed in the body. Mobilized movements tend to be more in the outer body in the extremities and less in the core of the body (Dion, 2018), although they still might be evident as an aspect of deeper bracing in the core. These incomplete movements are the cornerstone to dysregulation in the nervous system; the body stays mobilized to complete them (Somatic Experiencing Training®, personal communication, 2009–2011). Both tracking and identifying the incomplete movements are central to supporting the downregulation of the ANS.

We will now cover some examples of how this might be exhibited in a session.[20] Because the neck and head are involved in the physiology of the orienting reflex toward novelty in the environment, motor plans of the neck and head are very common (Levine, 1997, 2010; Ogden et al., 2006). These can include head movements of turning toward or away, replicating what occurred during the client's earlier experience that created the threat and need for the protective motor plan originally. This might look like a slight head movement on either side of the body. Impulses of turning away or toward something will be demonstrated by how the neck and head are moving. They also are seen in the neck extending as if trying to orient to a threat. Other neck and head movements can include, the head moving back, seemingly trying to get away as in a flight response (Levine, 1997, 2010; Ogden et al., 2006). Again, these are often not obvious or noticed by clients or clinicians until they are tracked as part of deactivating the nervous system. They are hiding in plain sight.

Mobilization motor plans often include movements of the arms and shoulders. The shoulders might be turning, as in a flight response for getting away. This can be indicated by a slight turn in the body. The hands could make a pushing away motion with arms in front of the body, almost as if pushing something out of one's space. This fight movement might be the whole movement or just the hands moving up in front of the body quickly. For a fight response in the hands themselves, you might see tensed fists or even a punching motion. The hands might be clenched and balled up.

Leg movements, including kicking or pushing as part of a fight response, are also common. As an indicator of this movement, you could notice the leg coming up or the foot moving as the beginning of a kick or pushing movement. A running motion is often the marker of the flight response in the legs; this is frequently exhibited by motions in the feet. Other sorts of leg movements are bracing and tightening in the legs, including holding the legs closed. There can be many variations of these movements as the body might need to mobilize to protect itself in various ways.

Body movements might seem more generalized, like tightening or bracing the whole body or possibly some parts of it. Any tightening that the client reports can be connected to a motor plan of protective action. There are many different variations of movements, and it is not necessarily important to know how they connect to a memory. It is more important to observe them and support the completion of the movement to deactivate the nervous system. Figuring out the motor plan's purpose and denoting whether it is fight or flight is also not necessary for deactivation even though I am offering some plausible ideas in this discussion. With that said, knowing the basic movements can sometimes help tie in the presenting issue with physiology. These are the most typical movements:

Fight: fists balled, leg moving up and down (like kicking), jaw tensing, pushing arms out in front, forward leaning, tense muscles
Flight: feet tapping (like running), backing away in the body or the head, turning away with the head or body, looking for exits

As stated, recognizing basic fight-or-flight movements can help the clinician decide which movements to focus on, particularly as they relate to the client's reported concerns in therapy. To demonstrate this, the clinician observes the movements, paying attention to the protective motor plan that seems most present and how it connects to the client's request for help. For example, a client with anger issues might show more movements that indicate a fight response. The anger is part of their fight response and reflects what is dominant in their nervous system at that moment. For this client, it is often useful to focus on any of the movements related to their symptoms over other movements. You might also note some running movements in the feet. Because of the client's explicit request for help (anger issues), you might hold off on exploring that movement at first. As you focus on completing fight motor plans if they are recognizable to you, this can be more useful to the client, as it ties in with their presenting issue. As these movements are worked with in session, the client will exhibit less anger over time; this occurs as they are no longer stuck in fight response. Similarly, for the client who is in treatment for anxiety, anxiety is often reduced as flight motor plans are complete. With the anxious client, the clinician wants to observe any incomplete flight response that is recognizable. This includes the movements listed that would indicate wanting to flee. Connecting the movements of fight-or-flight to the presenting problem of anger or anxiety will offer the most effective intervention for the client as they offer a way to directly work with the fixed state in the nervous system.

The completion of their fight-or-flight movements will result in the downregulation of the ANS to the VVC. A spontaneous breath and/or some reported body relaxation are recognizable signals from the ANS that deactivation to the green zone has occurred. This green zone physiology will include more softening in the body, fuller breaths, spontaneously looking around, and/or connecting more to the clinician. This marks a shift in state; tracking state change reinforces the effectiveness of the intervention, letting the clinician know they are right on track. The clinician will want to experiment a few more times with these movement patterns as they support deactivation by utilizing the completion of motor plans of action.

Following the impulse of the body to take the needed protective action will signal the body to downregulate because the protective action is complete. The essential element is, as always, doing an intervention and tracking, including checking in for what helps deactivate the nervous system most effectively. As noted earlier, in the animal world, trauma symptoms are nonexistent after these movements are completed (Levine, 1997). Finding ways to complete protective motor plans can deactivate the ANS for this same reduction of symptom (Berceli et al., 2014; Dion, 2018; Levine, 1997, 2010; Ogden et al., 2006; Porges, 2011).

The first step is to bring the movement into awareness by directing attention to the movement. "Notice the way your body turns slightly to the right," or "I wonder if you could feel how your neck wants to back away at this moment," or "Can you feel that tension in your fist as you are talking now?" or "Can you feel how your body is bracing as you talk about this?" These statements to the client are designed to have the client mindfully notice the movement that is already occurring in their body; highlighting this observation makes contact with the motor plan of protective action.

The next step is to direct the client to do the movement, often slowly, while demonstrating the movement to them. Because clients can often feel self-conscious, joining them in the movement and normalizing the action can make it safer to explore. It helps to mirror the movement to them by saying, "Let's do this together, and I will show this to you for you to see." Then, after modeling, do the action with the client while describing it. "Let yourself feel that slight turn in your body and slowly turn more to the right; I wonder what that feels like as you slow that movement down." Or "Let yourself have your neck slowly back up." "Can you just clench and unclench your fist right now?" "Is it okay to bring awareness to your body bracing?" This awareness brings attention to the body to its mobilization of fight-or-flight protective actions and starts the completion process. Mirroring helps the client begin to see how the movement is already occurring, in addition to mitigating any self-consciousness. Because these movements so easily are part of everyday conversations, they are generally below one's level of awareness until the clinician both notices them and works directly with them in sessions.

In working with movements, there can be a range to include working with the whole movement, working with only its impulse, or titrating the movement through bite-sizing the motor plan. For the movement of working with the body turning away as part of the flight response:

- Working with the whole movement: "Feel your body fully slowly turning to the right." In this example, the whole body would turn as the clinician mirrors this to the client.
- Working with only the impulse of the movement: "Feel the impulse in your body to turn away to the right." In this case, the movement would be very small and even imperceptible as the client taps into noticing the impulse.
- Working with titrating the movement: "Feel the body wanting to move right and try a very small micro movement of going to the right." With this direction, the client would experiment with a small movement.

After trying these different options, it is important to observe deactivation and consider the client's report on which version feels best as you proceed. The option that offers the most deactivation will be useful to repeat in that session and out of the session as it can be key to the deactivation process for the client, particularly when clients report anger or anxiety issues, as this works with the fight-or-flight system.

> *Reflection:* I find it most useful to start with the whole movement slowly as it helps the client make contact with the movement they are doing. Then, I generally move to feeling the impulse of the movement. That is more subtle and

often more accessible after first feeling the general movement. Some clinicians approach this differently with success, so it is fine to experiment.

Other examples of language and directing might be for the whole body, "Can you feel your legs wanting to move?" or "See if you can feel the impulse of running" for working with the impulse of the movement. Another example of titration of the movement is, "Feel how your feet want to run. Let's just try the very beginning of that movement" as a titrated movement. This range will depend on what feels best for the client; this requires checking in with the client. As discussed with the attunement cycle, any intervention (response) needs follow-up (tracking) to see if it works for the client. Checking in with the client is part of attunement. With attunement, the purpose is deactivation, so the clinician is tracking if there is a shift in physiology. Does anything look more relaxed? Is breathing easier? Is there a shift in the face and eyes looking more present? This shift in physiology is the indicator that the deactivation pathway is attuned for access to the VVC.

Motor plans look different for different movements, and the clinician being willing to be experimental is helpful. For hands balling into a fist, the clinician might say, "Let yourself notice the impulse to ball your fist, tightening it and letting it go." This might immediately lead to a spontaneous breath, indicating completion and downregulation in the nervous system. The client sometimes reports wanting to do the whole movement, which could be a punching movement. The real goal here is to start moving into more regulation through the completion of motor plans, shifting the fixed state of stuckness.

When the right plan is clear, more ease is evident in the body. With this knowledge, the clinician can encourage the client to repeat the movement as homework to support deactivation. Encouraging clients to practice the motor plan that was in their session is useful; it helps to complete the movement several times a day. It is important to emphasize not just the movement but also to take 10 to 20 seconds to notice the shift in the nervous system state, as indicated by deeper breath and/or less tension; these are markers of VVC. Noticing this shift reinforces the positive state and strengthens the VVC. You will also notice that the movements in sessions change over time as there is more completion in the nervous system. They can also switch around to different states of fight-or-flight, freeze, or shutdown. Although the motor plans do not fully go away, the movements along with the dominant state tend to become less of the automatic response in the ANS as they complete and deactivate the nervous system (Scaer, 2005).

Occasionally, you might observe two motor plans at once that almost seem to be fused together. An example might be wanting to turn away on one side of the body and trying to push back on the other side of the body. Another might be in the neck, where you see it backing away on one side and lifting on the other. It is not important to figure it out, but you can break down what you see and have the client try both. The feedback from the client and the ANS response will guide you on which might be more potent for their deactivation process. Clients will generally have a preference as to which motor plan they find most settling for their nervous system.

> *Reflection:* Clients and clinicians can get caught up in wanting to figure out the meaning of the movement, wondering what it is connected to in their earlier life or experiences. Assigning meaning to movement is not necessary and does not tend to be helpful, as the true meaning and connection to memory is often not known anyway. Trying to find the meaning can interrupt the process of moving the client to an authentic regulation, as it can be an attempt at faux deactivation, as discussed in Chapter 2. The purpose of motor plan completion is to restore more regulation. Because of this, focusing on the resulting shift in states is more useful to clients than trying to figure out the meaning. If clients seem to want to do this, offering this information can provide the understanding of why you are not exploring it with them.

If the meaning is important, it will often spontaneously show up as the client experiments. The client might hold their legs tightly closed. As the movement is supported to completion by tightening it and letting it go, occasionally a client might remember an earlier sexual assault and how their body wanted to be able to protect itself by blocking sexual contact. This spontaneous memory arising as the movement is explored is a type of integration; when this happens, the meaning and memory often hold a necessary piece of information from the body. In this case, the meaning and memory offer how the client had tried to protect themselves during a traumatic event. This linkage of meaning and memory creates integration as these aspects come together; the story is more authentically complete.

Examples

Motor plan of mobilization completion example (fight). The client is reporting anger at a family member for not respecting their boundaries about something important. As they talk, they speed up, and their body tension increases visibly. The clinician notices that the client's arms are particularly tense, and their fist is also balled up. The clinician might say, "Feel the tension in your fist right now and see if it is okay to tighten it, and then let it go." As this movement is completed, the client might visibly relax their arm, and the whole body might also relax. The clinician might direct this movement a few times, resulting in more access to the VVC.

In this example, anger is a signal from the body for the need for boundaries. This work with the motor plan for protective action will support the boundaries, and the client is often able to increase their skills in setting them as their body settles. With the tension softening in the body, the client can be more regulated while speaking, while also incorporating the information from the body that setting the boundaries is necessary. Anger from fight response is often a healthy signal of needing a boundary.

Clients can sometimes feel some anxiety about following the impulse of a fight response. This occurs most often if there is a history of exposure to abusive anger in the past, as well as a fear that they will act out inappropriately. They often need to be reassured that when they do the work of shifting their physiology, they bring in more skillful choices as they shift. I often share with clients that anger overreactions primarily occur when someone is stuck in the fight response; this helps them feel more comfortable with engaging with the movements. Motor plan completion shifts the body from fight response to VVC, leading to more competency in interactions as a result of a more regulated ANS.

Motor plan of mobilization completion example (flight). The client brings up dating a new person and states they feel "pretty anxious" about how it is going, adding they are uncertain about what they want in a relationship. As they talk, their head moves back on the right side, subtly almost appearing to be backing away. The clinician intervenes by saying, "I wonder if it is okay to notice that your head seems to back away as you talk. Can you feel this?" As the client does feel it, the clinician demonstrates the movement to the client. The protective movement is backing away, followed by the head returning to a neutral position; the client intentionally recreates the same movement. As the nervous system feels the completion, body tension also releases, resulting in more ease and regulation.

As noted before, the meaning may not be known but the resulting regulation in the body will often lead the client to know how they feel about the relationship. This anxiety could be connected to several things, including having red flags about the relationship, hesitation about simply being in a relationship at all, or possibly having a core belief surfacing. Working with and attending to the movement completion will shift the physiology, which is the goal. If the meaning is important, it will unfold in a more direct way.

SNS AND IMMOBILIZATION HYBRID: FREEZE

When attending to freeze, working with any obvious motor plans observed first will be useful. Doing so will lower activation, making it a good place to start if it is available. It is important to be mindful that freeze has immobilization as part of its blended physiology; it can easily move to shutdown, and an impulse for another action is also present.

Competing Impulses

Competing impulses are often at the base of freeze states; actions are interrupted and are not complete (Somatic Experiencing Training®, personal communication, 2009–2011). Examples of competing impulses are "I want to get out of my job, and I am too afraid to make a change," or "I want to set my boundaries with my partner, but I am afraid of rocking the boat." Inherent in these examples are two different impulses, which are often at the heart of working with freeze. Simply naming the competing impulses can result in identifying and underlining the movements of impulses for inhibited actions, shifting the physiology. If necessary, this can be followed by embodying and differentiating the two impulses; this includes feeling the different places in the body where the impulses lie, as well as the different kinds of sensations they hold. Usually, the impulse for not speaking up is familiar and might need less of a focus because the client already has this awareness; it is generally the less familiar impulse that is stuck. Bringing awareness to the other inhibited impulse (where the action is not being taken) often shifts the freeze state. This results in freeze losing its grip on the physiology and thus leads to deactivating. Other times, the client is not even aware that they are stuck in two competing impulses; therefore, identifying both is often useful.

As an example of working with competing impulses: "Notice if you can feel the impulse to get out of your job while noticing there is a fear of making change." The fear of making a change is already present, as it is the action the client is *not* taking. Because the lack of action is where the stuckness lies, the fear of change might not need to be explored and embodied as fully; it is the familiar sensation that is already present. Instead, the new impulse to change jobs is stuck, so embodying it helps to bring it forward as an action. This type of defusing by having the client feel them as two different impulses is helpful. "Notice that these are two separate impulses in your body right now. They are fused at this moment, but they are separate impulses. See if you can feel how they are different." Working with only the competing impulses in this manner might free up and shift the physiology as the less prominent impulse is embodied and felt. The client sometimes feels capable of taking the actions they desire to take when this defusing occurs; in this case, it is to change jobs. As the client experiences "I can" from the SNS, there is a shift to from orange to yellow; the impulse for the action is now present, including feeling anxiety about making the change. If this is the case, it might require an additional deactivation pathway to shift the ANS to work with the anxiety, such as pendulation or offering a reparative experience. At other times, working with competing impulses can sometimes elicit a sense of some sort of action that will give the ANS a sense of completion, downregulating the ANS; in this example, the client could simply get clearer on needing to change jobs, which might feel complete.

DVC: IMMOBILIZATION

With shutdown, there can be more complexity in addressing what might shift the state. Because of the underlying immobility, the primary focus is restoring movement. With DVC physiology dominance, there is often difficulty with interoception; part of its protective feature is not being present in the here and now, including, is not feeling one's body discussed in Chapter 4. To address this survival feature, the initial work includes the development of interoception. This is supported by being present in the here and now through orientation to the environment; orientation supports the nervous system in focusing outward. Because shutdown can be an inward state, learning to manage attention outwardly through orientation is useful, as it provides a shift. It also allows a type of being present in the here and now to be available.

Orientation, discussed in Chapter 4 (sensing the environment through the senses), can also be safer initially for the client than learning to feel sensations, as overwhelming sensations are underneath this state. Along with this, the deactivation pathway of embodiment of positive states encourages feeling safe sensations. This strengthens the capacity for holding positive sensations and begins to build a container to hold more challenging sensations. This process takes time and does not directly address the protective motor plan. However, the embodiment of positive states is the platform that needs to be in place to support its completion. It is crucial to have some ability for awareness of one's experiences through orientation, the embodiment of positive states, or completion of a fight-or-flight motor plan; when this is in place, shutdown motor plans can be addressed.

Shutdown completion is indicated as an intervention when the client is able to have some shifts as described earlier but continues unchanged with low energy, feelings of stuckness, and/or heaviness. To enable shutdown completion, some basic conditions are required. As noted, these conditions include having some ability to have some shifts in state. Both being able to stay in the present moment and being able to hold positive sensations are indicators of a general ability to shift. If these components are in place, the clinician can move forward with DVC completion, and the client has the foundation to uncouple or defuse the shutdown from terror, which is often necessary (Levine, 1997, 2010). Defusing shutdown begins as helping the client deactivate by using both orientation and embodiment of a resilient state to have small touches into the green zone. This starts building capacity.

Because the red zone of DVC inherently has a neuroception of a life threat at the core of its nervous system response, this step is important. Being able to reorient to the present moment and participate in social engagement also supports the client in having more VVC access; this is a foundational requirement needed for completion of shutdown. This starts building capacity, and at times it will defuse on its own with these interventions as terror softens through building the capacity; it is then no longer the primary internal experience. Being present in the here and now also reorients the nervous system to support feeling less terror. Other times, it needs a direct intervention of defusing; this is accomplished by having the client feel the terror while holding the shutdown state, which might feel like stillness, stuckness, quietness, lack of movement, or heaviness.[21] As the client does this, the clinician directs them to be in the environment through orientation and to find a place in the body that feels safe or the clinician uses any other intervention that allows an antidote to the terror to also be present. This often initiates the change in the shutdown and into the VVC.

When working with the shutdown state, it is helpful to hold the vision of the biological process of its completion in order to have an understanding of the process. As an example, imagine the deer being chased by the mountain lion and falling to the ground, shaking, and then rebounding and getting up and moving out of the field. This image helps to hold the blueprint of the outcome and the necessary steps of completion. It illustrates an example of the motor plan process of shutdown as the deer falls to the ground, discharging the energy with shaking, and then rebounds by returning to the herd afterward with restored energy. In this motor plan completion, the goal is to follow the shutdown-to-completion steps by making room for the process. The general recipe for completion is to first build capacity as stated above, then defuse the immobilization from terror (Levine, 1997, 2011), and finally allow the sensations and follow the movements in the body that are part of the process. This leads to rebounding with the restoration of energy, movement, and agency. Miller describes the DVC state as "not gaiety or the absence of pain, but vitality: the freedom to experience spontaneous feelings" (2008, pp. 60–61). Spontaneous feelings are often lost in DVC dominance. This freedom described here refers to the rebound, which is the reconnection to vitality after the completion of DVC protective motor plans.

As an example, the client might state that their feet cannot move, or they bring up the feeling of depression and heaviness; these symptoms can indicate DVC physiology. If the conditions are in place that the shutdown can be completed, as noted above, the clinician can move forward with these steps. Because movement in the nervous system is so important, the clinician might say, "Notice that heaviness, and what happens next?" This statement of "what happens next" primes the nervous system to keep moving. It implies that there *is* a "next" after stuckness. Although trauma happens fast, this process is often slow, and it needs space and quiet to complete. Sometimes next there is shaking, similar to the deer, and sometimes the client simply feels another kind of sensation in the feet.

Shaking is a natural process that sometimes occurs to release the energy of a high arousal state. Its function is to restore equilibrium and homeostasis to the nervous system (Berceli et al., 2014; Levine, 1997, 2010; Ogden et al., 2006). Berceli (2025) states that disinhibition regarding shaking supports nervous system regulation. Because shaking can feel awkward or embarrassing, affirming and encouraging clients' shaking supports the disinhibition of this natural response. "That is great that your body is shaking; just let that happen." That encouragement helps the clients stay with the process without inhibiting themselves.

As the shutdown completion continues, the clinician follows each awareness the client has, encouraging the process with "and what do you notice next?" In each step of working with completion, there is a movement toward a return of energy. The client usually reports feeling less tired or depressed or feeling different from what they had previously described. It is helpful to end with being present in the here and now with orientation and interoception, as the present moment has now been reestablished.

> *Practice tip:* Peter Levine often suggests using the "Voo" sound to support the completion of freeze (Somatic Experiencing Training®, personal communication, 2009–2011). I often suggest his recommendation as homework to clients to support their shifts into these new states after practicing in sessions. The "Voo" sound sounds like a foghorn. One takes a breath and with the exhale, makes this sound. This idea fits with Porges's concepts of chanting as supporting access to the VVC.

Example of the Completion of the Shutdown Process

CLINICIAN: *You know, you've been talking about this tiredness and all this lethargy in your body, and I want to go more toward this. Is that okay to do now?* (This is getting the agreement and permission for the intervention.)

CLIENT: *Yes, we have been talking about this. What do I need to do?*

CLINICIAN: *So let yourself just turn toward yourself. You may want to close your eyes. Let yourself bring awareness to how you identified that you have no energy and see if it feels okay to feel into it more in your body. What do you notice as you're with it?* (This is accessing the DVC physiology.)

CLIENT: *My limbs feel so heavy, yeah.* (Their body goes into a slump and they close their eyes.)

CLINICIAN: *So, take a moment and feel that heaviness and go toward it. We're going to follow it, if that's okay with you. So just notice it. One of the things I am really appreciating is that you naturally closed your eyes. It is really important that you do not feel any obligation to open them or engage with me in eye contact until your eyes want to open.* (Stating this prevents override in the client, as they often feeling obligated to look at the clinician. The eyes often want to be closed during work with the shutdown state.)

CLIENT: *My eyes feel sort of heavy so it feels good to close them.*

CLINICIAN: *Let yourself just notice that your eyes feels better. Just take your time noticing that.*

CLIENT: *I am just feeling the heaviness in my eyes and my body.* (Client yawns.)

CLINICIAN: *Can you just be with that heaviness?*

CLIENT: *Yeah.* (Client yawns more.)

CLINICIAN: *Take your time here.* (The clinician is giving space to the process.)

CLIENT: (Appears quiet and inward with eyes shut.)

CLINICIAN: *Let's go with this heaviness, and take your time here. We can see where things want to go next.* (The client might not interact much as this is a very internal process as they notice the heaviness and we are creating room for the shutdown to complete. This could take a few minutes or could go longer, 10–20 minutes.)

CLIENT: (Client continues to be very quiet and seems inside their own experience yawning occasionally, as the nervous system is deactivating. This is the completion of shutdown happening. After a time, breath starts to get deeper and bigger, and there are small movements in the hand and arm.)

CLINICIAN: *Just notice there is a little bit more breath and there is some movement beginning to happen. Keep noticing what wants to happen next, and just take your time.*

CLIENT: *My arms want to spread out.* (The client moves their arms outward while they also sit up taller and yawn. This is followed by breathing more deeply again.)

CLINICIAN: *Yeah, and then just notice how it is to feel your arms taking up more space. And, notice your head's a little more upright.* (Clinician is simply reflecting the rebound happening in the body.)

CLIENT: *My legs want to stretch out more.* (Client stretches out legs in front of them and eyes seem less heavy as they begin to open with more yawning.)

CLINICIAN: *Just noticing that, feel them stretch out. Notice your eyes are opening a little. Let yourself play with that, letting your eyes open and shut as they want to, listening to what feels right to your body.*

CLIENT: (Eyes open slightly and shut, almost fluttering and shifts in their seat, sitting up straighter.)

CLINICIAN: *Notice how your spine is a little different.* (This is reflecting the shift being observed.)

CLIENT: *I'm feeling more present here again.* (Client takes more deep breaths. Their body has more structure to it and they are sitting up taller.)

CLINICIAN: *Yeah. And what about the heaviness, the tiredness? What are you noticing about that now?*

CLIENT: *It feels less heavy.* (Client yawns a few more times with yawns being followed by deep breaths.)

CLINICIAN: *Yeah, so just be with the feeling of being less heavy.* (Waits a moment giving this awareness some time.) *What are you noticing?*

CLIENT: *I feel more awake.* (Eyes get bigger and client is more able to look around as orientation comes back on board, with more access to being present in the here and now.)

CLINICIAN: *Can you feel that change in your eyes?*

CLIENT: *Yeah, and my head's up a little bit more. I want to take that feeling in.* (The client has learned through embodiment of positive states to go toward what feels good.)

CLINICIAN: *As you notice the change in the head and the position, how do your eyes actually feel different?*

CLIENT: *They don't want to blink as much.* (Their eyes become more naturally open as opposed to the heaviness experienced earlier. Yawns continue followed by some deeper breaths.)

CLINICIAN: *Yeah. Can you feel they're a little wider open?*

CLIENT: *Yeah, wider open. My breath is deeper too.* (Breath is visibly fuller and deeper.)

CLINICIAN: *That's right. Go ahead and stay with that, notice your eyes and breath feeling different.* (Clinician is reinforcing VVC and positive states.)

CLIENT: *My limbs feel different; they are a little heavy but it is different kind of heavy. It is like they feel kind of restful. It's like they feel a little more relaxed.*

CLINICIAN: *Yeah, so, it is different kind of heavy, maybe more grounded?*

CLIENT: *Yes, definitely more grounded.*

CLINICIAN: *Go ahead and notice that grounding, feeling that there's a shift and it's different from being heavy. Maybe there's even more presence in your legs?*

CLIENT: *Absolutely, yeah, I want to soak that in. I feel like I can look at you more easily, now.* (The client looks directly at clinician, as more VVC is available.)

CLINICIAN: *Just notice how that is for us to be in connection again. What is that like in your body?*

CLIENT: *It feels more like, "Oh, you're here" and that feels good.* (Laughing at their comment.)

CLINICIAN: *So then let your body feel you are with me and that it feels good. Feel your own availability to connect now.*

CLIENT: *That's a nice feeling in my belly.*

Practice Tip: Although I started this example with focusing on the shutdown, I would only begin this after I had some access to the green zone (or the resilience vortex). It is crucial to focus on some access to the VVC for any intervention that is working with the trauma vortex, where shutdown would be held.

As an aside, yawns are often part of deactivation and often show up with DVC physiology. Because yawns can also be connected with moving into DVC, it is important to ask the question: Is the client getting more present or less present? If they are getting more present, continue with what you are doing. If they are getting less present, you probably need to consider a new intervention.

Because immobility is a nonmovement state, some clinicians find it useful to intervene with movements in session when treating DVC presentations (Berceli et al., 2014; Ogden et al., 2006). This could include working with TRE® (Tension & Trauma Release Exercises), developed by Berceli et al. (2014), or simply having the client stand up and move part of their body that feels still (Ogden et al., 2006). Berceli (2025) discusses the concept that neurogenic tremors (involuntary shaking movements) offer a functional process for the nervous system, leading it back to equilibrium. Equilibrium in the nervous system is a return to the VVC. Because shutdown is an immobilization state in the ANS, movements that promote the return to regulation in the body tend to be useful as it offers a contrast.

Beyond what is offered in this chapter, several great training programs teach about protective actions plans for trauma completion that delve deeply into more refined skills: the Somatic Experiencing® method, developed by Dr. Peter Levine; Sensorimotor Psychotherapy, developed by Dr. Pat Ogden; and Tension Release Training, developed by Dr. David Berceli. The Synergistic Play method, developed by Lisa Dion, is an approach used with children, applying nervous system techniques. I highly recommend that you check out these trainings if you are interested in getting more information about this topic.

> *Reflection*: In working with completion of motor plans, clients can definitely shift their physiology. With that said, I still observe that a person's "home away from home" (Dana, 2021) usually stays the same, but it is much softer. Typically, it continues to be the place the client goes to more in threat states.

SUMMARY

The body can utilize numerous movements to help the client shift their nervous system state to the ventral vagal complex (VVC). It's important to approach this process with an experimental and open mindset as you gain confidence in recognizing these movements. Motor plan completion of protective actions is typically most effective for addressing issues related to anger and anxiety as part of mobilization (SNS) and depression and disconnection from immobilization (DVC). While there may be other deactivation pathways required, motor plan completion is frequently used for these conditions when they are the primary presenting issue. It is not important to figure out the meaning or why it is showing up in session; it is more important to simply follow the body's impulse of completion for deactivation.

MOTOR PLAN OF PROTECTIVE ACTION EXERCISE

Two common movements that often support nervous system deactivation:

1. Let yourself experiment with your body now by doing a pretend running motion with your feet. Feel into the impulse to run as something your feet might want to do. As you move your feet into a running motion, have the movement be almost imperceptible as a very small movement. Do it for about 15 seconds, and then notice how your body feels now.
2. Experiment now with both hands up in front of your chest, mimicking that you are ready to push something away. Now, slowly move both hands in front of you, moving your arms and hands as if you are pushing something away from you. As you push, let your arms become as straight as they want to be and hold them out away from you. As you set them back down in your lap, notice what your body feels like now.

If either of these exercises brings more regulation, you can consider doing them to support your nervous system, as they could be useful protective motor plans in your body.

CHAPTER 11

Integration: Fused and Disconnected Experiences and the Coherent Narrative

Integration—the linkage of differentiated elements of a system—
illuminates a direct pathway towards health.

—Dan Siegel

Wholeness requires integration and honoring all aspects of oneself. The more an experience is integrated, the more it becomes part of one's life tapestry. An integrated experience does not stand out and feel in the way in life, nor is it denied and hidden. Having a full picture of life experiences and oneself that makes sense brings a sense of clarity in integration. Integration naturally involves either mindful acceptance or a neutral acknowledgment of different aspects of an experience, which in itself is regulating. This chapter explores integration as the process of linking and differentiating, as described by Siegel (2010a), as well as the role of one's personal narrative. These pathways foster a deep sense of being present, bringing access to the VVC by supporting deactivation.

DEACTIVATION PATHWAY: INTEGRATION OF FUSED AND DISCONNECTED EXPERIENCES

Integration, a core aspect of well-being, has been identified as the linkage of differentiated parts (Siegel, 2010a); this connotes that elements of experience are separated (differentiated) while in connection (linkage). Trauma experiences are hard to integrate if they are too fragmented (disconnected) or overly bound together (fused). Integration through linkage and differentiation leads to being fully present, as it includes holding all aspects of oneself (Siegel, 2010a). Clients either have too many things happening in their experience at one time, which can be defined as *fused* experiences, or they do not have access to their full experiences because they are *disconnected*. Integration is key in linking experiences or differentiating them, which leads to more wholeness. In trauma memory, the channels of experience include affect, image/memory, meaning/ beliefs, and somatic sensations (Kurtz, 1990; Levine, 2010); these aspects of experience become overly fused or disconnected when trauma occurs (Levine, 2010). Linking and differentiating occur in tandem, with linking requiring a level of differentiation first. In the nervous system, it is optimal for experiences to be both linked and differentiated to support wholeness and self-connection, leading to more regulation.

In SNS-yellow zone dominance, the tendency is for these aspects of experiences to be fused together. Fused realms of experience mean they are occurring all at the same time, operating as one unit of experience. Because these experiences also occur with the speediness of the SNS-yellow zone, it is often difficult to recognize that each aspect of these experiences is separate, rather than merged as one, when they appear. Differentiating is necessary to link the experiences. Conversely, with DVC-red zone dominance, experiences tend to be separated and disconnected from one another. Although they are part of one memory, the aspects are fragmented, with separated parts, and without a recognition of their linkages. Because fragmented experiences already have aspects of differentiation inherently, linking the experiences is key for integration. Both fused and disconnected experiences keep the nervous system in activation (Levine, 2010; Ogden et al., 2006).

Defusing in Integration for SNS States

In SNS-yellow zone dominance, fused experiences are demonstrated by a client who might report a quickening heartbeat along with a feeling of frustration while holding a belief that they do not feel they have value. Different realms of experience (sensations, emotions, and belief in this example) are all occurring quickly and at the same time, making them fused. The dysregulated fused state is the opposite of integration, where these realms of experience would be both connected and also individuated. Clients often have no awareness that different experiences are occurring at the same time as part of one pattern; all aspects are felt as one experience in the body. Adding to the difficulty in feeling the differentiated aspects that make up the pattern, the pattern often has an intensity to it. To support deactivation, these experiences need to be defused as differentiated but linked experiences, the foundation for integration and regulation (Levine, 2010; Siegel, 2010a).

This fusing of experiences can manifest in many ways. It can take time to learn to identify what might be fused and to see the pattern of fusing. Clinicians might need to ask themselves, "What is fused in this client because of other experiences?" This question helps to identify what might need to be defused. Clients might come in with chronic anxiety about taking tests. Test taking has become fused with anxiety—both realms of experience are occurring at the same time. There are countless examples. A job could get fused with pressure; they are two separate experiences, but as soon as the person goes to their job, they feel pressure. A partner could have early sexual abuse, which might fuse sexual feelings with a belief of being harmed. Again, sexual feelings and being harmed do not need to be linked, but early life experiences link these experiences together. These are examples of fusing, and this is occurring in many ways in the nervous system.

When strong experiences become fused, there is generally a nervous system component that needs addressing. The experiences are often overwhelming because they involve more than one channel of experience in the nervous system, and it is also harder to recognize the different fused experiences. Assisting the client in being mindful of these experiences as separated components, with corresponding differentiation of affect, image/memory, meaning/beliefs, and somatic sensations, supports the deactivation of the ANS (Somatic Experiencing Training®, personal communication, 2009–2011). This defusing will also create less intensity for the client as they focus on one aspect of their experiences rather than the whole experience or all aspects at once, which can be overwhelming. This threading apart of experiences also supports deactivation. Keeping this singular focus also helps the client tolerate the distress of their experiences more easily as it is broken down. The experience becomes less overwhelming in general.

As an example, a client might come into report feeling overwhelmed with frustration and hurt, also as part of their experience. All of these are aspects of emotion are fused. If the client feels somewhat stuck, the clinician could ask the client to notice each part of their experience as separate aspects. As the frustration is teased out, the clinician could say, "If you could notice the frustration as sensation only, what do you notice?" The client might report that their upper body is tense. The clinician has them notice this sensation. With this shift, the client might also notice the hurt moving to the foreground of their experience. They might begin to tear up. This shift in physiology can start the cascade of creating this separation from the other experiences. This can begin to deactivate the nervous system, and it also might underline what issue might need attention in the session; the frustration may be less important than the hurt. As this is addressed, the other realms of experience can tend to soften and sometimes separate on their own. The physiology is shifted as this occurs.

Defusing: Grief and Longing

One commonly fused experience is the combination of longing and grief. When a client identifies what they want in their life, grief often arises. Longing will be further discussed in Chapter 13; it is an important and positive step toward change, underlining impulses for a new direction of growth. It inherently feels good to know what one wants. As clarity brings knowledge of what one wants to pursue, grief often surfaces immediately. In these moments, the client primarily experiences the sadness of their grief as grief and longing have fused; they are unified as one experience, even though they are actually two different experiences. Separating these feelings is essential to identifying the emerging need expressed by the longing. Here is an example of defusing longing and grief:

> CLINICIAN: *Would it be okay to notice that there is both grief and longing here right now? Can you feel in your body that they are separate experiences? There is the longing for more intimacy, and there is also grief as you feel the loss from being taught to stay away from deeper connection in intimacy. Notice that they are separate. As you do this, what do you notice?*
>
> CLIENT: *The grief feels very heavy, and I keep feeling tears. I am so sad that avoiding intimacy and vulnerability has affected me so much in my life. It has been so hard on my relationships.*
>
> CLINICIAN: *And what do you notice about the longing for intimacy?*
>
> CLIENT: *It is hard to feel that with all of this sadness, but I think I feel it in my heart—like I get a feeling of reaching out or moving towards others more.* (As noted before, clients are often unclear about less developed or new experiences, so the clinician works with what the client does notice, even they are not fully able to describe it fully.)
>
> CLINICIAN: *Just let the sadness be here. I wonder if you can you pay more attention to noticing this feeling of reaching out.*
>
> CLIENT: *It has a warmth, and I feel some openness. I still feel sad, and that is in my heart also. But the reaching out feels warmer and I can really feel that in my heart too.* (As the client is more in the new experience, it becomes more solid for them and the grief is present with it.)
>
> CLINICIAN: *Can you take some time to just be with this now—paying more attention to this longing that has the warmth and openness? The grief might still be there, but let your attention go to the longing and how it feels good if that feels okay to you.*
>
> CLIENT: *Yes, it feels good to just want, as I sometimes stop myself from wanting or longing. I like feeling it. It feels good.*
>
> CLINICIAN: *Notice that right now you are allowing yourself to feel the longing and it does feel good.* (Having the client in real time notice that they are allowing the longing to be present is also a reparative experience, as it was not allowed as part of the old pattern. Underlining this to the client and guiding them toward noticing it is useful.)
>
> CLIENT: *I even feel some hope now as I do this—that I can make it different for myself now, even though I did not grow up learning this.*

CLINICIAN: *Let's take some time to stay with feeling the longing while also noticing the hope.* (The clinician could continue to strengthen these new experiences.)

In this example of defusing, the grief is not being directly dealt with at this moment as the focus is on identifying longing, which needs defusing first.

Linking in Integration

In DVC dominance, self-connection is challenging in general. Because of the red zone physiology, certain aspects of their experience are not linked in their nervous system. Clients demonstrate this by reporting somatic responses like feeling sad or having an upset stomach but having no sense of connection with the cause of these experiences. Or the client might have a traumatic memory with no affect; again, their experiences lack linkage. Their story might feel spotty and disconnected as they talk about it; they cannot report the details of their experience. This is a red zone indicator, and it underscores how aspects of experience like sensations, emotions, beliefs, and images are not connected.

> *Reflection:* As a reminder, memories are not essential to heal trauma even though they are listed as one aspect of experience. This section is simply underlining the disconnection in experiences when there is red zone dominance.

An example might be a client who reports feeling flat and depressed. This same client might have brought up a memory of feeling negated and dismissed by an experience as a child. Although this memory arises as the depression is explored, the client does not seem to feel any relevance to their feelings initially. As they discuss it more, these two experiences are linked as the client recognizes that they felt hurt by their early experiences; the memory of being negated and dismissed and the connection to sadness and pain now begin the linking process of integration. Because the experiences had become disconnected (therefore hidden) in their earlier life, there is no initial linkage. With the client in this example, the clinician might attempt to facilitate connection by helping the client to feel the pairing between these two experiences. "As you notice this memory that has surfaced, I am wondering if the sadness you mentioned earlier is also present. Is it okay to notice both of these things together?" This reconnecting of different facets supports more self-connection and integration. As these experiences are joined, both elements become a true "felt sense" (Gendlin, 1996) of integration. The client comes away with more of a sense of wholeness as parts come together internally. This is inherently regulating to the ANS.

Integration in Working With the Child Part

Working with the child part exemplifies the application of integration through both linkage and differentiation. Differentiation is essential when a painful experience arises, as it helps make the experience feel less overwhelming. Saying "let yourself feel the child part and their feelings, while the adult is present" creates awareness of the separate states of child and adult. This differentiation helps establish a connection to the adult self, while also distinguishing the two aspects. It shifts the merged state of child and adult, operating as one, into two distinct aspects. One foot is in the trauma vortex, and the other is in the resilience vortex. Here, the focus is more on differentiation, as the clinician emphasizes the separation of the two experiences, which provides greater stability and coherence. This differentiation also allows for linkage as both states are present and connected.

In linking, the goal of the clinician is attempting to bringing awareness to cut off experiences that are held in child states; these deeply rooted experiences are out of awareness. The clinician facilitates this process by bringing awareness to an adult (often thoughts) state versus the child (often emotions) state; these are held in present and past experiences respectively. Linking acknowledges the early experience is impacting the current response. In this approach, the child and adult parts are not unified but are encouraged to connect. By engaging both parts, the clinician uses the adult's resources to first differentiate the responses and then links them. The primary focus here is on linking, which facilitates the integration process.

Often clients report feeling upset with themselves for reacting in a way when they know better, referring to an overreaction with a partner or another relationship. The client's self-criticism is based on not having awareness of the earlier pain that brought out the emotional or child reaction to the situation. Linking this unintegrated aspect of the child state supports its integration. This requires first bringing awareness to the child aspect in order for there to be differentiation, which allows for the linkage to occur. It helps to say to the client: "I know you want to respond from a skilled adult place. What is it like to notice that there is a hurt child part here also? Can you take a moment to allow both to be present?" This underlines the hurt child in the emotional reaction and the awareness of the logical adult, both differentiating and linking these two aspects, providing an understanding of the judged behavior. In this intervention, the clinician is recognizing the child, which is differentiating, and then linking the experience that is below awareness that led to their overreaction. This can also promote agency, as the client can allow for the presence of the child part while supporting the goal of acting from the adult part.

Fragmented Responses

Similarly, clients can report fragmented responses when asked about their experience. This manifests as they state, "My mind feels. . . but my body says . . ." When this occurs, the client is referring to different aspects of themselves. Holding Siegel's description regarding linking differentiated parts (2010a), the clinician offers a link to the two experiences, saying, "Let's let both parts be here, noticing how it feels in the mind and how it is different in the body." This creates linkage and differentiation. This recognition of both parts often brings ease in the nervous system. Schwartz (2020, p. 58) says, "[T]he person will feel more unified, with a sense of continuity and integration."

Defusing is needed for:
- Separating aspects of experience that appear as one experience
- Differentiating the child part as a means to access the resource of the regulated adult part when the child part has overwhelming feelings

Linking is needed for:
- Connecting aspects of experience that are part of the same experience but are reported as separate
- Linking the child part for a more complete picture by acknowledging experience that has been cut off or is below the surface, which requires differentiating the child and adult physiological states first before linking
- Linking fragmented aspects that arise in sessions

DEACTIVATION PATHWAY: CREATING A COHERENT NARRATIVE

As Siegel says,

> When we can "make sense" of our lives in a deep, integrative manner, what emerges is a coherent narrative of our lives. . . . "Making sense" in the coherent narrative goes way beyond a logical understanding of past events, it involves all of our senses. (2010a, pp. 74, 178)

The coherent narrative is inherently integrative as all the aspects of the story are present and part of the tapestry; embodiment is implied with Siegel's emphasis on it involving all of our senses. This integration regulates and supports deactivation to the green zone as it leads to more presence—or being in the here and now, which is the bedrock of the VVC (Siegel, 2010a). This might seem obvious, but it is highly common for clients to come into therapy with an incoherent narrative. Clear examples of incoherency will include stating that issues are "not a big deal" or that "things were not that bad" or having no real memory and connection to their own life story. Misplaced blame and a lack of awareness about impact from experiences are all ways that the narrative of a client's story is not integrated. This disconnection and incoherency are linked to a lack of being fully present in current reality.

As discussed in earlier chapters, presence is one of the goals of trauma treatment; creating a coherent narrative is also key to supporting this process. To understand the coherent narrative more, we can explore the incoherent narrative. A narrative is incoherent when it is confusing, disjointed, or missing critical parts (Siegel, 2010a). This includes not having a sense of the whole story or having it mixed up. As noted earlier, challenging experiences might not be fully integrated and might be in red zone physiology and frozen off from awareness. A coherent narrative generally has most aspects of affect, image/memory, meaning/beliefs, and somatic sensations. When these aspects are absent, especially if there is more than one missing, the result often is an incoherent narrative. The clinician must observe how the client utilizes the channels of experience during their work.

Sometimes, this can mean the story is missing some realistic aspects in the autobiography. This lack of realism can include how the client accepts others' behaviors as acceptable when they are not acceptable. Examples of this could be a client who makes excuses for a partner's inattentiveness around an important relational need; another client could minimize the impact of a parent's alcoholism in their early life. The lack of realism and the denial can also include the client taking responsibility for aspects of the situation where they bear no responsibility. An example of this might be the client with a core belief of "I am a failure" as a result of being neglected and unattended to in their family. This is not reality, and it is an incoherent narrative. The clients in these scenarios are not in reality and, therefore, are not present. You might see how working with core beliefs can be part of this work, as offering reparative experiences (covered in Chapter 7) often shifts the narrative for the client, leading to more coherency. The therapeutic work is to support the coherent narrative for a reality-based version of their experience, which resides in green zone physiology.

The coherent narrative can occur spontaneously, or it can be targeted directly. In an example of the spontaneous version, the client might be talking about early childhood and suddenly say, "I can't believe no one helped me after I reported the abuse." This leads them to have their awareness shift from, "I thought it was my fault, that no one took care of me," to "That was not right to expect a child to cope on their own." This spontaneous integration of information leads to more presence as the client is in the reality of what happened. A new belief is being integrated as this awareness occurs. Along with that, the nervous system becomes regulated as the client embodies a new, coherent narrative. This new narrative includes, "It never was my fault." This produces a strong sense of relief that leads to more ease for the client and possibly even more self-compassion. The green zone is entered since the process of the integration of a spontaneous coherent narrative is downregulating. The shift in the narrative engenders deactivation into green zone physiology. The clinician often sees this as they observe changes in posture, tone of voice, breath, eye contact, and muscle tension. As with other deactivation pathways, the clinician encourages the client to embody the new way of being. "What is this like now to be with the sense that it never was your fault?" This encouragement into the new way of perceiving is felt and experienced as an integration of positive states, an earlier discussed deactivation pathway. It is critical to have this new narrative embodied. If the client says, "It feels great to know this now, and I can't believe how relieved I feel," the clinician directs the client by saying, "Let's take some time to notice what this feels like, to really take in that it was not your fault." In focusing this way with the client, deactivation occurs. The new coherent narrative creates access to the VVC.

In addition to a spontaneous coherent narrative, at other times the clinician is leading this client into a more coherent narrative. The client might be saying their "childhood was great" and that although their dad had anger issues, it was "not that big of a deal." Picking up on the possibility of an incoherent narrative, the clinician might explore the client's response to expressing and responding to anger from others. Through this exploration, the client might have awareness as they acknowledge strong anxiety over any kind of anger, including avoiding it. As they discuss these responses, the narrative shifts. The client begins to understand they were affected by their father's anger, changing the narrative. As they delve into their experience more, the client might have more feelings surface, as well as an understanding of the impact of their early experience. Difficult feelings and memories might surface, recalling how scared they felt around their parent. As they bring in this awareness, the real early childhood experience is integrated on a nervous system level, leading to more regulation. With this integration, they become grounded in their real experience. Even if an experience has challenges to it, it is more regulating to the client to move them toward being able to be present with how it really is.

As memories become part of the narrative, the client might struggle with some connected emotions because the disconnected experiences are not frozen anymore. In the immediate aftermath, this could create some dysregulation as the nervous system needs time to integrate this new experience. In this same example of an angry father, this could include a grief process as the reality sets in over how challenging the experience really was for the client. In time, it becomes naturally regulating to bring in awareness of how the anger created a loss in their relationship. The client might have memories of wishing it felt safer to connect with their father. Even though this grief feels bad, it can lead to green zone physiology, as grief becomes part of the story. As the client integrates the loss, regulation can occur. As the experience moves to having less charge or intensity, the client can stay present with the reality of what is happening.

The coherent narrative is always embodied, and there is ease with this embodiment. Clients naturally have more connection with Essence as they step into the coherent narrative. The goal of trauma treatment is to have the story as part of who the person is, and it is woven into the fabric of their Essence. All parts of memory, including the emotions and the true impact of the memory, can be part of the fabric of their life; this embodiment is integration.

Working Through Grief as Part of the Coherent Narrative

Part of developing a coherent narrative is the integration of the grief. All trauma will have an aspect of some type of loss in the experience. It is not uncommon to avoid grief, if possible, because of the pain of it. We do this by turning away from grief or minimizing its impact. *Trauma identity*, discussed earlier, is one way to avoid the feeling of early losses; the adaptation itself minimizes the feeling of loss. For the coherent narrative to be fully integrated, it requires that grief is acknowledged and felt.

Grief seems to prefer a direct focus to move through it, or a "dedicated time" (Kessler, 2019). Moving through grief does not mean it is never felt again, but instead that it is felt in a way that moves into the coherent narrative as part of the story. It no longer hijacks one's life, and it is not actively avoided. Instead, the losses are recognized and part of the story. Because grief can stay in the background at times, it requires a dedicated time, as well as a specificity in identifying what is lost. It helps to have clients do both things—set aside time for feeling their loss in or out of session and also to acknowledge and name the losses that have occurred. This supports the integration of grief. There can be quite a range of losses:

- Recognition of needs—safety/belonging, connection/reciprocity, inherent lovability/worth, differentiation/agency
- Access to regulation
- Innocence and/or childhood
- Trust
- Sense of self
- Hopefulness or optimism
- Freedom
- Limiting life experiences and relationships

As the losses are recognized and felt, they often soften. It does not mean they go away, as a loss is always a loss. Working through grief is a necessary component for movement into the coherent narrative.

SUMMARY

Integration is a key component for regulation. It includes awareness of experiences through linking and differentiating them as well as developing a coherent narrative to have experiences internalized as part of one's sense of self. As elements of experiences become both linked and differentiated, more regulation is available. This includes both channels of experiences as well as fragmented and child parts. Like other nervous system regulation experiences, more presence is the outcome. Both defusing (differentiating) and connecting (linking) aspects of experience settle the nervous system bringing in more regulation. Clients also benefit tremendously from integrating their story in a complete way; this assists in developing their coherent narrative, which can steer the nervous system to green zone physiology. Having a coherent narrative is a needed baseline to access resilience and post-traumatic growth. It is the foundation of the green zone of VVC and provides the neural platform for expansion. As the big picture unfolds and shifts the earlier understanding and beliefs, physiology holds fertile conditions for resilience and potential post-traumatic growth.

INTEGRATION EXERCISE OF DEFUSING

Take a moment to orient to your surroundings, noticing what your senses are drawn to. This can be what you see, noticing details of what you are observing, the sounds you are hearing, or perhaps the textures of where you might be seated. Bring into awareness anything in your body that might feel more settled in you as you take in things around you. Observe any kind of settling or change in your experience now, taking a moment to just savor that shift.

If it feels okay, take a moment to bring in an irrational fear that you struggle with at times, some behavior that you would like to do, but get too afraid to try. It might be something such as speaking out your feelings or asking for what you need. As you think of this fear, have your attention go toward noting the sensations in your body that come up, and notice that the behavior you fear is *completely different* from the fear itself, as they are two separate experiences. Let your body recognize and feel this distinction between these two aspects. See if you can bring in awareness of how the fear is something that got linked with the behavior and it is not necessarily something to be fearful about. Allow your body to sit with the experience of the desire of the behavior you have feared and the fear itself as separate. Take time to feel this differentiation.

This is an example of defusing an irrational fear as it differentiates fear and a non-life-threatening behavior.

CHAPTER 12

Embodied Agency

In some ways, suffering ceases to be suffering at the moment it finds meaning . . .

—Viktor Frankl

Many people find mastery after trauma through their reconnection with *agency*. Agency refers to empowerment and efficacy. In the aftermath of trauma, where helplessness and powerlessness are foundational experiences, the recovery of agency is a crucial part of trauma recovery. It is always powerful to witness a client recovering their sense of agency. Agency brings forth Essence as it connects to one's innate and unique purpose. This aspect of the treatment often occurs after clients move from victim to survivor and then evolve to being a thriver. Thriving can be post-traumatic growth, or it might be simply finding one's life more fully after trauma, no longer encumbered by trauma symptoms on any regular basis, and finding vitality and enlivenment for fullhearted living. The purpose of all trauma therapy is to expand one's sense of agency to have a better life. This chapter focuses on key aspects of developing and/or restoring personal agency to shift the nervous system toward the VVC. Personal agency assists the client toward living more fully; this includes evolving from victim physiology, integrating the *challenge response*, and finding embodied meaning.

In the context of trauma, agency refers to a person's ability to make choices and take actions that influence their life, despite having experienced traumatic events. It encompasses having a sense of control over one's actions, decisions, and the course of one's life, which can often be disrupted or diminished in the aftermath of trauma. When a person experiences trauma, particularly in situations where they feel helpless or powerless (e.g., abuse, violence, or loss), their sense of agency can be undermined. Rebuilding agency is an important part of trauma recovery, as it helps individuals regain a sense of autonomy, empowerment, and self-efficacy. Fully restored agency can involve regaining control over one's body, emotions, decisions, and personal boundaries, which is key to healing and moving forward.

VICTIMIZATION AND LOCUS OF CONTROL

It is natural to feel victimized when experiencing trauma. Victimization feelings will be fixed in threat response, and the lack of agency impacts these states. Even though victim thinking can be a barrier to post-traumatic growth and resilience, it can also often be necessary as it supports the client feeling the impact of what happened, including the grief. Truly integrating the trauma or loss requires feeling the victimization of the experience, including the reality of all of the feelings about the required changes needed in life. Needing time is normal while a client comes to terms with accepting what happened and how their life is different; this time period takes as long as it takes. During this time, the integration of the loss and/or changes in life can lead to the necessary question, "Who am I now?" This process is often part of finding one's way through their journey. Finding the path forward does not mean that it is a nice and neat story. It is more important to be able to live in a way that integrates one's experiences to promote finding a sense of life force and vitality.

Early work in trauma often includes both denial and "Why me?" This victimization of questioning "Why me?" has a blend of yellow and red zone physiology at its core because of the powerlessness of that state. This can lead to stuckness. Trauma is not yet accepted, and there is little internal locus of control. This is an *internalized fight* response as one is resisting the trauma. There could also be avoidance of trauma, which is an *internalized flight* response. Both of these responses can lead to stuckness. At the heart of the resistance and the avoidance is often a belief of "I just can't do this." As noted in Figure 1.3, "I can't" is part of the DVC. As the client shifts their focus from "Why me?" to acceptance, they seem to benefit greatly from moving to this different lens of seeing their trauma (see Figure 12.1). Their life becomes less about what happened to them and more about how to find a path forward. "When we are no longer able to change a situation, . . . we are challenged to change ourselves" (Frankl, 1992, p. 116). Changing ourselves includes looking at what we *can* do. This requires a type of doing that stems from the "I can" response, which is based on choices. This accesses the green zone, the neural platform to support the possibility of moving through the trauma with support, finding one's resources, and potentially moving into post-traumatic growth.

DVC dominance and victim thinking go hand in hand. As discussed early on, DVC dominance is the neural platform of "I can't." With this in mind, one of the first steps the clinician can take is to assist the client in embodying any sense of "I can" occurring in the session. This means actively looking for examples live in session, as the client will not likely notice them when they occur.

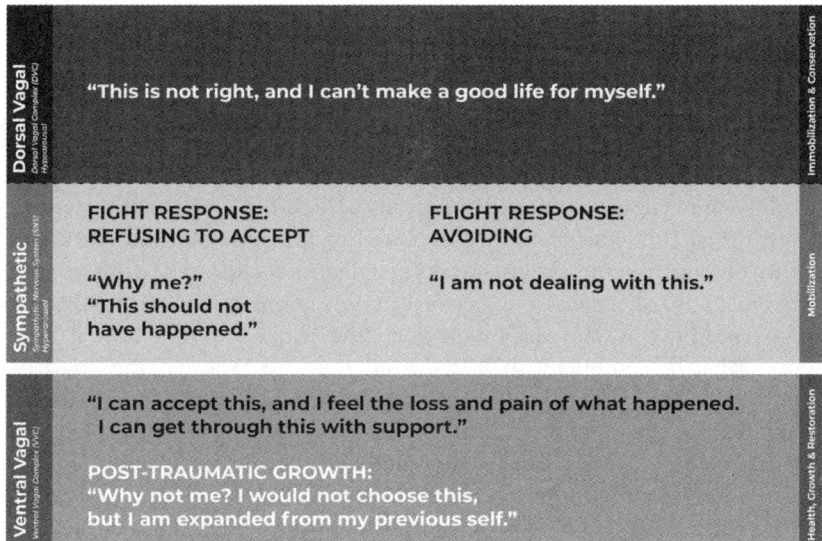

FIGURE 12.1: Victimization to Post-Traumatic Growth Credit: Ruby Jo Walker; graphic by Cindy Miller Atchison Design & Art

It also means starting very small. Examples could include any area of their life where they are demonstrating a small or large sense of "I can":

- They got the kids off to school that morning without a struggle.
- They finished a project, meeting a deadline at work.
- They had a supportive conversation with their partner.
- They finished going through the cards after the funeral.
- They were able to deal with cleaning out clothes in the closet (after a death).
- They got through a day at work without needing an extra break to process emotions.
- They were able to accomplish a task they had put off doing.
- They were able to talk to a friend about their feelings.
- They could explain to their children the appropriate details of the situation.
- They went through the life insurance paperwork.
- They ate dinner every night that week.
- They did a form of self-care, like a massage or haircut.

These may seem like small examples, yet they are crucial to the recovery of agency. Clients need to embody and take in what they *are* doing and what they *can* do. The clinician then listens closely, having clients embody any of these examples as part of their emerging agency. The "I can" here is the opposite of so much of the client's experience that it is important to not just recognize, but amplify this state. To accomplish this, the clinician slows the client down to embody the "I can." The clinician says, "Can we just take a moment to notice this . . . (identifying the agency that is coming forth) happened?" Applying embodiment of positive states is important here as the client will benefit from integrating in this experience. After noticing the physiological shift, which often involves sitting up straighter, taking a deeper breath, or feeling expansion in the chest, the client feels and savors the sensations, further embodying this change. Additionally, the clinician directs the client to notice how it feels in the body that the body *can* shift states—as they are experiencing an "I can." Strengthening the VVC by utilizing the embodiment of positive states deactivation pathway again supports building capacity by shifting the physiology. Over time, these physiological shifts from embodied experiences of "I can" will often build more of a sense of internal locus of control. This happens with repetition and over time. This "I can" practice also brings the client out of the trauma vortex and into the resilience vortex. This is the first step toward more resilience or the potential movement into post-traumatic growth.

Locus of control is defined as the degree to which someone believes that they have control over the outcomes in their life (Rotter, 1966). A person with an internal locus of control believes they can control their life situations, while a person with an external locus of control believes life is mostly controlled by outside factors. Internal locus of control is often associated with post-traumatic growth and resilience because clients have more ownership in their life outcomes, thereby using agency for changes.

Internal and external locus of control have different underlying physiology. In the internal locus of control, the green zone is available, even in the struggle; as noted earlier, in the green zone, "I can" is present. In the external locus of control, the DVC state is more dominant because "I can't" is more present. External locus of control is the basis of victim thinking, as it leads clients to believe they cannot take control of their lives. Because the red zone physiology is dominant, the "I can't" mentality that goes along with that state makes efforts to change one's life very difficult. This difficulty continues to perpetuate victim thinking; the underlying red zone physiology becomes a vicious cycle as it is reinforced by the inability to take the action steps they might want to take. This inaction leads only to more DVC dominance. It is not surprising that clients can easily get stuck in this state. Victim thinking is very obviously a barrier to resilience and post-traumatic growth because it embeds one further in the dysregulated states.

Clinicians also seem to have an intuitive sense of knowing when a client is actually stuck or when they are simply in the process of where they need to be. Understanding any early childhood trauma identity stemming from inaccurate and limiting core beliefs is often at the core of stuckness, in addition to red zone physiology and both require interventions. General core beliefs that cement victim physiology include:

- It is my fault.
- I can never have what I need.
- I am not allowed to feel good.
- I deserved this.
- If I were better, this would not have happened.

These beliefs need to be targeted to support shifting out of victim physiology.

After engaging over time with clients in this way, direct conversations about locus of control ideas can also be part of the therapy. Talking directly about the impact of early childhood and physiological state on feelings of agency, as well as personal responsibility, can be useful and helpful. Introducing this too early can be ineffective if it feels like misattunement and judgment. With more regulation, clinicians can gently explore the use of words with clients—"I can" versus "I can't" and the idea of strengthening their sense of agency, including leading them toward awareness of the challenge response.

THE CHALLENGE RESPONSE

The *challenge response* (McGonigal, 2016) is also useful in supporting agency. The challenge response is a top-down intervention to shift bottom-up physiology; the person is encouraged to see what is happening as a challenge rather than a threat. This also reinforces one's internal locus of control. It can also be evoked to shift physiology and build resilience. This response uses non-threat-mobilization physiology for action rather than for fight-or-flight. McGonigal's research (2016) described how getting excited about an event can feel similar to preparing for a challenge. The physiology for both experiences is in the SNS, as excitement and preparation are nonthreat SNS states. She noted in her research that when the focus was changed to "the body's stress response mobilizes energy to meet the demands of the situation" (McGonigal, 2016, p. 117), the students came to understand their body was getting them ready for the challenge they were undertaking. With this new lens, they were able to have a physiological shift into empowerment and readiness to face the challenge. Using a top-down reframe of the body's threat state shifted the physiology from being in a threat state. The challenge response underlines how top-down work and bottom-up work can both be supportive.

This kind of intervention needs to be carefully used; if it is ill-timed, clients feel the clinician is "tone deaf" and misattuned. To alleviate this, the clinician can address this concern with a preface. Examples might be: "Now, this might feel off, but I wanted to offer something to you . . ." "I want to say something that might feel edgy, so please let me know if this does not feel right . . ." or "I am not really sure about this, but it keeps coming up, so I would like to share with you this thought . . ." or "It is okay if you feel this won't work as it is just an idea . . ." This kind of prelude assists the client in not needing to agree and to have a true choice in their interest and response to the idea of post-traumatic growth. This helps them in the empowerment of their own choices.

To go a little further with this idea, the clinician can connect this notion with post-traumatic growth also as a challenge. The clinician could add, "I know this is hard, but I am curious if you would want to look at this time as an opportunity to grow and strengthen your resilience" or even what my clinician said to me: "You have simply gotten through things before, so I wonder if you focused on expanding yourself this time if it would be helpful to you." This invitation into expansion is also another way to introduce the challenge response. Clients generally react favorably to this if they are not too steeped in red zone physiology; some doing is accessible to them. Inherent in this challenge for expansion, the client is in a state of agency and out of the powerlessness of trauma.

EMBODIED MEANING

Finding meaning after trauma is viewed as a key feature of post-traumatic growth and is another avenue toward agency. This includes doing good works, loving and caring for others, and facing challenges by expansion (Frankl, 2015). Frankl states, "[F]acing a fate he cannot change, he may rise above himself, may grow beyond himself, and by doing so may change himself" (2015, p. 237). Finding embodied meaning can be a healing impulse towards expansion as the person moves to a deeper sense of purpose. This process supports the neurobiology of resilience because it accesses green zone physiology and brings in a sense of mastery as meaning is embodied with a "felt sense" (Gendlin, 1996) of "I can." When clients discover a sense of purpose or meaning, it magnifies their sense of agency. From there, things seem to shift in profound ways. This shift moves the nervous system from the red or yellow zone physiology to the green zone.

Living with an anchor in meaning seems to redirect the energy and focus of the nervous system away from the past and the trauma vortex. It does not end suffering, but it does shift attention, which shifts physiology. Embodied meaning is geared toward utilizing the suffering of one's experiences for the good of others and oneself. An example of finding meaning could include a caseworker who seeks employment in human services after suffering abuse as a child; they take a job to support clients recovering from abuse as an empowering use of their early life experience. Another example is a parent whose child died in a school shooting. After this horrific event, the parent becomes a political advocate for gun control. In these situations, the client uses their traumatic situation to focus on change for others. This sense of purpose creates regulation in the nervous system, creating mastery and efficacy. Because traumatic events often feel out of control, through finding meaning, the client moves into more agency; the embodied experience of meaning offers this to their life. The client moves from victim to survivor and then to being a thriver; this is post-traumatic growth. The person is not held back by their experience because they focus on transcendence, inherent in purpose and meaning.

In addition to the mastery this shift in focus brings to the client, altruism is also present. In altruism, as the client moves toward helping others, more green zone physiology is available. Remembering that altruism is part of the VVC, "transcendence to something vast" is also regulating to the nervous system (Keltner, 2024). Trauma experiences become a way to help and understand others. This evolution to a different perspective is inherently empowering, bringing feelings of mastery to the nervous system and leading to a metamorphosis. The client is now more than their trauma, expanding their sense of self. The client's challenging experience becomes a catalyst to support another person or a social cause, eliciting VVC physiology. Additionally, there is often satisfaction gained from taking action for others when it was not available for oneself; this becomes a restoration of control of one's life, evoking agency.

Clients can also feel a profound shift in their being. They report that things are different; what they value and prioritize has transformed into a new way of living. Oftentimes, this is their Essence manifesting—their best version of themselves, as it brings in more intentionality in living. Questions come up that are ripe for exploring: "Who do I want to be now?" "How do I want to live?" "How do I live more fully now?" The hard-earned and eclipsing wisdom of trauma is now deeply and profoundly cemented as the cornerstone for living in a new way. This is the heart of post-traumatic growth.

Porges states, "We have a quest for safety, but it is not our sole goal. . . . Safety is the facilitator of our internalized personal goals. The concept of purpose is deeply rooted in our nature, and potentially, biological" (2021, p. 245). It is lovely to consider the concept that "safety is not our sole goal." Instead, internalized personal goals grow out of regulation, and from this cultivated regulation, expansion becomes possible. Expansion can occur naturally when there is a connection to Essence. There seems to be a circular relationship that more safety leads to more purpose and meaning, and more meaning and purpose lead to more safety while strengthening agency.

SUMMARY

Recovering agency is crucial in trauma recovery, and is supported by shifting victim physiology, applying the challenge response, and discovering embodied meaning. The placement of the locus of control can impact agency, and supporting the transition from victimization states to "I can" physiology can be beneficial for achieving a sense of mastery. The challenge response also serves as a means to shift physiology and can act as a bridge to developing greater agency.

Transitioning to find embodied meaning can redirect the focus from trauma toward expansion, fostering a connection to resilience and post-traumatic growth. Clinicians can collaborate with clients, guiding them to uncover purpose and meaning, cultivate challenge responses, and strengthen their internal locus of control.

AGENCY EXERCISE

Allow yourself to turn toward your experience in your body right now, focusing on whatever might feel settled in your body, taking the time you need. If it is available to you, bring up a moment in your life when you felt you met a challenge in a way that felt good to you. It does not mean that it was easy, but that there was even a small sense of mastery. Let yourself notice any sensations of empowerment or agency, noticing what it feels like in your body. You can note if there are also images that arise. Allow yourself to savor the body sensations that accompany this experience, taking your time to feel it. Take some time to notice your body overall now. Savor again whatever feels good, as you are with your sense of agency.

SECTION III

INTEGRATION IN THERAPY

CHAPTER 13

The Change Process

It's only after you've stepped outside your comfort zone that you begin to change, grow, and transform.

—Roy T. Bennett

Transformation in our clients is inherently nourishing to us as clinicians. Watching clients shift their nervous systems, their relationships, and their self-connection is heartwarming to witness. As clients step more into their true selves, Essence, it often feels rewarding as it highlights the reciprocity of the therapeutic process. Understanding the change process is important because clients can become discouraged if they do not grasp how it occurs. In addition to the crucial step of clarifying what the client desires, it is also vital to recognize the indicators of the change process. This chapter will explore the journey of transformation as it relates to the unfolding of the therapeutic process.

All clinical work starts with the client seeking change. A guideline for the process is to know exactly what a client wants. A helpful question to ask is, "What do you want to be different that would make you feel your time, money, and work here are worth it to you?" This obvious question is a critical element in therapy; its answer directs the treatment. Fundamental to the agreement of the therapeutic process, it shapes the therapy process.. In therapeutic work, the answers range from shifts in anxiety, anger, depression, relational issues, core beliefs, and wanting more fulfillment. These desired changes focus on areas of life that are underlined by the maps of *general nervous system functioning, co-regulation capacity, and limiting core beliefs,* which have been discussed throughout this book (see Figure 2.2). The client's identified goal serves as the guiding force for therapeutic interventions. Clearly defining the desired change is the first step; without it, there is no road map for treatment.

Change starts with building self-connection in service of nervous system regulation. This change process leads to agency and feeling more in charge of one's life. Initially, it helps clients to familiarize themselves with their nervous system, as well as how nervous system states are connected to the process of change. Having an understanding of the deactivation process is important for the client's buy-in of nervous system work. Using the list of indicators on the chart (see Figure 1.3) coupled with the client's self-report, it is often quite easy to pinpoint their state, the beginning step in self-connection. This gives a marker of where they are, and it can be a reference for seeing changes as symptoms change through deactivation processes over time. As discussed, almost any presenting issue can be identified by its physiological underpinnings of the red and yellow threat states. Additionally, clients need psychoeducation explaining that nervous system dysregulation is normal so they are realistically aware that they will not be in green states all the time. Instead, they need the knowledge that they will shift throughout the day; this provides understanding so that clients are both realistic and nonjudgmental toward themselves. Additionally, knowing how to track their own nervous system is key to being able to change responses as they acquire ways to shift their state.

> *Practice Tip:* I show every client the Polyvagal Theory Chart of Trauma Response (Figure 1.3), and I educate them on nervous system information as it connects to behavior and emotions. Together, we reflect where their issue places them on the chart. Explaining the non-pathologizing and biological association between threat's impact on state supports strengthening safety, and this can start in the first session. Clients can feel the safety to both examine and understand their responses using the lens of neurobiology. Additionally, we explore how to begin the process of shifting their state for their desired outcomes. This includes discussing the deactivation pathways I am aware of at that moment. We often come back to visit the chart and identify where they currently see themselves. With clients presenting with anxiety, we might identify them as high yellow. As this changes, I make a point of showing them where they are when they shift their nervous system set point to mid-to-low yellow and/or more regular green zone access. This supports their engagement in therapy, and they feel a sense of accomplishment by seeing changes in their nervous system.

It is imperative to have clients learn right away about the necessity of tracking their state through their self-awareness. It helps to take time to identify the particular sensations they associate with each state; clients generally can describe this very quickly as the chart is explained to them. Discussing this is a way to map their nervous system (Dana, 2018). Clients tend to like the idea of understanding nervous system states and are eager to track their state, particularly when it is tied in with their therapy goal. For example, if a client is struggling with defensive responses in their marriage by identifying their increased heartbeat, voice change, or muscle tension, you can support them in recognizing that they have moved to mobilization (the yellow zone), which creates the defensiveness. Grasping the connection between state and behavior provides them with the sense of how the communication pattern needs to be shifted through physiology as they sense their body. Tracking in live time how it feels to communicate from the green zone can be eye-opening as they have the "felt sense" (Gendlin, 1996) of the differences.

This process of tracking one's states becomes the cornerstone of self-attunement and learning how to attend to oneself. Questions from the clinician modeled in session help with this information, as asking questions about the client's experiences in their body is the bridge to self-attunement. Self-attunement does require the availability of interoception. Embodiment through interoception is intertwined with self-attunement for regulation. This results in having embodiment as a therapeutic goal of nervous system work. (This goal is imbedded in a nonpathologizing lens toward the reasons for difficulty with embodiment due to low interoceptive feedback.) Having interoception skills is essential for real agency in one's life, as discussed in Chapter 4. It is critical to feel how one is affected in life, as well as what is truly important.

Interoception is also key for being in the present moment to access the signals from the body that can provide the necessary cues for attending to oneself; this helps attain regulation. Additionally, clients can learn to recognize that their newfound ability to feel and tolerate emotions and experiences without losing their emotional balance is a sign of resilience and potential post-traumatic growth. It is not a dip into trauma to have uncomfortable feelings; being able to be with the experiences is a reflection of capacity. Increased capacity is no small thing, as it is part of flexibility in the nervous system.

Also, part of this signaling is feeling new healing impulses not just toward what will regulate them more but also toward Essence, which holds aliveness and vitality. As the client pays attention to where they are truly drawn in their lives, they are in touch with their true self. Following these impulses supports regulation and vitality and can result in expansion. Examples of this extend beyond nervous system signals around boundaries and needs that support regulation. These examples include career changes, relationships, hobbies and interests, and everything in between. There are no limits on what might support a client to flourish more; it includes incorporating what one wants and does not want in their life. This kind of listening often evokes the road map of the client's thwarted impulses that are rising to awareness to be restored. Clinicians need to listen closely to learn where their clients are feeling called, as it offers rich information for their expansion into Essence.

As discussed in other parts of this book, clients are often assigned homework in the form of neural exercises that arise from their sessions. These neural exercises can include repetition of deactivation pathways applied during their sessions. If the client is working on changing a limiting core belief after a session in which reparative experiences were the focus, the homework would include working with this new non-limiting belief. and holding it along with the corresponding positive sensations; this embodiment is the neural exercise which holds the new pattern of being in the world. As an example it could be holding the words, "I have the right to my feelings" as they feel the warmth in their belly. Each deactivation pathway will have associated homework of its unique application that occurred in session. Clients are encouraged to replicate this on their own to support the development of the new neural pathways that access the VVC. Homework can include other activities that support regulation such as breath work, yoga, time outdoors, time with trusted others, or any known activity that will facilitate downregulation.

EXERCISE FOR CONNECTION TO A RESTORED IMPULSE

Let yourself check in and feel yourself, asking the questions, "What makes me feel more alive? What am I drawn to?" What comes up might be a hobby you have let go of or one you want to start. It might include a spiritual practice or an activity that nurtures your sense of vitality. It could even be a person or pet you want to spend more time with in your life. Allow yourself to feel this as a new signal to pay attention to for yourself. Notice what this is like and what you might be drawn to. As we follow the thread of aliveness, we move into more regulation.

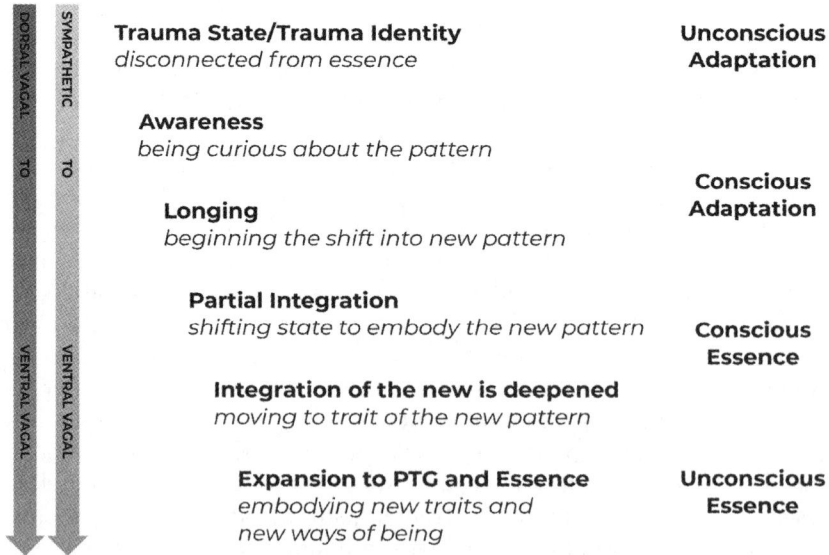

FIGURE 13.1: Continuum of Embodiment   Credit: Ruby Jo Walker with inspiration from Emily Newcomer; graphic by Cindy Miller Atchison Design & Art

THE CONTINUUM OF EMBODIMENT

For developmental wounding, the Continuum of Embodiment provides a unique map for the change process. The Continuum of Embodiment (see Figure 13.1 in the text and on the color insert) identifies six general phases in embodiment that are the path of the return to Essence. It is a continuum that starts with trauma identity with the associated dysregulation of red and yellow zone physiology in the nervous system; it ends in the expansion of self and post-traumatic growth and more access to the VVC. The time it takes to see progress varies depending on the client and the specific issue they are addressing. For some clients, previous therapy work combined with a focus on the nervous system and embodiment practices may lead to quick progress within eight to ten sessions. However, for other clients, especially when the issue is deeply rooted in their early developmental history, it may take years to attain full movement to Essence.

The first phase is trauma state or trauma identity. Trauma identity will hold dysregulated physiology and is often an *unconscious adaptation*; it is unconscious as the client is operating in an automated way as part of a pattern without conscious choice. The client is disconnected from Essence as they are in embedded in their childhood and life conditioning. In this phase, the client might come into therapy with an issue; their adaptation, discussed in Chapter 7, is often the reason they are seeking help, and they are often blind to that knowledge. Just like the fish in water, they do not see they have a pattern. They often have only a slight awareness of the adaptation's impact or none at all. Because the adaptation is unconscious and a default pattern, there is often no insight into the deeper issue how of their adaptation is playing out in their life.

An example is a client who was not attended to as a child and grew up with little support, doing things on their own. Their adaptation led to the development of a trauma identity of doing it alone in life and not expecting anyone to attend to their needs. As a default to their conditioning, this might not be conscious to the client. This unconscious adaptation means the client has no awareness of the patterning and does not see the limit in their life because of the patterning. They have no awareness that they are blocking experiences that could keep them feeling less alone. They might come into therapy with complaints of feeling tired and flat or with some feelings of sadness and/or frustration with the lack of reciprocity in their relationships. Any of these presentations could be connected to their adaptive trauma identity, and they are often unrecognized by the client.

The second phase includes awareness of the pattern. The pattern is now a *conscious adaptation*. It is conscious, as there is awareness of the behaviors associated with the pattern, but one still is in the adaptation. Because these patterns become automatic, changes the client desires are not yet integrated. In this phase, the client begins to see the adaptation and recognize their trauma identity; they often get curious as they become aware that they have a pattern.

In the example used above, in this phase, the client might notice that their *trauma identity* makes it hard to both ask for and accept help. This awareness does not lead to change yet, but the client begins to see the impact on their life. During therapy, the clinician encourages the client to notice the pattern and how it feels. The client is often curious to explore this idea and is open to examining the impact of earlier life events, as well as how the adaptation interfaces with relationships now.

In the third phase, the client starts to have *longing*. As previously mentioned, the client's journey toward wholeness will be guided by their sense of longing. Longing is the cry for a new way of being. It is very significant because the client is voicing, "I want out of the pattern I am in." This is a powerful message from the body to right the system. This righting of the system can lead to Essence, or who they are if they are not in their adaptation of their trauma identity. In this same example, the client might begin to say that they wish relationships were different. As in the example used above, they might notice that they are tired of doing it alone and not feeling attended to by others. This is the beginning of longing that precedes the reconditioning of this normal human impulse of needing more reciprocity and support or another identified emergence of a new way of being.

Clients will almost always know what they *do not* want before they know what they do want. Because of developmental wounding, the clinician might need to help the client get clear on what they want by inquiring. Simply ask, "I hear you do not want to feel so alone. Can you talk more about how you wish your relationships were different?" Or the clinician might help them recognize what they want by stating, "I think I hear you saying you want more connection in your life." Helping the client get clear is an important step. For clients, it could mean focusing on shifting the relationships they are in or finding new relationships. That needs to be determined. When they get to the point that they want their life to be different, "the longing for the new" is not very distant from them. As they tap into the wholeness of longing, it opens up possibilities of having life be different. As noted, longing often is the beginning of the restoration of a thwarted impulse. In this same example, the client might become aware that they feel a new impulse to have more connection in their life.

To review, we know that longing is often fused with grief. As the client feels the longing, they also immediately feel grief. This grief is the realization of the pain of not having the need met. As a reminder, longing in its pure form (and defused from grief discussed in Chapter 11) is a state to embrace because it is the path to making a change and a connection to Essence. Longing provides the road map for the client's new growth process. In addition to empowering, clients often find it regulating to be in the authentic and new awareness of "This is what I want." As this occurs, the threat state is deactivating, and the effort from SNS can lessen. There is a new right action toward differences in relationships with others, which is a foothold in the green zone of VVC.

In the fourth phase, *partial integration*, the client occasionally shifts their behaviors to try out the new pattern. They might regularly embody the new state associated with the phrase, "It is okay to want support." This state, which includes the positive sensations on how the client is integrating the new reparative experience, is now accessible part of the time. This is an indicator of partial integration and conscious Essence, as the client is intentionally committing to their Essence, which includes the new pattern. With awareness, the client is actively working on integrating the new way of being. Committing to a new pattern is a recognition and pledge to one's true self, Essence. With this same example, the client is regularly feeling attended to and integrating that things feel different through embodiment; they do commit to the new pattern of wanting more support. They still have the old habituation and past conditioning present that can lead to the inability to receive. They also will catch themselves not asking for or taking in help. They are regularly taking note of which relationships feed them and possibly making changes. This is the back-and-forth pathway of change. There is a sense of balance, including increased access to the co-regulation of the VVC.

In this fourth phase, the associated bodily sensations (state) are regularly embodied to support change. A client is encouraged to lean into the body's experience of how it feels to have support. This embodiment of sensations around support is the reinforcement of the state, leading to the development of *state to trait* discussed in Chapter 3. At this phase, the temporary states have developed more fully into traits, which are more enduring (Hanson, 2009). The client is more solidly planted in Essence than in the old pattern.

In the fifth phase, the old pattern has metamorphosed. *Integration* of the new pattern has deepened and occurs regularly and more often. There is an unconscious Essence that is sometimes available. In this transition, the client is regularly in the newness of Essence without actively working on the change, but it might be a stretch in challenging times. This practice of embodiment has shifted states into traits (Hanson, 2009). In this same example, the client in this phase is in their Essence with reciprocity in their relationships most of the time. As part of being in Essence, they have often shifted most of their relationships to include support and feeling attended to by others. They regularly ask for needs to be met. This is the state-to-trait change process (Hanson, 2009). Through the practice of embodying a state (the temporary aspect of taking in the new pattern), there is a shift to a trait (in which the pattern feels more enduring). The more stable quality of a trait supports the change process (Hanson, 2009). Clients might have to occasionally remind themselves it is okay to ask for help in some situations, particularly when they have learned the pattern; this can include family members or longer-term relationships. Traits have become more reliable yet still require some attention through practicing state work, which is the embodiment of being okay to have needs with others. This change is now integrated.

The last phase is an *expansion to post-traumatic growth* and Essence. This is the phase in which adaptations and conditioning are replaced with the new way of being. At this point, in unconscious Essence, there is no longer the work to stay in Essence. The client feels the transformation without effort; it is simply a new way of living. Relationships are very different from their original adaptation, and clients find the way they are negotiating needs is the new normal. True Essence is restored, and the client feels expanded. Parts are no longer frozen off, and the SNS is no longer operating regularly from past threat-based adaptations. This leads to relational balance and ANS fluidity and includes shifts in co-regulation capacity as part of it, as relationships are truly different. Expansion does not just mean post-traumatic growth; it also refers to the vitality and aliveness that are part of being deeply connected to themselves.

RECOGNITION OF GROWTH EXERCISE

Bring awareness to your personal experience of growth and the way it helped you be more yourself in your Essence. As you turn toward your Essence, allow yourself to bring up an image that resonates with a sense of your authentic self or feel this sense in your body. As you are with this, allow self-appreciation of your growth path and your commitment to Essence.

This process generally happens over time. The clinician stays aware of the phases to continue to support integration for the client. Clients also often think that simply knowing their needs and having permission to integrate them creates change. It does not, as insight rarely leads to change. True expansion is created over time and is a process with back-and-forth steps. Change is never a straight line. Oscillation in the change process is completely normal. Although clients often assume they are doing something wrong, the oscillation of change helps the process along its path. Psychoeducation is often necessary as clients need encouragement and understanding that change is a process, and it will take time, with toggling between the old pattern and the new direction.

For general change beyond the Continuum of Embodiment, it is crucial to understand that it tends to be gradual and nonlinear. Clients need time to fully integrate deep nervous system work as it involves repetition and practice. Change will always have turns and twists as clients find their way. It is also important to provide psychoeducation on the disequilibrium of the change process. This loss of emotional and pattern homeostasis occurs when the new is not integrated yet, and the old no longer works. Clients are standing in two worlds; it naturally brings uncertainty to the client, which adds to the disequilibrium. Uncertainty is challenging as humans have a strong need "to know." For this reason, clients benefit from the validation that it is difficult to be in the liminal space of change.

SUMMARY

Knowing what a client truly wants from therapy provides the road map for change. Psychoeducation on the nervous system and tracking states creates engagement and a reference for desired changes. Also, informing clients about the understanding that change occurs in phases over time helps normalize their process. Stressing the normalcy of finding the change process unsettling can be helpful. There is a Continuum of Embodiment that shifts the client from trauma identity to the blueprint of their true self, or Essence. It is necessary to support change outside of the sessions for deeper transformation.

LONGING EXERCISE

Take some time now to connect with yourself and let yourself feel your body. Notice how you are in this moment, and gently acknowledge whatever might be present. If it feels okay, see if there is any way you can settle your nervous system through orientation, breath, "taking in the good" (Hanson, 2009), or whatever appeals to you, taking the time you need. As you settle, allow yourself to notice the answer to this question: "What do I long for now in my life?" Notice what comes up, and notice how it feels in your body to name what you are longing for right now. Acknowledge any grief that might be present, noticing that the grief and the longing are two separate experiences. Take a moment to feel their differences. If it feels right, see if you can now go back to the longing. Notice where you feel it and what it feels like in your body, noticing the sensations. If any doubts creep in as you are with the longing, allow the doubt to be present while putting most of your attention on the longing, allowing yourself to feel the importance of the direction that this longing is offering you. Feel into how it is pointing you toward an important change in your life. Now, imagine your life with this longing fulfilled. Feel in your body what it would be like to have this longing met, bringing in your senses, including how it would look and what you might hear, smell, and feel around you. Take some time to just feel this, trusting your longing to take you back on your path to Essence.

CHAPTER 14

Phases of Treatment and Session Guide

A map helps you get where you're going, but it doesn't decide where you want to go. Every path we take carries the imprint of our past and the possibility of our becoming.

—Author unknown

In working therapeutically to apply a Polyvagal Theory lens with clients, it is important to understand the phases of treatment. This understanding informs which interventions will be most effective and useful to the client in their current state. The goal for every session is to be able to deactivate the nervous system. This process, which includes all the deactivation pathways that have been covered in previous chapters, supports a new template for the nervous system; this new template is downregulation for access to VVC in each session. This repeated experience begins to *teach* the nervous system to develop a pattern, rather than being stuck in red or yellow zones.

As discussed earlier, how quickly the nervous system can deactivate to the green zone of the VVC is a marker of resilience. The clinician keeps this purpose in the foreground to promote strengthening regulation. Working in this manner can be applied to any issues clients might bring to therapy, as presenting issues will generally have a nervous system as the focus of each session. Repeating the pattern of downregulation to VVC promotes "the new normal" that therapy is trying to achieve and is foundational to changing nervous system states. Autonomic flexibility is available only if clients are not in fixed nervous system states of red and yellow and have access to the green zone. As stated before, from the green zone of VVC, clients have the neural platform of health, growth, and restoration, which are the key components of post-traumatic growth and resilience.

PHASES OF TREATMENT

Clients will move back and forth between phases of treatment. This is a normal part of the change process, as discussed in the last chapter. Even in one session, a client can move between these phases.

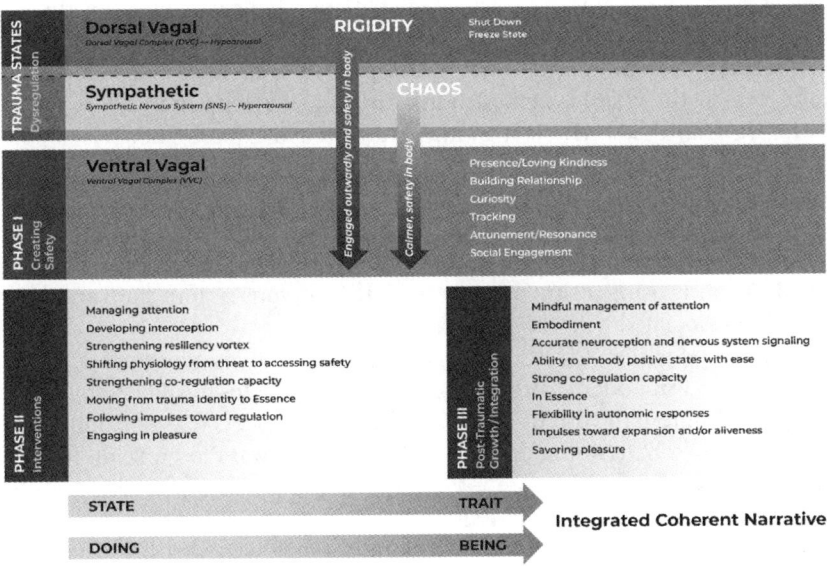

FIGURE 14.1:   Phases of Treatment   Credit: Ruby Jo Walker; graphic by Cindy Miller Atchison Design & Art

Phase 1

As noted in Figure 14.1, the client presents with a trauma state and trauma identity. Initially, the client exhibits yellow or red zone dominance; this occurs with both how the client defines their concern for seeking help and for the indicators from their nervous system. (See Polyvagal Theory Chart of Trauma Response, Figure 1.3.) Together, these two contexts provide communication for how the nervous system is attempting to expand. If the client states they want more intimacy in their relationships, this identifies which state is dominant, as well as the potential map that might be applied, which would be their co-regulation capacity. This is the tracking part of attunement that will lead to the necessary interventions or responses.

Remember that attunement is presence, tracking, perception, and response. These aspects are part of co-regulation and the route by which the clinician approaches interventions. If a client comes in edgy and upset and wants to feel less reactive in a work situation, their nervous system indicators are in the yellow zone. Asking for help to be less reactive is also an indication of yellow zone nervous system dominance, as reactivity is an indicator of the SNS. The treatment goal is aligned with what the clinician is tracking through attunement. Another client might state they want help with their communication in their relationships. The clinician might be tracking that the client is expressing themself very clearly. In this case, there is no alignment between the client's goals and the information from interpersonal tracking. This underlines a need for further exploration as the client is demonstrating incongruence in their self-report versus the clinician's experience; it an important area to explore since it is not obvious. This is different from a client who brings up communication issues and struggles within the session to communicate effectively. In both cases, the tracking gives valuable information to get curious about for further clarity. Getting clarity is the perception part of the attunement cycle that informs interventions. The clinician is using attunement to track the nervous system state and how it is or is not associated with their goals.

As discussed earlier, to have clarity on the goals, it is always important to ask, "What do you want out of working together?" It also helps to add, "What do you want to be different in your life that will make this process feel worth it to you?" This points the client in the direction of where they want to grow, discussed in the last chapter. As stated before, having this direction clearly defined becomes a central point to come back to regularly to ensure the client's needs are being met; it can also be beneficial for a check-in if a new goal arises. This also promotes more agency and responsibility with the client in the therapeutic process.

After bringing awareness to the state of the nervous system by identifying the underlying physiological state, Phase 1 of treatment is to create safety. The clinician does this first by offering their own VVC presence by being grounded, embodied, and in loving-kindness, to send the signal of safety to the client. The clinician is actively building a relationship with the client using social engagement, curiosity, and attunement. This creates resonance, so the client can feel joined and understood. The connection through resonance supports the "felt sense" (Gendlin, 1996) of safety for the client, critical to changing the physiological state. All through this process, the clinician is actively tracking the client and their sense of safety and relationship.

Tracking is very broad, and it includes:

- Nervous system states
- Body posture and movements
- Facial expressions
- Speech and prosody
- Co-regulation capacity—in the session and self-reports

- Limiting core beliefs from trauma identity—both directly expressed as well as observed in behaviors
- Indicators of Essence
- Body presentations
- The process of relating to the clinician
- Congruence with words and affect
- Developmental themes

All this tracking begins to inform interventions that will be most beneficial to the client. It is also the means to support creating safety for the client. As the client feels seen, heard, and understood, more safety is created as part of that resonance. All treatment is focused on cultivating safety (Porges, 2003, 2021, 2022), as internalized safety restores access to VVC. In the early stages of treatment, being "safe enough" in sessions might be all that is obtainable; this capacity is built over time.

It is important to be aware that clients often label their struggles with inaccurate judgment. This can be focused on almost anything. Examples are: "I guess I am just being resistant." "I have no right to feel so angry." "I am just being too cognitive, I guess." When you, as the clinician, observe this, it helps to immediately ask yourself, "What is the wisdom here?" There is often an organic impulse trying to emerge, and it is key to the client process (Kurtz, 1990). In applying to these examples:

- *"I guess I am just being resistant."* Often, the client has a very important "no" that needs exploration. Trusting the "no" will lead to something else unfolding that will benefit the client, because the therapy sometimes wants to take a new direction, or a new detail that needs addressing is present.
- *"I have no right to feel so angry."* Anger can regularly unfold into a new boundary or need. When this is explored fully, the client's anger will lead to an action that can produce regulation.
- *"I am just being too cognitive, I guess."* In doing somatic work, sometimes clients need a break while they are building tolerance toward being in their body. Additionally, sometimes the cognitive information is a new direction of the therapy or an important aspect of integration.

Practice Tip: I have been taught by my best mentors not to believe in resistance. It is no longer a word I use to describe clients. Having this attitude is nervous system friendly, promoting safety, as it removes judgment. This concept ties right in with seeing behaviors as adaptive. This approach not only depathologizes behaviors, but it also supports the most effective therapy, as there truly is a wisdom that will unfold with the right attention.

Phase 2

Because Phase 2 is about interventions, all the deactivation pathways are part of this phase of treatment, as well as regulation activities. Phase 2 revolves around *doing* as opposed to *being* (which is the focus later in Phase 3). As discussed earlier, the more there is dysregulation in the nervous system, the more doing is required. As the nervous system settles with more regulation, there is less need to do, since the nervous system is moving in the right direction and needs less instruction. The Phase 2 goals create changing states that lead to traits (Hanson, 2009), deepening the change process as the changes become more stabilized and more enduring. The outcome of this process is that there is more ease available. Additionally, the nervous system begins to move more easily into regulation after dysregulation.

Managing Attention. At the beginning of Phase 2, the intervention phase, the portal into the VVC is more established; strengthening that portal is also the goal. In trauma states, there is great difficulty in managing one's attention because attention is hijacked. In the red zone, attention is hard to attain, because of feeling more checked out. Rumination is often part of freeze response, as there is disconnection from the body, while also a fixation encompassing both DVC and SNS. Both red zone manifestations of attention struggles are born out of underlying physiology. Likewise, in yellow zone dominance, attention tends to go to focusing on what is wrong, as well as looking for what might go wrong. Therefore, a primary intervention includes teaching the management of attention. The two main deactivation pathways to support this are: the embodiment of positive states (see Chapter 3) and being present in the here and now (see Chapter 4). The goal of this work is for clients to have mindful management of attention, resulting in more access to the VVC.

Developing Interoception. Developing interoception is key for receiving body signals that lead to attending to one's needs, but also to having agency and empowerment over time. Trauma can disconnect one from one's body, disabling the needed information for fully living one's life, particularly when there is red zone dominance. It results in more emotional dysregulation because impulses for regulation and nourishment are thwarted. The recovery of interoception (discussed in Chapter 4), is critical for following impulses that lead to living one's life from Essence, not conditioning. This leads to embodiment over time.

Strengthening the Resiliency Vortex. Strengthening the resiliency vortex (Chapter 3) develops the capacity for resilience, as one is able to hold more of their experiences. It becomes a way to be more in flow in life and less hindered by challenges that occur. The embodiment of positive states is the primary pathway to support the nervous system in this way. With practice, strengthening the resiliency vortex will prime clients to notice positive states with ease, providing deeper shifts toward the VVC.

Shift Physiology From Threat to Accessing Safety. Shifting physiology to access safety is crucial for true nervous system regulation and is the foundation of resilience and post-traumatic growth. All of the deactivation pathways are interventions to support this in therapy. More regular access to safety often supports accurate neuroception. Developing accurate neuroception and nervous system signaling supports the process of accessing safety as well as regulation. Regular access to safety (the green zone) results in flexibility in autonomic responses, a foundational aspect of resilience and post-traumatic growth.

Strengthening Co-Regulation Capacity. Co-regulation is a natural way to develop resilience and post-traumatic growth, as it is in our wiring to co-regulate to support the nervous system. Although it is natural, life experiences can make this a resource that is difficult to access. The good news is that the capacity for co-regulation can be recovered and is already an inherent aspect of all therapeutic processes. Developing this in the context of therapy supports co-regulation in other relationships.

Moving From Trauma Identity to Essence. Renewing the connection to Essence supports a sense of vitality. The process is critical for truly receiving nourishment. This shift provides learning to live from one's most authentic self, not being held back by the limits of adaptations and nervous system dysregulation. As clients have more access to their Essence, they inherently have more freedom and aliveness.

Impulses Toward Regulation. Discussed throughout this book, threat states of red and yellow can limit behavioral repertoire. Life-enhancing impulses are inhibited, as threat states narrow one's life. As clients learn to follow new healing impulses, there is more access to the VVC. Restoring these thwarted impulses is at the heart of regulation and one's avenue into Essence. As discussed in Chapter 2, as these impulses are restored, agency becomes more available. Through this process, healthy new patterns create deeper access to the VVC and one's Essence, along with aliveness and vitality.

Engaging in Pleasure. When survival is the primary focus, experiencing pleasure goes offline in service of survival. Joy, true intimacy, and bodily pleasure become muted as body sensations are subdued or deemed unsafe. Effective trauma treatment goes beyond reducing trauma symptoms and includes engaging in pleasure as a means for more fullhearted living. Savoring pleasure is a mark of increased regulation, as it accesses the VVC (Bryant & Veroff, 2006; Dana, 2018). Both the embodiment of positive states and being present in the here and now are necessary deactivation pathways to develop engagement with pleasure.

> *Practice Tip*: As part of Phase 2 in treatment and doing, developing contracts with clients has been discussed for various aspects of treatment. As a reminder for any of these goals, it is often useful to ask the client if you can contract to work with a specific barrier you feel would help stretch the client into having more regulation. For example, in development of interoception, I often ask clients if we can agree to spend 5–10 minutes per session working on this. The process of developing interoception is often challenging to clients. Making an agreement often supports the process of the stretch; it becomes a focal point to do the work that is necessary for change. Any of these areas of intervention could be considered to do a contract with the client.

Phase 3

In Phase 3, there is more regular access to the VVC. The nervous system has shifted from "doing" as part of needing safety to "being," with an increased ability to have rest and ease of the green zone. As a result of this, the nervous system is able "to be" more easily, as "being" is now a new and safe option. As this reorganization is occurring, the clinician is mostly encouraging the client to *embody the positive state* of the expansion occurring. This includes more presence through being in the here and now, as well as noticing what is going well or even okay. Increased capacity and agency in challenges, self-compassion, increased co-regulation availability, embodying and following longing impulses, connection with Essence, and finding authentic meaning are all markers that indicate a measurement of growth and expansion. The nervous system has regular access to the VVC with a broader range of autonomic flexibility. The client often reports feeling more responsive rather than reactive. Through the work of deactivating the nervous system and learning to truly be in the present moment, the client now has an integrated coherent narrative. As with most of the presentations in Phase 3, the client is encouraged to embody these changes. It is through this embodiment that changes are cemented. Increased resilience and post-traumatic growth can be anchored deeply through embodiment.

> *Practice Tip*: Clients need time for integration after deep nervous system work. This can be a range for clients, and there is no right amount of time between sessions. It is helpful to talk about this concept of integration as clients decide what they feel best supports them.

THE SESSION GUIDE: PROGRESSION
OF A SESSION AND TRACKING

The Session Guide (Figure 14.2) is a companion for the clinician as they integrate the PVT approach in their work. The guide offers an overview of the session, including the beginning, middle, and end, as well as useful concepts to hold while working with a PVT-informed approach.

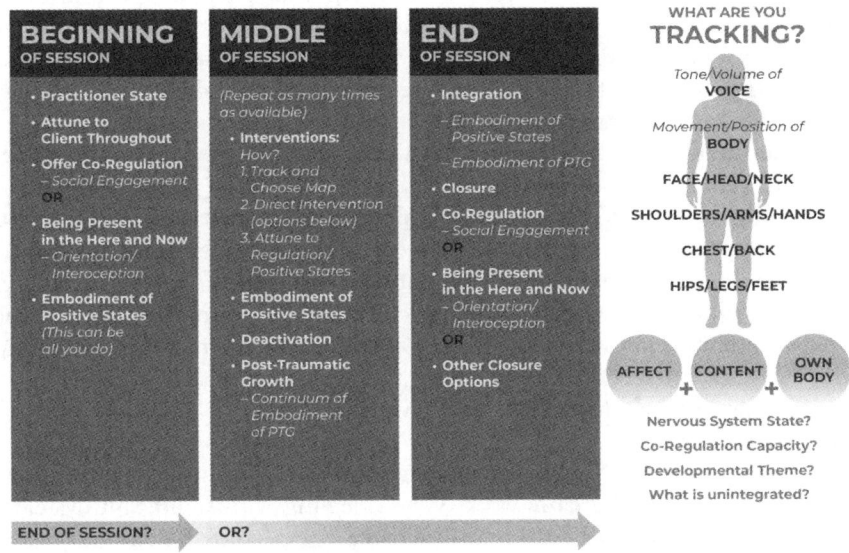

FIGURE 14.2: Session Guide Credit: Emily Newcomer with input from Mia Carrasco-Songer based on content from Ruby Jo Walker; graphic by Cindy Miller Atchison Design & Art

Beginning of Session

As described throughout this book, everything starts with the clinician in presence, signaling safety to the client and creating the container for any therapeutic work. It is the first aspect of the attunement cycle, building co-regulation through presence, tracking, perception, and response. Initially, the clinician starts by utilizing the deactivation pathways of co-regulation and/or being present in the here and now through orientation and interoception. Both interventions intiate green zone physiology access. They can be nonthreatening ways to begin working with clients to settle their nervous system safely without bringing in any material that is disruptive to the physiology, which will be attended to later as the ANS is supported to the VVC.

For some clients, social engagement is challenging, and for others, it settles them immediately. Having these two options for settling the nervous system through social engagement or being present in the here and now through orientation provides a move toward VVC immediately for the client. With some clients, engaging socially with whatever they brought up as they come to the session or another known safe content promotes more safety. A start to a brief social interaction designed to settle the nervous system can be, "You mentioned that you went on a walk before you came here today. Where is the trail you took today?" Another client might find even that amount of social engagement challenging instead, the clinician might say, "Can we take a moment and just let your eyes go where they want?" The client might describe the trees they see outside the window. This orientation to the environment supports VVC. Both of these interventions sometimes require psychoeducation, so the client does not find it unexpected and therefore activating to their ANS.

From the beginning, the clinician is always tracking nervous system states. As they see the nervous system settle more, as indicated by shifts in breath, muscle tension, facial expression, and outward social engagement availability, clinicians can direct the client to the deactivation pathway of the embodiment of positive states. They might say, "Can you take a moment to notice your body now?" or "Can you feel the shift to feeling the green zone at this moment?" The client is then directed to embody and savor the change. This strengthens the connection to the VVC.

As indicated on the Session Guide (Figure 14.2), this might be all that happens in a session in the early work. When dealing with significant dysregulation, this is a safe intervention to deactivate the nervous system and begin teaching about shifting nervous system states. Tracking states becomes a critical aspect of therapy. It helps clients understand the therapy process, and it teaches the relationship between states and regulation. It also outlines the therapy process as the clinician ties in the client's particular therapeutic goal to the concept of the nervous system state. Clients readily understand this and become very engaged in applying this PVT approach.

Example for the Beginning of a Session

CLIENT: (After hurriedly entering the room) *I got stuck in traffic and was so busy this morning. I almost did not get here on time.* (Client is in the SNS dominant state, which includes the client not being in a relational state.)

CLINICIAN: (Smiling) *I am glad you made it. Do you want to take a moment to just let yourself land here?* (Acknowledging the state of the client, while offering some time to settle.)

CLIENT: *Yes, I was worried about getting here.*

CLINICIAN: *See if it feels okay to take some time to notice that you made it on time.* (Clinician is offering an entry into the green zone for more deactivation.)

CLIENT: *Yes, it is a relief.* (Breathing shallowly and showing tenseness in their body/posture.)

CLINICIAN: *Can we take a moment and have you feel the relief . . . and notice how it feels in your body now as you do?* (Directing the client toward deactivation to green zone physiology as the client is reporting relief, but it is not embodied yet.)

CLIENT: *I feel myself slowing down, and I am breathing differently.* (Moving to the VVC.)

CLINICIAN: *Let's just stay with this relief for a moment if that feels okay, and not hurry through it.* (Supporting VVC and shifting states.)

CLIENT: *I have a lot to talk about, but I feel a little better. I have had a big week.*

CLINICIAN: (Does not respond to the client's conversational lead quickly; this is to give the client time to just feel the relief. Instead, nods in acknowledgment and focuses on staying in the green zone of therapeutic presence.)

CLIENT: *I had a lot happen with my partner and at work, so I really want to talk about this.* (Quickly shifting states back to SNS dominance.)

CLINICIAN: *Take your time and notice we have the whole session. There is time for you . . .* (Checking to see if the client can take this in.)

CLIENT: (Slows down again.) *Yes, I have just been anxious all week.*

CLINICIAN: (With the attuned awareness that getting more into the content will support deactivation, the clinician brings relational warmth and presence to the client, signaling being with the client.) *"Let me know where you want to start today . . ."*

In this example, the clinician does a combination of settling the nervous system but also recognizing that deactivation will be supported by the client getting into the content. The clinician also perceives that it is hard for the client to be relational in this state, so focuses on providing regulation with space initially. In this example, there was not availability to be relational at the beginning of the session with more typical greetings because of the client's state. Sometimes, using co-regulation will feel irritating to the client as in urgency, they simply want to get to their agenda for the session. This is often part of SNS dominance; the focus is instead on urgency and getting to "work" on the client issues. This often changes over time as the client has more regular access to the green zone. At other times, the work might be focused on having the client take in the developmental repair so that there is space for their feelings, and/or maybe that they can get what they need. With attunement, the clinician understands what is going to be most effective in supporting the client toward green zone physiology. As with all interventions, it is always a good idea to try one and go in a different direction through attunement with the client.

Middle of the Session

In the middle of the session, the clinician uses attunement to determine the intervention. On the right side of Figure 14.2, tracking focus is noted. In the body, this tracking includes voice (tone/volume), body (movement/position), face/head/neck (aspects of VVC physiology), shoulders/arms/hands, chest/back, and hips/legs/feet. Tracking of the body, with affect, content, and the clinician's body, leads to the most effective interventions.

An example of tracking for potential interventions might include a client who is moving their body a lot as they talk, and their voice might be high. The client appears tense. Their affect seems to be anxious. The content might include a recent interaction with their mother, who has expressed disappointment in their new job choice. This disapproval from their mom made the client feel confused just when the client was excited about this new possibility. Additionally, the client was also experiencing both doubt and self-criticism as they struggled with their mother's judgments.

Interventions could go in many different directions to support deactivation. One deactivation pathway might be to simply direct toward being present in the here and now (orientation and interoception) to settle the nervous system to see if coming into regulation changes the self-criticism. Another deactivation pathway might be to try pendulation between the anxiety in the body and another place of ease. The clinician could also go toward the developmental wound by offering a reparative experience. With this intervention, they could work with the client in identifying and embodying their knowledge of "I did the right thing," or "I have a right to do what feels best for me in my life," or even work with the child part around the criticism.

Many times, the clinician is going to have information from their own body that informs them of the best intervention (Siegel, 2010b). All roads really do lead to Rome, so any intervention can be useful; even when the information does not work the way the clinician hopes it might, it is informative. The more clinicians learn to work with themselves, including their nervous system and their developmental wounding, the clearer they are in their perceptions. The sensing from their own body tends to get more accurate and attuned. (Ways to work with this will be covered in Chapter 15.)

It is important in the process of utilizing interventions to know that when anything is offered in the spirit of an experiment as something to try, clients are generally not negatively affected unless a clinician locks in to their own ideas without being open to feedback. A nonattached and invitational approach provides safety, eliciting the VVC.

> *Practice Tip*: When offering non-attached feedback to the client, certain language can help support the attunement. Saying things like, "I have an imagining that (and naming what you think might be going on.)" You could also say, "I am

bringing up (something you are wondering about), and this might be projection as I am not sure." This kind of language helps the client feel the clinician's non-attachment that enhances the attunement.

In the middle of the session, the clinician picks one of the three maps to use: general nervous system functioning, co-regulation capacity, or limiting core beliefs from developmental wounding. They then pick the deactivation pathway(s) that will best address this map. If deactivation occurs, it is followed by embodying the resulting regulation and/or positive state. The clinician can utilize Figure 13.1, the Continuum of Embodiment chart, to see where the client is in their integration process.

Example of the Middle of the Session (Same Client)

CLIENT: (Talking quickly again) *I had such a tough time with my partner. I felt things had been getting better, and then he did nothing for our anniversary, even though he knows this was important to me. I felt awful, and we got into a big fight. He says he shows me he loves me every day, and this one day is not that important. It felt really bad, and I was mad as I have talked about this so many times. And then, at work, the whole team got recognition except for me on the project we worked on. I did so much of the work to get it done. It was just an awful week for me.*

CLINICIAN: *There is a lot here. And I hear it feels so bad to be overlooked, and I am wondering how it is to tell me about this?* (The clinician is moving toward the trauma vortex as some regulation has already occurred in the session, creating more capacity to go toward the difficulty the client is experiencing, as a lead-in to a deactivation pathway. The clinician is also naming the potential theme of "being overlooked.")

CLIENT: *I feel like I am not important . . . like I do not matter . . .* (Getting tearful.)

CLINICIAN: (After taking a moment.) *Let me just say something, and let's just see what happens . . . "You matter even if you are not recognized in a way that you want." . . . Can this go into your body at all?* The clinician has now refined the theme to the words the client is using.

CLIENT: *It does not go in too much, just a little in my heart area. I still feel pretty tense, and I am so sad about both of these things happening in one week.* (Client begins to tear up.) (As noted, it is typical for a new belief to be integrated only slightly.)

CLINICIAN: *Let the sadness be there around your partner and the work situation, while also noticing the place in your heart where you can begin to take in that you matter. See if you can put most of your attention on the place in your heart that is taking it in.* (The therapeutic direction is to the resilience vortex.)

CLIENT: (After taking some time.) *Well, it feels like it expands a bit, and I do feel less tense, and I am still sad, but it is less.*

CLINICIAN: *Is it ok to just stay with this expansion, while noticing less tension?* (Further embodiment of the positive state.)

CLIENT: (Pausing and then taking a deeper breath.) *It feels better and I feel it more in my body now. Mostly, I start feeling mad that these things do not feel very fair to me, and I think I want to speak up more.*

CLINICIAN: *And what is that like to feel that you want to speak up more?* (Accessing "I can," resilience, a restored healing impulse to speak up, and access to green zone.)

CLIENT: *It feels good.* (Straightening up in the chair.) *It feels important, actually. I do not want to be overlooked.* (The clinician had used these words earlier but they did not quite fit then. Now, they have more resonance, as the words "I matter" were key to begin integrating first.)

CLINICIAN: *Can you take time to feel the shift in your spine and feel those words you just said: "I do not want to be overlooked."* (The clinician is reflecting the change in posture that may or may not be in the client's awareness.)

CLIENT: *I do not want to be overlooked.* (Said in a neutral tone.)

CLINICIAN: *Can you repeat that, really feeling how important those words are, while again noticing how your spine is straighter?* (The client is integrating those words, but they are not fully embodied, so repeating helps to cultivate the embodiment.)

CLIENT: *I do not want to be overlooked.* (Said in a strong tone of voice.) *I feel stronger and more upright. It feels a lot better, actually.* (The client looks settled, less tearful, with a clear shift in their body as the words become more embodied.)

CLINICIAN: *Take some time to feel the change as you feel those words.*

CLIENT: *I feel much better.*

This session could reinforce this new pattern more or it could move to how to talk with their partner and boss and work with any barriers to that communication.

Middle of the Session: General Deactivation Information

Deactivation pathways can vary, depending on the client. There is no one-size-fits-all as attunement is key; one issue can be worked with in multiple ways. The following is an example of potential deactivation pathways that could be used with a client presenting with depression. Attuning to the particular presentation provides an understanding of the optimum deactivation pathways that will benefit the client:

- *The client needs more capacity to hold positive feelings due to a history of abuse or current trauma:* **embodiment of positive states.** This will help the client safely embody positive states, strengthening the capacity for resilience, and shifting the depression.

- *The client presents with a disconnect from their body and experiences:* **being present in the here and now** and/or **integration of fused and disconnected experiences** can be helpful. The client could learn to be in their body through interoception by being present in the here and now. They could also benefit from having aspects of their memory, emotions, body sensations, and beliefs integrated through linking them because of the disconnection, which could be underlying the depression.
- *The client is feeling alone and unworthy:* **co-regulation** and **offering reparative experiences.** The clinician would provide co-regulation to alleviate the loneliness and offer a reparative experience to support the sense of unworthiness to shift the limiting core belief. Both regulation and reparative experiences can shift the physiology to the green zone, alleviating the depression.
- *The client is feeling self-critical:* **self-compassion.** The client learns to hold their experiences with kindness, while feeling less alone as they connect to common humanity in self-compassion. This shifts the client to the ventral vagal complex of the green zone. As self-compassion is integrated, depressive symptoms are sometimes decreased.
- *Feeling overwhelmed and just going through the motions:* **motor plan completion of protective actions** and **pendulation.** The client deactivates freeze/shutdown in their body through the motor plan completion of protective movements. They could also pendulate between two states, like ease and overwhelm. Both of these interventions often metabolize the sense of the heaviness of depressive symptoms.
- *The client is not present with how they were affected in their life, including having unintegrated grief around a loss:* **the coherent narrative** supports the client integrating grief (or another experience), leading to more coherency and lessening depression symptoms.
- *The client is struggling and in a victim state, leading to being stuck in DVC:* **embodying agency.** The client would find agency through focusing on meaning in shifting the victimization of their experience by advocating for a cause connected to their trauma. This often leads to deactivation because mobilization is used for a purpose. The change of focus often provides a lifeline that can relieve depressive distress.

Ending of the Session

As deactivation occurs and the embodiment of the VVC reinforces that state, the clinician can look to ending the session. Embodiment is key to strengthening that state, and it is often settling to close sessions with the relatively neutral interventions of using social engagement or accessing presence with orientation again, as was done at the beginning. This can be a good place to end for some clients.

When there has been strong content or major physiological shifts, it can be useful to bring in some cognition to support the ending of the session. It might be saying, "What felt important here today?" or "What are you taking from today?" Additionally, it can be useful when there is some tenderness present to say, "I am wondering if there is something you need to say or hear before we stop today?" This is particularly useful if you sense that the client feels somewhat incomplete. Other times, it might be important not to add any content or overlay, particularly when the client might still be integrating. You can be transparent about it. "I know a lot happened today, so we can talk more next time as you take some time to integrate this."

There are also times when ending a session is simply not ideal because of the state of the client. Ending on time is a signal of safety, so it is mostly important to follow the guidelines of time boundaries. It is also important to be relational around that process. Examples of phrasing that might help with these kinds of situations that offer options help:

- "How is it to stop here, even though it is not quite ideal?"
- "Let's just take a moment and see if you need to say or hear anything before we stop."
- "It is time to close our session, and I know there are still some things here; can we just take a moment to orient?"
- "Is there anything that might make you feel a little more complete at this moment?"
- "Can we take a moment to just do a couple of 3-3-5 breaths as we move into closing?"
- "Let's bookmark this for next time."
- The clinician could go back to an earlier embodied positive state, reinforcing it as a way to end the session: "Let's bring up again that feeling you had earlier today in your body when you felt . . ." (any positive state).

It is also important to follow up the next time you meet if you use the interventions. Checking in with how it was after the session, as well as noting if they did anything that did help their nervous system can support more embodiment of positive states.

As mentioned, homework is often helpful in applying the lens of the nervous system. Because experience is what changes the brain, strengthening the new pattern or growth edge is useful for deepening the new neural pathways (Hanson, 2018). Strengthening includes having the client repeat deactivation pathways that supported deactivation in their session. Of particular importance is the embodiment of VVC physiological states that come from any deactivation pathway. Brain change is also what Linda Graham (2013) calls "little and often" 10–20 seconds, 10–20 times per day; this is doable for clients. It is helpful to give this information as psychoeducation so clients understand the importance of repetition and embodiment in shifting their nervous systems; it will only change if they work on it. Applying the embodiment of positive states as a deactivation pathway strengthens the new state into a trait (Hanson, 2009).

Any of the deactivation pathways that have arisen from session work are useful to embody to support the ongoing trait change and provide more access to VVC physiology. This is a critical aspect of PVT-applied therapy because it teaches shifting the state. An example might be to have the client feel the new belief they are working to embody as a new trait or way of being. "I would like you to practice taking in the new belief 'I matter' multiple times per day to support this change you are working on here." This could be encouraged with any of the pathways named, letting the client know that practice and embodiment are the most effective ways to change the pattern. Clients usually find it empowering that they can work on the changes they want on their own.

Example of the End of the Session (Same Client)

CLINICIAN: *It is getting close to needing to stop for today. I am wondering how you are doing right now.*

CLIENT: *I feel much better. I guess I really needed to get that "I matter," especially in the hard situations.* (The client has clariified what is most important to integrate.)

CLINICIAN: *So, for this week, I wonder if you could work with these words that came up today and embody them multiple times per day: "I matter and it does not depend on how I am responded to . . ." You seemed to feel those words in your heart area, so it would help to add in those words, while feeling that same sensation in your heart.*

CLIENT: *It continues to feel good. Yes, I want to work on this. I am also glad we talked about how to talk to my partner and my boss at work. I feel I have a way to do that now.*

CLINICIAN: *Take a moment to feel that—that you can do that now.* (This promotes more agency, as it touches into "I can" physiology.)

CLIENT: *That also feels great—I feel that shift in my spine again. And there is some relief.*

CLINICIAN: *Nice.*

CLIENT: *See you next week.*

Reflection: For many years, I was against homework, believing that clients do not need more to do. I also thought it led to too much doing for clients. Now, I give everyone homework, with the recognition that changing the nervous system takes intention and attention. Nervous system change can happen, but there needs to be awareness and commitment to make that change.

SUMMARY

Understanding the phases of treatment and the session guide can be useful to have an understanding of the overall process and where to keep the therapeutic focus. Additionally, having a map for the session process in an outlined form leads to more spontaneity in applying it as it is ingrained in the therapy process. The treatment process is about creating the neural platform for both more resilience and post-traumatic growth, and these guides provide the guidelines for this process. Some clinicians report using the session guide while in session.

INTEGRATION OF ONE'S VALUE EXERCISE

Take a moment to feel you have much to offer your clients. Feel this in your body, noticing how it feels to claim this for yourself. Bring up a time that you felt that you were effective with your client and how your work felt useful to them. As you feel this sense of being helpful and effective, notice what it is like in your body as you hold the feeling that what you have to offer is valuable to your client. Feel a sense of your worth and value with this one client. Allow yourself to take in what feeling value is like in your body, noticing the sensations. Allow yourself to savor how it feels, taking some time here to really feel into this. As you savor this experience, bring in the awareness that your own body can guide you into offering what your clients might need as you listen to the whispers of information coming from your body in resonance. Feel the sense that listening to your own wisdom, along with your willingness to support your client, can be enough to help your client. Allow yourself to take time to take this in, feeling how you have value right now.

CHAPTER 15

The Clinician's Expansion of Self: The Parallel Process of Deepening Presence

Know yourself—your clients can only go as far as you can take them and where you have been able to go within yourself.

Most clinicians have a range of effectiveness. This range will be informed by their ability to work with both their nervous system state and the adaptations from their developmental wounding. In the same way that clients are less present while in adaptations and nervous system dysregulation, so are clinicians. Their range of effectiveness can be increased with awareness, coupled with their ability to work with themselves. This chapter will discuss the common themes that can limit a clinician, as well as ways to support moving toward their wholeness and embodied presence.

MY JOURNEY

Early in my career, I began to see that if I struggled with clients in any way in sessions, from being upset with them, judging them, not liking them, or feeling anything about their journey, it was all about a problem with a limit in myself, not the client. I began to bring my struggles to supervision to find ways to get more present and back into unconditional positive regard and loving-kindness. I explored the questions: "What made me upset?" "What made me judge?" "What made me not like someone?" Any struggle with a client's journey became my limitation in being effective. Using this lens, I began to see that my struggles with clients were my opportunity to grow. Because I am on a path of passion for growth, this invitation for self-examination was very welcome to me. As discussed in the chapter on cultivating presence, I could see that learning to be in the most authentic loving place in myself with my clients seemed to be where I felt most effective.

I sometimes used to joke that I was getting paid to work on myself. I have found that tracking my ability to be in a loving presence is the key to my own expansion. If I have lost track of the loving presence and am not able to offer true presence, I taught myself to realize that I had hit a barrier and wound in myself. Rather than feeling pressure or hardship, it was nourishing to me to use this approach. I could hold my limitations with compassion, curiosity, and an interest in expansion. My limitation became my opportunity.

I did not know it at the time, but I was actually on the journey of post-traumatic growth in a polyvagal-informed way. I was using limits and struggles with my clients for expansion, as my clients did in their post-traumatic growth. Working this way, I was unwittingly trying to get back to VVC and safety, for me and the client; doing so is inherently regulating. I did not have the language, but I had the knowledge that it was up to me. I worked in supervision to attain the relational human-to-human connection of offering a loving connection with my clients. I feel honored to have been in this process and truly grateful for the growth I have had as a result of working with my clients. I received more regulation myself in this process, the gift of working in this manner.

Over time, I also feel I moved more into my Essence with clients. I certainly understood my professional role, but I have also been able to bring myself forward more. Providing therapy is both easy and nourishing for me as a result of this path; I feel my authenticity and Essence as I sit with clients. In my education, besides the usual positive regard for clients, there was also an emphasis on being a blank slate with clients. Again, without having the defining language at the time, my work with my limitations led me to a path of bringing my true self to sessions in a VVC way. I do not mean this in an unprofessional, unboundaried way. Infusing my work with my humanness has become a primary way of being with clients now.

Decades of this kind of practice have led me to a place in which staying in loving-kindness is pretty easy. I know very well what bumps my nervous system and the particular issues that lead me to struggle. Because these limits are about my developmental wounding and not the client, I have explored the realms of how to work with myself. I rarely get surprised these days as most of the patterns are well-known terrain and easily workable for me. That leads to much enjoyment in providing therapy to my clients, leading to more VVC in the connection as I revel in the reciprocity of the work.

I feel that reciprocity in my enjoyment of their processes and their growth. In my caseload today, I enjoy each of my clients immensely. Their edges, issues, and struggles are things I know about from my personal journey. It is easy to hold them with loving-kindness and tenderness as well as appreciation of their courage. It truly touches me, and I feel the privilege of being part of their healing journey. It is an honor that brings me deep fulfillment to be able to work this way.

PRESENCE: IT IS EVERYTHING

Everything truly goes back to the clinician's presence, and as discussed throughout this book, it is always where the session starts. This requires being grounded and embodied, with benevolence and loving-kindness as the foundation of presence. Having an embodied "felt sense" (Gendlin, 1996) of presence provides the guideposts that help to recognize when presence is lost. This lays the groundwork for the dual presence of holding your experience while tracking another's experience. Simply put, the more you do this, the better you get at it. It is crucial to track yourself to develop this skill.

The emphasis on tracking your state is critical as it provides information on where you are in the process. This requires a type of dual mindfulness, tracking the client as well as tracking yourself. Examples of this might be tracking the client's anger while mindfully noting your bodily reaction to the anger. Reactions can range from fear about the anger to relief: "Ah, finally, you are feeling anger!" This range will be based on your nervous system state, your experiences with anger, and your core beliefs. If you had painful experiences with anger, your neuroception could create threat states of SNS or DVC. This manifests as wanting to get away from the anger (mobilization-flight), feeling anger about the anger (mobilization-fight), or shutting down with being more checked out (DVC). Each of these reactions is a form of being less present. There are countless variations of how our experiences can affect our reactions. It is why tracking is so important.

In tracking yourself, certain topics discussed by clients can also trigger emotional responses affecting your ability to stay present. These topics may touch on sensitive areas, childhood beliefs, or even current life experiences. Consider a clinician who recently had a miscarriage and a client reports being unexpectedly pregnant. If the grief is raw, this might bring up pain for the clinician, making it hard to fully stay with the client. Or maybe the client reports having an affair, and the clinician is reminded of a painful memory of an affair happening years before in their marriage. These kinds of situations can happen regularly and can thwart the ability to stay in presence. Additionally, some topics might lead to judgment from the clinician. A client might discuss a way they parented that is not necessarily harmful to a child but does not fit the value system of the clinician. The client might bring up a political point of view that is very different from that of the clinician. Judgment creates less presence because it moves the clinician out of the connection of the green zone. These kinds of topics can cause the clinician to lose access to the green zone, and therefore, they lose the ability to be present with the client.

There are as many examples of losing presence as there are life experiences. Clinicians bring their human selves to their work, and that includes their nervous system and human responses. Because clinicians hold the container for the client processes, all of their experiences are part of the field of working with the client. This includes issues that might still be present, past triggers, and pains that are part of life's journey. Going back to the maps of the nervous system (Figure 2.2), the clinician's personal map will interface with the map of the client. Remembering that the three areas include *general nervous system functioning, co-regulation capacity,* and *limiting core beliefs,* there will be a crossover of experiences. Some areas will have challenges, and others will not. For this reason, the more clinicians know themselves, the more effective they can be. Let's examine each area with the clinician in mind.

THE THREE MAPS OF THE NERVOUS SYSTEM FOR CLINICIANS

General Nervous System Functioning

The clinician's nervous system dominance will be part of the therapy. If both nervous system dominant states tend to be matched, things can be fluid and smooth. However, if the clinician has more SNS dominance than the client, which entails speediness and energy in their state, that could be too much and too fast for a client with DVC dominance. Likewise, a clinician with DVC dominance might move slowly for a client with more SNS dominance. Working the edges of slowing down or speeding up a little, combined with an acknowledgment of the differences, can also help.

Co-Regulation Capacity

The clinician's relational patterning will show up in the therapeutic relationship. This requires that the clinician have awareness of how they are impacted by clients' relational adaptations.

Clinicians with external regulation adaptations might:
- merge with the client
- not allow enough space for the client's process
- feel left out if the client has autoregulation tendencies
- take the client's reactions personally

Clinicians with autoregulation adaptations might:
- stay too distant from clients
- extend too much space in sessions
- feel overwhelmed by the client's processes
- take the client's reactions personally

To avoid tendencies that might make the clinician less present requires fully tracking oneself and the client so that the client feels met, while the clinician is still being themself. This requires some flexibility in one's range to help the client feel met in their experiences.

Relationally, clinicians can struggle with what might be happening between the client and themself, including normal transference from the client. Even though clinicians are well-versed in understanding that transference is part of therapeutic work, a threat state can still be evoked. It is not unusual for a client to project negative feelings about someone else onto their clinician; even with this knowledge, it can still lead to dysregulation for the clinician. The client might feel the clinician is judging them because they experienced judgment or a lack of acceptance earlier in life. This perceived judgment might not be happening at all; it is the client's projection onto the clinician. Even though this is not uncommon for clients, because of our very human and threat-sensitive nature it is still challenging to receive negative feedback from another person. It often leads to the clinician "losing their seat," by becoming dysregulated or triggered themselves. It requires that clinicians work with their state when the interaction results in being less present. It is well documented that this kind of transference often offers good information about the experiences of the client. In that vein, it can provide an opportunity to work through earlier childhood issues with reparative experiences while strengthening the therapeutic relationship.

Also, relationally, for some clinicians, the client expressing any feeling toward the clinician can be difficult. This includes not just having anger expressed, but also positive feelings can evoke red or yellow zone physiology. Depending on one's history, both can be difficult. If there were challenges with anger in the clinician's background, anger from a client might be an issue. This can lead the clinician to be less present when anger surfaces. Similarly, a lack of positive emotional expression early in life might bring up a threat state when clients bring up either positive or negative feelings about the relationship. The clinician might get dysregulated and begin wondering about their worth because the client is upset. Similarly, the clinician might feel the pain of wondering if they deserve positive feelings when those feelings are brought up by the client. Expression of either positive or negative feelings can bring up feelings of unworthiness that were part of earlier life experiences; the clinician's nervous system might move into a threat state when these things are touched on in sessions. Because of their threat reactions, the clinician's developmental wounding can affect how present they can be in their relationship with clients. (This example demonstrates the crossover as co-regulation capacity and limiting beliefs are often connected.)

Being in a relationship with the client can touch on relational issues in the clinician. This is normal as clinicians are the instruments in the therapy. Again, the goal is simply to track this effectively enough that the clinician can return to being present once again with the client.

Limiting Core Beliefs

We all have many personal examples of how our early life experiences offer us gifts in working with clients; they can also undermine aspects of our attunement with clients. We all have patterns that affect our therapeutic work, and they tend to be connected to our early childhood wounding experiences. Developmental wounding leads to patterns. This patterning also affects clinicians into habituated responses based on their personal history. If the clinician never had safety in childhood, they might create so much safety in sessions that they do not appropriately challenge the client. Or maybe the clinicians' needs were never met in childhood, so they might overly caretake the client, not promoting differentiation and/or independence, as it was an adaptation from their history. The various patterns all move away from true presence because they do not fully attune to the specific needs of the client; the clinician is responding from their own adaptation rather than the client's needs. This is a form of not being present. Learning to undertake the work with one's patterns enhances presence and paves the way for deeper work with clients. The more one knows one's tendencies with clients, the more effective one can become (Hakomi Advanced Training, personal communication, 2006).

These patterns we have in our lives will limit our range of options in working with our clients. The clinician's core beliefs tends to be the area most affected in therapy. Rooted in trauma identity, choices are limited similarly to clients. Just like clients, clinicians have default responses that are part of their default way of working with clients. Questions to ask oneself regarding the main themes include:

Safety-belonging:
- To keep safety, do I avoid bringing up challenges to the client's process?
- Am I focusing so much on the client that I lose contact with my own body?
- Do I find myself being too careful?
- Do I need to show agreement with everything the client says?
- Am I being more intellectual as part of playing it safe and not getting into feelings too much?
- Do I try overly hard to belong and connect so I feel safer?

Connection-reciprocity:
- Do I work too hard to connect with the client?
- Am I avoiding bringing in conflict?
- Do I take it personally if the client is upset?
- Do I try to meet the needs of the client rather than helping them explore their struggle?
- Do I get impatient with the client not meeting their own needs?
- Do I feel tired because I am working so hard with the client?

- Am I more invested in client progress than the client is?
- Do I have my agenda about what the client needs to do in their life?
- Am I focused on keeping the client liking me, changing how I might respond at times?

Inherent lovability-worth:
- Is my value connected with how well I perceive the client is doing?
- Do I work hard to prove my value to the client?
- Do I need the client to tell me I am doing good work with them?
- Is it hard to feel my value if the client is not doing well?
- Do I take the client's lack of progress in therapy personally?
- Do I tend to please the client and avoid my authentic responses?
- Do I need compliments from the client to feel my worth?
- Am I afraid of compliments from the client?
- Do I feel pressure to be perfect?
- Do I feel I need to know the answer when I do not?

Agency-differentiation:
- Do I feel I have to know everything or be right?
- Do I feel I know best?
- Do I hide my true perspective at times from clients?
- Do I tend to promote dependence or independence?
- Can I be okay if the client has different values from me?
- Do I feel the client needs to see things my way?
- Is it hard to have the client move on in their progress?
- Do I feel disempowered to speak about what feels important?
- Do I tend to judge a client's behavior or emotions?

These questions reflect areas of potential growth for the clinician. There is crossover between the four categories of needs, and it is less important to pay attention to the category itself as much as identifying automated behaviors that might be occurring. Automated behaviors will always limit the clinician's presence and skills. When the clinician becomes aware of their limit, they must develop an internal response to losing the course of their presence. Similar to the client, it requires looking at the question: *What wants to be integrated?*

The clinician's finding their antidote to losing presence will depend on whether they can find what they need to integrate for more effectiveness. We will explore just a few from each need category.

Some examples of integration are:

Safety-belonging:
- Allow yourself to feel a sense of safety in the connection with the client.
- Working on an embodiment practice, particularly in sessions.

- Expand yourself by moving from "playing it safe" to stretching the client with challenges when appropriate.
- Trust yourself to go deeper with clients, rather than simply staying cognitive.
- Possible mantras to try: "It is okay to take a risk." "There are always options." "I am safe right now."

Connection-reciprocity:
- Notice the fear of conflict; focus on a sense of safety with the client.
- Bring in acceptance and compassion around any sense of neediness.
- Trust the client more by exploring rather than fixing things.
- Bring awareness to working harder than the client.
- Possible mantras to try: "I can be okay even if we are not as connected as I want to be." "I do not have to fix anything; I can just be." "I can get support if I need it."

Inherent lovability-worth:
- Take in the sense of your own value including noticing what you are doing well.
- Allow your authentic self to be present.
- Feel your value even when there is disagreement or conflict.
- Embody that your value is separate from the client's progress.
- Possible mantras: "My value is not dependent on how the client is doing." "I do not have to prove myself." "It is okay to be real."

Agency-differentiation:
- Work with your own identity in differentiation.
- Allow yourself to feel okay even if you do not know something.
- Support the goal of agency with clients.
- Bring in curiosity instead of taking it personally regarding what the client is doing or not doing.
- Possible mantras: "I can be curious when I feel fear." "I am okay even if the client and I see this differently." "It is okay for me not to have answers."

Reflection: For me personally, as a clinician, my session dysregulation came from not feeling I was enough. Being worried about my value is an old and lifelong theme from childhood. With this trigger in place, I would then work too hard to fix things; my attempt to fix led me into not being with someone, moving away from a sense of presence. With attention to this pattern, I now know my body cues that indicate that this old theme is alive in me; I tend to speed up and feel a tightness in my chest. I now remind myself of a mantra that I learned from Phil Del Prince in my advanced Hakomi training. Whenever I get these sensations I repeat: "There is nothing to do, nothing to fix." My nervous system settles, and I can move back to being more present again. This has improved over time, taking moments to do now, but it required more work earlier on in my learning. As with most things, practice helps. Another struggle I had early on as a young clinician was saying what I really thought. I would hold back my authentic response in an attempt to be liked. Another wise Hakomi trainer, Deepesh Faucheux, said, "You can say anything to your clients if you say it with love." That had a profound effect on me. When I felt afraid to speak about something, I would move into even more loving-kindness and speak. I found he was right about this perspective as clients seem to know I was speaking because of my care for them. I found it very freeing and it gave me a way to be more present.

We all have patterns that affect our therapeutic work, and they tend to be connected to our early childhood wounding experiences. The more we know our patterns, the more effective we will be. It is essential to work on our patterns to be more in service of clients.

It is also just important to note that we have gifts, also from earlier wounding. Each limit has an associated strength. If being overly safe in choices in therapy is a limit, it also means you are good at creating safety. If you need to always feel connected with the client, one associated strength is being good at building relationships. If proving yourself to ensure your value is a limit, you are likely a strong learner to support your clients. If you have struggled with agency, you often have a strength of empowering others naturally. There are as many gifts as there are limits. Recognizing your unique gifts is as important as recognizing your limits.

> *Reflection:* What is one of your unique gifts from wounding? Take a moment to bring it up and name it to yourself. Allow any gratitude to be present of the gift you have developed. Allow yourself to feel that in your body.

SUMMARY

There are many ways clinicians lose presence, and there are just as many ways to return to presence. Learning how to return to presence might require supportive supervision or therapy, depending on what might feel more useful. However, attending to these experiences (general nervous system functioning, co-regulation capacity, and limiting core beliefs) will open the therapeutic process. It will also increase a clinician's range of efficacy. The work clinicians do with themselves around these three areas will benefit them both professionally and personally. When the process is approached with a sense of being able to grow oneself, there can be enjoyment and self-appreciation. This supports the clinician's resilience—and sometimes even a path into one's own post-traumatic growth.

EXPANSION EXERCISE

First, bring attention to your desire to be more present. Notice how this stems from a deep desire from within your Essence as a benevolence toward another. Notice how this feels in your body, particularly noting whatever feels good. Take a moment to just be with this. As you sit with this, allow your attention to go toward whatever way you might be struggling right now with not feeling effective. Allow yourself to note this to yourself. As you do this, feel into your body, and ask the question, "What do I need to embody right now to support myself?" Listen closely with your heart. Whatever shows up, allow yourself to feel it in your body, bringing a sense of self-compassion and kindness toward whatever arises. Allow some time to take this in with embodying the sensations and words that feel nourishing to you.

Notes

Chapter 1

1. This is not a cognitive perception, as it happens before thought.
2. Freeze is technically a hybrid state of SNS and DVC and is orange in the Polyvagal Theory Chart of Trauma Response. It includes the physiology of the SNS and the immobility of the DVC. Because treatment generally addresses immobilization similarly, freeze and shutdown are generally being grouped together in this book except when aspects of treatment are different.
3. Faulty neuroception occurs frequently after experiences of nervous system dysregulation such as childhood trauma, events, illnesses, or any experience that creates threat states.
4. In a regulated dorsal vagal state, the body supports homeostasis, which is essential for digestion and the automatic functions of organs and glands. It is only in threat physiology that the physiology, behaviors, and emotions listed on the Polyvagal Theory Chart of Trauma Response are present.
5. Ogden et al. (2006) discuss freeze and shutdown as "tonic immobility" and "immobility," respectively.
6. Perceived danger and life threat create the same physiology as real danger or life threat. The nervous system does not make the distinction between these two concepts. Perceiving on this level is not cognitive.
7. This is referring to challenging experiences that are not resolved by mobilization strategies. Oftentimes in longer-term challenges, mobilization either does not occur or not broadly enough to shift the ANS out of DVC physiology.
8. In a nonthreat state, the SNS is responsible for mobilization in the body for taking actions. It is only in threat physiology that the physiology, behaviors, and emotions listed on the Polyvagal Theory Chart of Trauma Response are present.
9. To be clearer, a stuck person has a tendency toward a particular threat state. While they may experience VVC-green zone; their nervous system state dominance can lead to difficulties in accessing the VVC-green zone; the oscillation between the VVC and the fixed threat state is less fluid.

Chapter 2

10 Deactivation is sometimes used to describe parasympathetic activity in general, encompassing both the dorsal vagal complex (DVC) and the ventral vagal complex (VVC). In this text, however, I am specifically using *deactivation* to mean downregulation as it relates to the VVC. Since the DVC represents the most extreme state of arousal, my focus will be on deactivation toward the VVC, which reflects a lower and more regulated level of arousal.

11 Ron Kurtz (1990) originally used the term "strategies" for understanding patterns that occur in developmental wounding. Using the same concept, I have changed this term to "adaptations" as it seems to fit better because the patterns from developmental wounding rarely feel like a choice.

12 The SNS-yellow zone can be obvious as activation in the nervous system. The DVC-red zone also has activation and is a higher level of arousal. In referring to nervous system deactivation, I am referring to the downregulation of both threat states.

13 Kain and Terrell (2018) identify the "faux window of tolerance," describing defensive accommodations for making experiences manageable. Borrowing this idea, I have named the concept "faux deactivation" to contrast deactivation and management, which appears to be deactivation; the process does not truly downregulate the nervous system. Before finding this term from Kain and Terrell, I had referred to this concept as "management." Our two concepts do have some crossover, with Kain and Terrell using the window of tolerance as their overlay; instead, I am using deactivation pathways as my overlay.

Chapter 3

14 This process of strengthening positive states occurring organically in real time is different from resourcing, which is more generalized. In general resourcing, clinicians are looking to develop internal and external resources as an adjunct to supporting trauma processing. In this organic approach, the focus is on the resources that are present right in the moment as they are occurring. Although both approaches support the nervous system, finding unintegrated resources as they occur is a naturalistic way to support deactivation and is often easier to access because what is being integrated is immediately available to the client.

15 These terms refer to trying to be positive at all times, even in tragic and challenging situations. These coping techniques tend to be a way to bypass the actual experience and are often rooted in anxiety. They tend to create disconnection with oneself as they deny the struggle.

Chapter 5

16 Tatkin uses the term "avoidant" in describing partners who generally "auto-regulate." He uses the term "angry-resistant" to describe partners who tend to use "only external regulation." For this book, we are using the adaptive terms of "autoregulators" and "external regulators" as substitutes while referring to his work, as he also uses these terms intermittently.

Chapter 7

17 In this book, we primarily discuss relational trauma. Other types of trauma such as medical issues, falls, and natural disasters often require different deactivation pathways, but they can evoke relational needs depending on how others respond to them.

18 I learned working with the child through Hakomi Mindfulness Training, developed by Ron Kurtz and Voice Dialogue, developed by Hal and Sidra Stone. This work is an adaptation of both of these models.

19 Having the adult state while talking to the child state strengthens the resilience vortex. The adult is often more connected to the resilience vortex, while the child is part of the trauma vortex, particularly when there are barriers in integrating a new belief. Because the adult can hold regulation and other skills, this links and differentiates these two states.

Chapter 10

20 Unless otherwise noted, these examples and content evolved from Somatic Experiencing Training® I received almost 20 years ago. I have been applying and adapting these techniques for the last two decades and they might not reflect current Somatic Experiencing® curriculum today.

21 Peter Levine, Pat Ogden, and Somatic Experiencing® use the terms "coupling" and "uncoupling." I have renamed this "fusing" and "defusing."

References

Badenoch, B. (2018). *The heart of trauma: Healing the embodied brain in the context of relationships.* Norton.

Beck, A. T. (1979). *Cognitive therapy of depression.* Guilford.

Beck, J. S. (1995). *Cognitive therapy: Basics and beyond.* Guilford Press.

Beck, J. S., & Beck, A. T. (2011). *Cognitive behavior therapy: Basics and beyond.* Guilford.

Berceli, D. (2025). Body tremors. In H. Grassman, M. Stupiggia, & S. W. Porges (Eds.), *Somatic-oriented therapies: Embodiment, trauma, and a polyvagal perspective* (pp. 161–168). Norton.

Berceli, D., Salmon, M., Bonifas, R., & Ndefo, N. (2014). Effects of self-induced unclassified therapeutic tremors on quality of life among non-professional caregivers: A pilot study. *Global Advances in Health and Medicine, 3*(5) 45–48. https://pmc.ncbi.nlm.nih.gov/articles/PMC4268601/

Blaustein, M. E. (2019). *2-Day certificate course: ARC trauma treatment for children and adolescents.* PESI *[Handout materials].* https://catalog.pesi.com/documents?DocumentId=38989&DocumentStatus=2&programRegistrantid=2269854

Brunet, J., McDonough, M. H., Hadd, V., Crocker, P. R. E., & Sabiston, C. M. (2010). The posttraumatic growth inventory: An examination of the factor structure and invariance among breast cancer survivors. *Psycho-Oncology, 19,* 830–838.

Bryant, F. B., & Veroff, J. (2006). *Savoring: A new model of positive experience.* Psychology Press.

Calhoun, L. G., & Tedeschi, R. G. (1999). *Facilitating posttraumatic growth: A clinician's guide.* Lawrence Erlbaum Associates.

Calhoun, L. G., & Tedeschi, R. G. (2013). *Posttraumatic growth in clinical practice.* Routledge.

Carter, D. (2011). *Thaw: Freedom from frozen feelings.* Create Space Independent Publishing.

Cozolino, L. J. (2006). *The neuroscience of human relationships: Attachment and the developing social brain.* Norton.

Craig, A. (2002). How do you feel? Interoception: The sense of the physiological condition of the body. *Nature Reviews Neuroscience, 3,* 655–666. https://doi.org/10.1038/nrn894

Dana, D. (2018). *The Polyvagal Theory in therapy: Engaging the rhythm of regulation.* Norton.

Dana, D. (2020). *Polyvagal exercises for safety and connection: 50 client-centered practices.* Norton.

Dana, D. (2021). *Anchored: How to befriend your nervous system using Polyvagal Theory.* Sounds True.

Dion, L. (2018). *Aggression in play therapy: A neurobiological approach for integrating intensity.* Norton.

Divecha, D. (2020, August 12). *Rifts and repairs in the fabric of family life.* Developmental Science. https://www.developmentalscience.com/blog/2020/8/12/rifts-and-repairs-in-the-fabric-of-family-life

Eisenberg, N., Fabes, R. A., & Spinrad, T. L. (2006). Prosocial development. In N. Eisenberg, W. Damon, and R. M. Lerner (Eds.), *Handbook of child psychology: Social, emotional, and personality development* (6th ed., pp. 646–718). John Wiley & Sons.

Eisman, J. (2015). Hakomi character theory. In H. Weiss, G. Johanson, & L. Monda (Eds.), *Hakomi mindfulness-centered somatic psychotherapy: A comprehensive guide to theory and practice* (pp. 76–90). Norton.

Fischer, A. (2015). The role of core organizing beliefs in Hakomi therapy. In H. Weiss, G. Johanson, & L. Monda (Eds.), *Hakomi mindfulness-centered somatic psychotherapy: A comprehensive guide to theory and practice* (pp. 66–75). W. W. Norton & Company.

Frankl, V. E. (1992). Man's search for meaning: An introduction to logotherapy (4th ed.). Beacon Press.

Geller, S. M. (2018). Therapeutic presence and Polyvagal Theory: Principles and practices for cultivating effective therapeutic relationships. In S. W. Porges & D. Dana (Eds.), *Clinical applications of the Polyvagal Theory: The emergence of polyvagal-informed therapies* (pp. 106–126). Norton.

Frankl, V. E.(2015). *Man's search for meaning* (Gift ed.). Beacon Press. (Original work published 1963).

Geller, S. M., & Porges, S. W. (2014). Therapeutic presence: Neurophysiological mechanisms mediating feeling safe in therapeutic relationships. *Journal of Psychotherapy Integration, 24*(3), 178–192. https://doi.org/10.1037/a0037511

Gendlin, E. T. (1996). *Focusing-oriented psychotherapy: A manual of the experiential method.* Guilford.

Germer, C. (2009). *The mindful path of self-compassion: Freeing yourself from destructive thoughts and emotions.* Guilford.

Gilbert, P. (2010). *The compassionate mind: A new approach to life's challenges.* New Harbinger.

Graham, L. (2013). *Bouncing back: Rewiring your brain for maximum resilience and well-being.* New World Library.

Hanson, R. (2009). *Buddha's brain: The practical neuroscience of happiness, love & wisdom.* New Harbinger.

Hanson, R. (2018). *Positive neuroplasticity: The mindful cultivation of resilient well-being [PowerPoint slides].* http://media.rickhanson.net/slides/9.11.18Google_Pos_NP_Hanson.pdf

Hanson, R., & Hanson. F. (2018). *Resilient: How to grow an unshakable core of calm, strength, and happiness.* Harmony.

Hatcher, R. L. (2015). Interpersonal competencies: Responsiveness, technique, and training in psychotherapy. *American Psychologist, 70*(8), 747–757. https://doi.org/10.1037/a0039803

Kain, K. L., & Terrell, S. J. (2018). *Nurturing resilience: Helping clients move forward from developmental trauma*. North Atlantic Books.

Kalisvaart, H., & Ogden, P. (2025). Sensorimotor psychotherapy: Processing trauma and attachment through the body. In H. Grassman, M. Stupiggia, & S. W. Porges (Eds.), *Somatic-oriented therapies: Embodiment, trauma, and a polyvagal perspective* (pp. 209–220). Norton.

Keltner, D. (2024). *Awe: The new science of everyday wonder and how it can transform your life*. Penguin.

Kessler, D. (2019). *Finding meaning: The sixth stage of grief*. Scribner.

Kurtz, R. (1990). *Body-centered psychotherapy: The Hakomi method: The integrated use of mindfulness, nonviolence, and the body*. LifeRhythm.

Kurtz, R. (2015). The essential method. In H. Weiss, G. Johanson, & L. Monda (Eds.), *Hakomi mindfulness-centered somatic psychotherapy: A comprehensive guide to theory and practice* (pp. 19–30). Norton.

Kurtz, R. (n.d.) On being good with people. *Inside Out Journal*. Irish Association of Humanistic and Integrative Psychotherapy. https://iahip.org/page-1075745

Lanius, R. A., Harricharan, S., & Kearney, S. (2023). *Sensory pathways to healing from trauma*. Guilford.

Levine, P. A. (1997). *Waking the tiger: Healing trauma: The innate capacity to transform overwhelming experiences*. North Atlantic Books.

Levine, P. A. (2010). *In an unspoken voice: How the body releases trauma and restores goodness*. North Atlantic Books.

Levine, P. A. (2015). *Trauma and memory: Brain and body in a search for the living past: A practical guide for understanding and working with the traumatic memory*. North Atlantic Books.

Linehan, M. M. (1993). *Skills training manual for treating borderline personality disorder*. Guilford.

Lukin, K. (2019, August 1). Toxic positivity: Don't always look on the bright side: Truly process your emotions instead. Psychology Today. https://www.psychologytoday.com/us/blog/the-man-cave/201908/toxic-positivity-dont-always-look-the-bright-side

Mahler, K. (2017). *Interoception: The eighth sensory system: Practical solutions for improving self-regulation, self-awareness, and social understanding*. AAPC.

Marriott, S., & Kelley, A. (2024). *Secure relating: Holding your own in an insecure world*. HarperCollins.

Maslow, A. H. (1968). *Toward a psychology of being* (2nd ed.). Van Nostrand Reinhold.

Miller, A. (2008). *The drama of the gifted child: The search for the true self*. Basic Books.

Murphy, J. (2015). The therapeutic relationship in Hakomi therapy. In H. Weiss, G. Johanson, & L. Monda (Eds.), *Hakomi mindfulness-centered somatic psychotherapy: A comprehensive guide to theory and practice* (pp. 93–107). Norton.

Neff, K., & Germer, C. (2018). *The mindful self-compassion workbook: A proven way to accept yourself, build inner strength, and thrive*. Guilford.

O'Connor, V., Langhinrichsen-Rohling, J. & Peterman, A. H. (2022). When core beliefs get stuck: Distinct routes to posttraumatic growth and depreciation. *Personality and Individual Differences, 197*, 111787. https://doi.org/10.1016/j.paid.2022.111787

Ogden, P., Minton, K., & Pain, C. (2006). *Trauma and the body: A sensorimotor approach to psychotherapy.* Norton.

Ord, A. S., Stranahan, K. R., Hurley, R. A., & Taber, K. H. (2020). Stress-Related growth: Building a more resilient brain. *Journal of Neuropsychiatry and Clinical Neurosciences, 32*(3), A4-212. https://doi.org/10.1176/appi.neuropsych.20050111

Paulsen, S. L., & Lanius, U. F. (2014). Fractionating trauma processing: TOTEM-SPOTS and other attenuating tactics. In Lanius, U. F., Paulsen, S. L., Corrigan F. M. (Eds.), *Neurobiology and treatment of traumatic dissociation towards an embodied self* (pp. 367–382). Springer.

Poole Heller, D. (2019). *The power of attachment: How to create deep and lasting relationships.* Sounds True.

Porges, S. W. (2003). Social engagement and attachment: A phylogenetic perspective. *Annals of the New York Academy of Sciences, 1008*(1), 31–47. https://doi.org/10.1196/annals.1301.004

Porges, S. W. (2011). *The Polyvagal Theory: Neurophysiological foundations of emotions, attachment, communication, and self-regulation.* Norton.

Porges, S. W. (2012). *Polyvagal theory: Why this changes everything* [Webinar transcript]. The National Institute for the Clinical Application of Behavioral Medicine. https://www.flexiblemindtherapy.com/uploads/6/5/5/2/65520823/nicabm-porges-2012.pdf?utm_source=chatgpt.com"https://www.flexiblemindtherapy.com/uploads/6/5/5/2/65520823/nicabm-porges-2012.pdf

Porges, S. W. (2021). *Polyvagal safety: Attachment, communication, self-regulation.* Norton.

Porges, S. W. (2022). Polyvagal Theory: A science of safety. *Frontiers in Integrative Neuroscience, 16,* 871227. https://doi.org/10.3389/fnint.2022.871227

Porges, S. W. (2024). *Polyvagal perspectives: Interventions, practices, and strategies.* Norton.

Porges, S. W., & Porges, S. (2023). *Our polyvagal world: How safety and trauma change us.* Norton.

Rahman, T. (2016). *Being in my body: What you might not have known about trauma, dissociation, and the brain.* Open Sesame.

Reeds, M. M. (2015). The therapeutic relationship in Hakomi therapy. In H. Weiss, G. Johanson, & L. Monda (Eds.), *Hakomi mindfulness-centered somatic psychotherapy: A comprehensive guide to theory and practice* (pp. 217–226). Norton.

Roberts, B. W., Luo, J., Briley, D. A., Chow, P. I., Su, R., & Hill, P. L. (2017). A systematic review of personality trait change through intervention. *Psychological Bulletin, 143*(2), 117–141. https://doi.org/10.1037/bul0000088

Rotter, J. B. (1966). Generalized expectancies for internal versus external control of reinforcement. *Psychological Monographs: General and Applied, 80*(1), 1–28. https://doi.org/10.1037/h0092976

Scaer, R. (2005). *The trauma spectrum: Hidden wounds and human resiliency.* Norton.

Schwarts, R. C. (1995). *Internal Family Systems.* Guilford.

Schwartz, A. (2020). *The post-traumatic growth guidebook: Practical mind-body tools to heal trauma, foster resilience and awaken your potential.* PESI.

Seligman, M. E. P. (2011). *Flourish: A visionary new understanding of happiness and well-being.* Atria Paperback.

Shepperd, J. A., Waters, E. A., Weinstein, N. D., & Klein, W. M. P. (2015). A primer on unrealistic optimism. *Current Directions in Psychological Science*, 24(3), 232–237. https://doi.org/10.1177/0963721414568341

Siegel, D. J. (1999). *The developing mind: How relationships and the brain interact to shape who we are*. Guilford.

Siegel, D. J. (2010a). *Mindsight: The new science of personal transformation*. Bantam Books.

Siegel, D. J. (2010b). *The mindful clinician: A clinician's guide to mindsight and neural integration*. Norton.

Siegel, D. J. (2012a). *The whole-brain child: 12 revolutionary strategies to nurture your child's developing mind*. Bantam.

Siegel, D. J. (2012b). *Pocket guide to interpersonal neurobiology: An integrative handbook of the mind*. Norton.

Siegel, D. J. (2013). Presence, attunement, and resonance are the way we clinically create the essential condition of trust. As our patients feel this [Status update]. Facebook.

Siegel, D. J. (2017). *Mind: A journey to the heart of being human*. Norton.

Siegel, D. J., & Hartzell, M. (2014). *Parenting from the inside out: How a deeper self-understanding can help you raise children who thrive* (10th anniversary ed.). TarcherPerigee.

Siegel, D. J. (2023, April 4). Presence, attunement, and resonance are the way we clinically create the essential condition of trust. Facebook.

Stevens, L., & Woodruff, C. C. (2018). What is this feeling that I have for myself and for others? Contemporary perspectives on empathy, compassion, and self-compassion and their absence. In L. Stevens & C. C. Woodruff (Eds.), *The neuroscience of empathy, compassion, and self-compassion* (pp. 1–21). Elsevier. https://doi.org/10.1016/B978-0-12-809837-0.00001-5

Taku, K., Cann, A., Calhoun, L. G., & Tedeschi, R. G. (2008). The factor structure of the posttraumatic growth inventory: A comparison of five models using confirmatory factor analysis. *Journal of Traumatic Stress*, 21, 158–164.

Tatkin, S. (2015, April 2). Our automatic brain: Everything new will soon be old. Stan Tatkin Blog. https://stantatkinblog.wordpress.com/2015/04/02/our-automatic-brain-everything-new-will-soon-be-old/

Tatkin, S. (2023). *In each other's care: A guide to the most common relationship conflicts and how to work through them*. Sounds True.

Tedeschi, R. G., & Calhoun, L. G. (1996). The posttraumatic growth inventory: Measuring the positive legacy of trauma. *Journal of Traumatic Stress*, 9, 455–471.

Vaish, A., Grossmann, T., & Woodward, A. (2008). Not all emotions are created equal: The negativity bias in social–emotional development. *Psychological Bulletin*, 134(3), 383–403. https://doi.org/10.1037/0033-2909.134.3.383

van der Kolk, B. A. (2014). *The body keeps the score: Brain, mind, and body in the healing of trauma*. Penguin.

Walker, R. J., & Newcomer, E. (2025). Applying the neurobiology of resilience. In H. Grassman, M. Stupiggia, & S. W. Porges (Eds.), *Somatic-oriented therapies: Embodiment, trauma, and a polyvagal perspective* (pp. 112–122). Norton.

Weiss, H. (2015). Transformation. In H. Weiss, G. Johanson, & L. Monda (Eds.), *Hakomi mindfulness-centered somatic psychotherapy: A comprehensive guide to theory and practice* (pp. 225–236). Norton.

Weiss, H., Johanson, G., & Monda, L. (Eds.). (2015). *Hakomi mindfulness-centered somatic psychotherapy: A comprehensive guide to theory and practice.* Norton.

Wetherford, R. (2011). *Stan Tatkin on a psychobiological approach to couples therapy.* psychotherapy.net. https://www.psychotherapy.net/interview/couples/stan-tatkin#section -avoidant-and-angry-resistant-styles

Winfrey, O., & Perry, B. D. (2021). *What happened to you? Conversations on trauma, resilience, and healing.* Flatiron Books.

Wood, K. (2024). Trauma and the impact of misattunement in early childhood. *Journal of Psychiatry Reform, 11*(1). https://journalofpsychiatryreform.com/2024/01/05/ trauma-and-the-impact-of-misattunement-in-early-childhood/

Index

In this index, *f* denotes figure and *n* denotes note.

About the Author

Ruby Jo Walker, LCSW, is an author, speaker, trainer, and nationally recognized leader in Applied Polyvagal Theory for trauma treatment. As an education partner with the Polyvagal Institute (PVI), she plays a central role in bringing Polyvagal Theory to life through clinical applications—transforming the neurobiology of the nervous system into accessible, embodied, and relational practices that support clinicians and organizations.

Ruby Jo is the founder of Southwest Trauma Training and has more than three decades of clinical and training experience. She is certified in Somatic Experiencing™ and Hakomi Mindfulness Somatic Therapy and is widely respected for her clarity, depth, and clinical integrity.

Additionally, Ruby Jo is a leader in trauma-support organizations across the United States, is a frequent presenter at national and regional sexual assault and domestic violence conferences, and has previously served in a leadership role on the Colorado statewide task force, developing supportive resources for healthcare workers during the COVID-19 pandemic.

Ruby Jo was a contributing author to *Somatic-Oriented Therapies: Embodiment, Trauma, and the Polyvagal Perspective* (Norton, 2025), and *Applied Polyvagal Theory for Resilience and Post-Traumatic Growth: A Clinician's Guide* is her first solo-authored book.